*'Everest for me, and I believe for the world, is the physical and symbolic
manifestation of overcoming odds to achieve a dream.'*
— Tom Whittaker

Many Everests

An inspiring journey of transforming dreams into reality

Ravindra Kumar

BLOOMSBURY
NEW DELHI • LONDON • OXFORD • NEW YORK • SYDNEY

Bloomsbury Publishing India Pvt. Ltd
Second Floor, LSC Building No. 4
DDA Complex, Pocket C – 6 & 7, Vasant Kunj
New Delhi 110070

BLOOMSBURY, BLOOMSBURY INDIA and the Diana logo are trademarks of
Bloomsbury Publishing Plc

First published in India 2017

ISBN 978 93 86141 32 3

15 14 13 12 11

Typeset by Manipal Digital Systems
Printed at Gopsons Papers Pvt. Ltd., Noida

To find out more about our authors and books visit www. bloomsbury. com.
Here you will find extracts, author interviews, details of forthcoming
events and the option to sign up for our newsletters.

Many Everests

❖ "What a captivating account ! It inspired me to know that as I have been accepting bigger and bigger challenges in my life and moving up and up, realizing that even the most ordinary people can scale the highest peaks of achievements by surmounting bigger and bigger challenges, there are many others in the new generation like me.

Capt. M.S. Kohli ,
The Leader of The First Indian Everest Expedition Team to climb Mt. Everest in 1965.

❖ I am sending it to our library so that many of our staff and faculty can read the book. I am sure your inspiring story can bring change in many of their lives.

Prof. Devang V. Khakhar ,
Director, IIT Bombay.

❖ 'It is start to finish book. I have found the book absorbing and written in good flow. Link to "will power" and "positive attitude" is well illustrated through the anecdotes. I am confident, the book will go a long way in shaping the life of young aspirants who want to excel in their life.

Dr. Aruna Sharma, I.A.S.,
Secretary, Ministry of Steel, Government of India.

❖ "The book "Many Everests" will be a source of inspiration to millions of youths with parents living in poverty & deprivations to aspire & achieve a life of prosperity, affluence & fame-their dream by overcoming hurdles coming their ways through commitment, willpower and Advance Positive Visualizations as suggested by the author."

Col Subodh Kumar,
Indian Army.

❖ "I read it in two night sessions. It was so fascinating that I felt I must immediately convey my reactions."

Sri Vivek Channa,
Retd. I.A.S.

Dedicated to:

All the common people still struggling to realize their unfulfilled dreams—
May you swim in the ocean of perfect health, wealth, peace, and prosperity.

Acknowledgements

When eating bamboo sprouts, remember the man who planted them. —
Chinese proverb.

I feel this book will never be complete without expressing my
gratitude to the people involved in shaping and realising my
dreams in life, and in the making of this book.

I am sincerely grateful to all those, who have directly or
indirectly contributed, even to the minor extent, in covering
the journey of my life so beautifully and successfully. It is due
to their assistance and support that I have reached so far and
am standing here today. I am especially grateful to my parents,
maternal grandparents, and maternal great grandparents for
their teachings and their hopes on me.

Further, my heartfelt gratitude goes to all those, who contributed
in making my journey to Mt. Everest successful, especially both
my District Collectors, Sri D. Anandan and Sri A K Singh, both
the Superintendents of Police, Sri Mandeep Singh Tuli and Sri
Manoj Tiwari, Inspector   eneral of Police Sri Vineet Vinayak
and Principal Secretary (Forest) Sri Arkind Kumar. All other

important contributors are mentioned in appropriate contexts in the concerned chapters of this book.

My humble gratitude goes to my seniors in the Indian Administrative Services: Sri Champak Chatterjee, Sri Robin Gupta, Sri P K Jha, Sri B K Prasad, Sri Dharmendra Singh Gangwar and Sri Chanchal Kumar for motivating me to take up the assignment of documenting my journey. Some of them also guided me in shaping this book, especially Sri Robin Gupta and Sri Dharmendra Singh Gangwar.

I had faired the daily routine of journey to Mt. Everest while I was posted as Sub-Divisional Magistrate in South Sikkim District under District Magistrate Sri Prabhakar Verma, but this book took present shape during my posting as the Additional District Magistrate in North Sikkim District under the District Magistrate Sri Chewang Gyatso Bhutia. My sincere gratitude goes out to both of them. I can't ignore the silent support from my helpers, Jeevan and Phurden, in Sikkim. They had been a constant support during my stay in North Sikkim and had helped me to devote myself to this book completely by taking care of the domestic front.

Further, I can't miss to express my deep affection to my wife, Diksha, who read the final script and gave me valuable inputs on minor modifications required, while I was busy in my day-to-day job in Sitapur District of Uttar Pradesh, my posting at the time of publishing this book.

I also wish to extend my gratitude to my service senior Sri Abhijit Sinha, my cousin Mrs. Abha Rani Singh & her husband Sri B R R Kumar for helping me approaching the publishers. I deeply acknowledge the constant support of Sri Praveen Tiwari, who enabled me to get this book published by Bloomsbury Publishing.

Finally, I am grateful to the Government of Sikkim as well as the people of Sikkim for providing a peaceful work environment and zero political interference, without which, neither I could have saved sufficient time to devote for this book nor could write with a cool and focused mind.

Contents

Introduction

More than two years have passed since I ascended the Everest. Many people suggested that I should write a book about my journey. I had penned down my daily activities during my mountaineering training at HMI Darjeeling, at the pre-Everest training camp in Chemchey, as well as during the two months of my Everest expedition. I had made this a habit to cater to my own reference in the future, just so I could relive those sweet memories.

As I would ponder about the suggestions to me for writing a book, I would think of what it would contribute to the world. But I had have my answers: the daily schedule of an Everest summiteer, the climbing skills, precautions to be taken while climbing, etc. The only problem was that the answers for these are already available on the internet as well as in the books and biographies of many legendary mountaineers, who have successfully climbed the Everest many times. And I believe they are more experienced mountaineers than I am. Of course they are, they're professionals! I am just an amateur who was zealous enough to learn the skills of mountaineering few years ago. I had my motives behind this venture. Learning from the Sikkim earthquake of September 2011, I knew it would make me able to overcome the physical barriers of connectivity like the disruption of roads in case of a natural calamity in the hilly state of Sikkim. I was brimming with this idea to help the locals in times of need and hardships. Later my eagerness to learn mountaineering turned into a passion to climb any peak. And from that passion stemmed wild desire to climb Mount Everest, the highest peak in the world! So, in a year, during which I thought, planned and trained, I reached the zenith, without attempting any intermediate peaks. I had no history of climbing and no one in my family did it either. So, if I write a book as a mountaineer then honestly, it would be writing a book for the sake of writing one and not to contribute something new to the world.

I had once thought of writing a motivational book but there are thousands of those available in the market and on the internet. Then what could I possibly do? I had also wondered if I should give up the idea of writing the book. But, no, I couldn't.

The pressure from the near and dear ones kept on rising. It culminated in the form of questions and queries, 'When are you coming up with your write-up on your Everest experience?' 'When are you completing your book?' 'When you publish your book, please send me a copy as I want to show my children how an IAS officer climbed Mount Everest.' And there were many more. So one day, I finally, decided to move ahead with an idea of writing a book as soon as I got the answer to my mental dilemna. I would not only document my life's journey till now, but also share the tricks to success, to pass many milestones and to overcome difficult hurdles in life.

On a deeper analysis, I also discovered that I was in a good position to offer something new to readers. The world is full of people with certain principles in life but only a few of them actually abide by them. We should become someone who lives the principles than merely preaching it. While writing motivational theories, most writers describe other people's experiences whether they are eminent personalities of the world or unknown unique achievers. There are very few books in which writers have shared experiences and events from their own lives and have shared the techniques which they used to make it through their difficulties. Here I would document and bring to the people, the technique I have tried and tested well in my own life. It has given me a tremendous output in terms of many significant successes I have achieved so far.

I chose to tell my own story and not to write about the big achievers. This is because the readers might not consider themselves as achievers at all, and might lose the connection between themselves and the great personality. I feel that the mass relate to a person born and brought up in similar conditions to their own,who has struggled through the same problems and hardships in life which they are also struggling through, and who is living in the same society as they are, but could still overcome many milestones. So they would be compelled to think about their own prospects that, if they use this trick, they can also transform their lives.

So, what is this technique to success I have been talking of? How did this trick transform my life, and how can it bring transformation in your life likewise? Before proceeding on this, I give you examples of the three major transformational journeys out of the many, which I have taken so far.

The first one is my long journey from being born in a poor farmer's family, with my father's income being extremely modest. I went from living in a one-room house built by our great grandfather to working in one of the highest paid jobs in the world. Shipping pays a very handsome salary in comparison to many other well paid jobs in the world. It was the job that I got immediately after completing my basic education and it exposed me to quite a decent amount of money as compared to the acute scarcity that I had witnessed in my childhood. I went from a one room house in one of the most remote villages of India to having my own deluxe house in the metro like Mumbai.

The second is the journey from my early education in a Hindi-medium school in my village to clearing the toughest engineering examination in India, IIT JEE, in my first attempt, right after I passed the higher secondary examination. I went on to crack what is considered as one of the toughest examination in India, the civil services examination. In fact, being born in a poor family, my father couldn't afford educating me in a private English medium school in a nearby town despite my wish was to study there like my cousin, Tej Pratap.

The final one is my journey from being a lean and physically weak, under-weight and malnourished boy from a farmer's family (often falling sick in my childhood) to earning a Black Belt in karate during my training in T S Chanakya. I had gained a stout weight of 85 Kgs during my well-paying job in shipping. I had to come back in a proper shape again in order to be able to climb Mount Everest, the highest peak of the world, which is the ultimate test of one's stamina and physical strength.

I still think of my childhood, and my unadulterated life. While studying in a Hindi-medium school in a village, I used to visualise and fantasize that I was studying in an English Medium school in town and was going to class everyday dressed well in a uniform with a tie, like my cousin. My visualization then brought me to Navodaya Vidyalaya in reality in the town of Begusarai only a few years later.

As I was physically weak and usually was beaten up by my classmates, I really wished that one day I become very strong and in a position to protect myself as well as others who are weak. I used to dream of being strong someday. That one day, I would possess a strong body. Subsequently, I had a chance to learn karate during my college years and received a Black Belt. I was pretty well known for my physical strength during my training of three years in T S Chanakya and also led the winning tug of war team, the ultimate test of physical strength.

Thus, wandering in imagination, visualization and fantasizing about future was my inherent habit since childhood. As I grew older and gained consciousness of the world, I came to know that I am not the only one who is in the habit of dreaming and fantasizing and living under continuous waves of imagination and visualization. There had been many people in the world including the famous scientist Albert Einstein, the legendary psychiatrist Carl Jung, painter Pablo Picasso, the well-known cosmologist Stephen Hawking, philosopher Ludwig Andreas von Feuerbach etc., who had similar habits and had already accepted the hidden power of fantasy and imagination and had also mentioned them in different contexts. It has also been referred to, directly or indirectly in the religious texts of all the major religions of the world including Hinduism, Islam and Christianity. Thus, this miraculous power has been used for centuries in different forms, but still, the vast majority of the population is not aware of the power of imagination and visualization.

I was convinced with the power of imagination and visualization as a very effective tool for success in life after witnessing its power in achieving many such milestones in my life. At several occasions in my life, when I used this technique to bring changes in life, I clearly noticed that it worked well and gave the desired outcomes. After deep observation about events and successes in my life, I started believing that positive visualization about something turns it into reality and brings it to you in real life. I became fully convinced of its miraculous power after scaling the Everest in my maiden attempt, despite tremendous hindrance during the whole journey. It removed all the doubts in my mind regarding its effectiveness. I realised that my habit of fantasizing and continuously imagining over many months, a scene where I visualised myself climbing the last stretch of slope of Everest and finally standing on its peak, really made the main contribution behind my success of reaching the highest peak of the world.

But how does imagination and visualization work and affect your future? Let us look at the example of an elephant.

Baby elephants are constrained by being chained to a post. They fight with all their might to break free. Day in and day out they try to escape, but eventually they give up. When the baby elephants become adults, they no longer need chains to be tied at their place; just a thin rope will do. Of course, an adult elephant is perfectly capable of breaking the rope, but since its experience as a baby have convinced it that it can't break the rope, it never tries. It never goes beyond the visualization of its childhood instances of failure and thus, it remains constrained by a thin rope throughout life.

Being born and brought up in economically backward region of Bihar, I observed that most of the youth of this generation in our region, especially those from an economically lower strata of the society, continue to do the same job in which their ancestors had been struggling to earn their livelihood for generations. The son continues his father's occupation (becoming a barber, a vendor, or a washerman, etc.) although if he had tried, he could have got better work. After their ancestors' repeated failures or their own initial failures, they have accepted that they are not capable of doing any better. Thus, they give up before even trying, like the elephant. They are thus, devoid of dreams, of imagination, and have never visualised themselves out of the deplorable condition they are in right now.

Being born in a middle class family, my concern goes out to the mass. I am an integral part of the mass myself, having a deep sentiment and attachment tied to the common mass. By penning down my life experiences, I want them to realise their dreams, cherish their wishes, advance, and scale many heights. I will explain in detail about the effectiveness of imagination and visualization in different situations of life by the anecdotage and real-life events from my own life to show how this technique worked well in different situations to bring great success in my life as well as to come out of hopeless situations of multiple failures. This would definitely inspire everybody to take up challenges head on and fight with absolute confidence to fulfil their long-cherished dreams. It would be easy for them to realise their dreams using this well-tried and tested simple technique.

I have a strong belief that there are ample resources, ample wealth, and happiness in the world and that there won't be any scarcity even if everyone gets everything they want. By helping common people to realise that they can also get what they want, I am not losing anything, but gaining huge satisfaction by being exposed to the positive environment and the increased level of happiness in the society that will be created with this act of sharing.

With these thoughts and visions, I have tried to bring my own real life events in front of you and have tried to convey my experiences and learnings in life to you. Your valuable comments or suggestions to improve this book will be heartily appreciated.

With warm regards,
Ravindra Kumar

How This Book Can Help You Realize Your Long-Cherished Dream

Thinking, Imagination, Visualization

The power to imagine or create an image of something, real or virtual, on the screen of mind is an inherent capacity of the human brain. We, in our day-to-day life, visualise about the things of our choice. Every human being uses it on regular basis and plans and carries out his life based on the images that exist in the mind. Many of us use it as a habit without being aware that we are using it.

This is a wonderful gift given to the human being. Whenever we create a perception about a person or place or thing, we create a picture of it on the screen of our mind. Even if we recall a speech given by a famous person say Prime minister of our country, then what comes first in our mind is just the picture and animation of the scene, where we see prime minister giving speech. Here, important thing to notice is that we see the mental imagery of process of giving speech by our mind's eye, and recall the content of speech or hear the speech in mind. It never happens that we recall the content of speech from darkness i. e. without any picture.

Similarly, while reading about any topic, you might have observed that whenever you read with full concentration, a mental movie about the content of topic is created in your mind. The following day, what you recall is the movie or scene, which was created in your mind the previous day and you reproduce it in your words. Whenever you try to memorise by heart the content of a topic word by word, then a picture of page, which you read, is stored in your mind and you recall that picture. So, it is picture, which prevails in your mind and not merely the text.

On the same line, when you recall about your favourite delicacy, a picture of that particular dish comes to your mind, which you may have seen somewhere in a restaurant or in a party in the past. Although you like the particular dish because of its delicious taste, what comes first in your mind is its picture. You may recall the taste subsequently focusing further on the mental picture of the dish. It never happens that you recall the taste of your favourite dish without seeing its picture in your mind.

That's why Aristotle, the famous Greek Philosopher of fourth century B.C. said, 'The soul never thinks without a mental picture.' This means, human being has been using the mental picture since time immemorial and there is nothing new about it.

It is truly said, a picture is worth thousands words. A picture can explain us worth more than what a thousand words can explain. What we can understand from a picture, can't be explained properly even in thousand words. Cave paintings from ancient times depict the culture and lifestyle of early men to us. In today's world, corporate emphasizes more on visual presentation to attract the attention of customers and to sell the product than the long speech as a tool.

USA is using computer programs to retrieve mental images of faces from human brain in criminal investigation. Earlier, artists were engaged for drawing manually picture of such faces as described by witnesses, which lacked accuracy but presently, with computer software, better and accurate images of faces can be directly extracted from the brain of witness.

It is because the human mind captures a picture or a visual image more than any other sensory perception. Picture is more inherent to human mind than speech or any other perception. Our history also tells that human beings or the *Homo sapiens* used symbols, a visual mode, to communicate with each other for quite a long time before they learnt using verbal mode of communication.

That's why, I have emphasized the power of visualization over the process of thinking or the power of imagination although there is lot of debate and discussion about clear cut meaning and description of these three words.

Thought can be understood as an idea, opinion, view, impression, perception, image etc., which is created by the process of thinking. With this tool, we interpret the world around us as we perceive it and also discuss, debate, plan, introspect, analyze, and speculate about the world or surroundings. Thinking includes all our sensory perceptions of sight, sound, smell, flavour, etc. and the power to interpret, analyze, and speculate etc.

Imagination may be understood as the perception of appearance or picture, feel, smell, sound, taste, etc. It is the ability to create a mental image of something (some object, event or scene) that doesn't actually exist right at that moment and thus, are not perceived through our senses but the created mental image simulates all these sensory perceptions. This means, we can imagine about something and see, listen, taste, smell, touch and feel its texture, temperature or pressure or its other characteristics in our mind without actually having that thing in front of us. We imagine about eating a sweet savoury like gulabjamun, we imagine its original appearance, colour as well as feel its softness, sweet taste and fragrance.

Imagination is also the ability to come up with new and creative ideas. Painting is an art, which thrives mostly on imagination. In this form, controlled and targeted imagination is used to discover better and easy ways to accomplish complex and new tasks. Uncontrolled imagination or dreaming without any specific purpose, when you get carried away in a dream, is generally kept in the category of day dreaming.

Visualization is the pictorial aspect of a visual image, graph, map, diagrams, sketches, animations, etc. of something, which is not actually present at that moment. Visualization is generally associated with the sensory perception of sight.

We can also say that visualization is more focused and serious kind of imagination with a purpose. During imagination, the object of imagination may seem far away from you and you don't see the details but when you pay serious attention to it and visualize it then it is drawn towards you and you go into more details. When you go in details then it is easier to perceive it as real and generate emotions and feelings attached with it, which ultimately sends signal to subconscious mind to start working to materialise it. Unlike visualization, imagination is not always concerned about the intricacies of details.

For example, you have missed to watch a crucial cricket match between India and Pakistan but your mind imagines the match. You imagine a scene where Pakistan team is bowling and Indian cricketer M. S. Dhoni and Virat Kohli are batting. Both are taking strike one by one and are scoring fast. This is imagination where you are watching the cricket from some distance. Now, suddenly you zoom in the whole scene in your mind's screen where Pakistan cricketer Shahid Afridi is bowling and *you* are batting, with M. S. Dhoni on other side of the pitch. You carefully watch the movement of the ball thrown by Afridi and quickly strike with your bat and then run for the score. You are witnessing your swift movement from one side of pitch and the movement of Dhoni from opposite side to ensure a risk free score while being aware about the whereabouts of ball. You see this whole thing quite vividly and get so absorbed in it that sometimes you forget about your actual physical whereabouts. Later, when you come out of this mental movie, you feel like you were in a dream. This is visualization. Your mind witnesses the whole scene with your involvement in it as if it was really happening in your life.

Thus, the word *thinking* is wider than imagination and the word *imagination* is wider than *visualization*. The process of thinking includes both the processes of imagination and visualization. The process of imagination includes the process of visualization but visualization goes much deeper than imagination.

Human mind has an unlimited capacity to visualize. But every visualization doesn't turn into reality. Human needs and desires are unlimited. People dream about having numerous things in a short time. In spite of making hundreds of wishes and dreaming about them day and night, what people get in reality is just a few wishes fulfilled. If we go by the principle that imagination and visualization create reality, then every desire of human being should have been fulfilled but it doesn't happen. So, either the principle is wrong or there are some shortcomings in the process.

Theories Supporting Visualization

The power of imagination and visualization in the human mind and its conversion to reality can be justified on the basis of many modern scientific research and their findings.

In 1905, Einstein propounded his famous mass energy equivalence theory $E= mc^2$ and said that both mass and energy are present in every physical object. These, both, are equivalent in every physical object in such a manner that they are always present in same (constant) proportion to one another and in such a way that total physical quantity in the object remains constant. The constant proportion between equivalent amounts of energy and mass is equal to the square of speed of light. If we add certain amount of external energy to any physical object then its mass will increase by an amount, which is equivalent to the energy added. For example, adding 25 kilowatt-hours (or 90 mega joules) of any form of energy to any object will increase its mass by 1 microgram, even though no matter has been added. In simple language, we can say that mass and energy are interchangeable, i. e. both can be changed into each other. The principle on which, the hydrogen bomb works, is one such example of conversion of mass into energy.

In 1927, the Davisson-Germer experiment (electron scattering experiment on crystalline solid) carried out by American physicists Clinton Davisson and Lester Germer in Bell Labs found that the electron has dual personality. It has characteristics of both particle and wave i. e. both mass and energy. The wave quality gave the electron the characteristics of light. Thus, this experiment confirmed the earlier de Broglie hypothesis that all matter displays wave-particle duality and the entire realm of physical nature has a dual personality that is, both mass and energy.

Similarly, the human body as a physical object also has dual characteristics of mass and energy. The physical body represents mass whereas thought, imagination and visualization represents a form of energy. As stated earlier, in Einstein's mass-energy equivalence theory, mass and energy are interchangeable, so the energy in the form of thought, imagination and visualization are interchangeable into mass and it gets converted into physical form or mass in future as the outcome of our present desire or dream.

Let's consider the opinions of ancient yogis and munis on the subject.

In the 1940's, Sri Paramahansa Yogananda in his book *Autobiography of a Yogi* wrote, 'On the epochal Theory of Relativity have arisen the mathematical possibilities of exploring the ultimate atom. Great scientists are now boldly asserting not only that the atom is energy rather than matter, but that atomic energy is essentially mind-stuff (see p. 267).'

In the 1970's, Swami Sivananda Radha, a German yogini and the founder of Yasodhara Ashram in Canada, wrote in her book *Kundalini Yoga for the West*:

'Mind is a miniature universe.
Universe is the expansion of the mind.' (p. 184)

The book further described, 'Mind and its many possible manifestations are an expression of that one power, Energy. The process of thinking is an energy process. How much energy is used to produce a thought? Where do we take it from? When thought is put into action, combined with emotion, we use the term 'energy expenditure', 'emotional investment' and so on, because we can measure our 'energy output' by our feeling of tiredness or exhaustion (p. 188).'

In the 1980's, Swami Satyananda Saraswati, the founder of the Bihar School of Yoga and author of over 80 books, wrote in his book *Kundalini Tantra*, 'It is also generally accepted by scientists that psychic energy, most widely known as bioenergy, is body-based and affects both the physical and mental spheres as indicated by yogis. It has also been measured as a force field surrounding the body up to a distance of twelve feet by Yale neuro-psychiatrist, Dr Leonard Ravitz. This seems to support the yogic concept of the subtle pranic body which interpenetrates and is interdependent with the physical structure, motivating it to function (p. 327).'

Swami ji continued, 'There is a considerable support for this hypothesis, gathered from the monitoring of the physiological changes experienced by psychics during laboratory tests of paranormal events. For instance, as part of his usual experimental procedure, Dr Grenady Sergeyev of the A. A. Utkomskii Physiological Institute (a Leningrad military laboratory), took readings of the brain waves, heartbeat and pulse rates of Neyla Mikhailova during her numerous demonstrations of psychokinesis. He found that while Mikhailova was causing objects to move without touching them, his instruments recorded a tremendous vibration throughout her body and its surrounding force field which pulsed in the direction of her gaze. Her heart and brain waves also pulsed in unison with this energy vibration, indicating that the energy Mikhailova used in her psychic feats is intimately connected with her whole body.'

Reports go on to state that: 'After doing these tests, Mrs Mikhailova was utterly exhausted. There was almost no pulse. She'd lost close to four pounds in half an hour…(p. 327).' The example of demonstration of psychokinesis (the moving of matter by mind power) by Mrs Mikhailova can be taken as a live example of mass-energy conversion.

The more surprising and miraculous examples of mass-energy conversion can be found in the book *Autobiography of a Yogi*, where author Sri Paramahansa Yogananda mentioned about a man named Swami Pranabananda, who used to appear in more than one body at different places at same time as witnessed by the author himself (see p. 24). He further mentioned, 'The power of appearing in more than one body is a siddhi (yogic power) mentioned in Patanjali's Yoga Sutras (see p. 227 n.). The phenomenon of bilocation has been exhibited in the lives of many saints down the ages.'

In the same book, he has also mentioned about another person named Lahiri Mahasaya, who had power to appear and disappear, i.e. the power to dematerialise and materialise himself at will (see p. 7). He further explained this miraculous power in terms of Einstein's theory of Mass Energy Equivalence:,'Masters who are able to materialise and dematerialise their bodies and other objects, and to move with velocity of light, and to utilize the creative light rays in bringing into instant visibility any physical manifestation, have fulfilled lawful condition: their mass is infinite (see p. 269).'

Sri Paramahansa Yogananda scientifically explained the above miraculous power. According to him, the perfect yogi is liberated from all delusions concerning matter and its gravitational weight and he sees the universe as an undifferentiated mass of light. He sees no difference between light rays composing water and the light rays composing land. Free from matter-consciousness, free from three dimensions of space and fourth dimension of time, a master transfers his body of light with equal ease over or through the light rays of earth, water, fire and air.

This explanation of Sri Paramahansa Yogananda can be better understood if we relate it with previously mentioned Davisson-Germer experiment where electron (a constituent of atom of which our body is made of) demonstrates dual characteristics of particle and wave and the wave quality gave the electron the characteristics of light. [*1]

---

1   *How the wave quality gave the electron the characteristics of light can be practically found in your old TV, which had a cathode ray tube. In a cathode ray tube, electron is fired at a phosphor surface (phosphor coated inner side of the TV Screen) with the help of big magnet and each electron makes a lighted pixel when it hits the back of the screen. It has means to accelerate and deflect the electron beams onto the screen to create the images. This fired electron beams makes the picture on the TV Screen consisting of millions of those lighted pixels.*

He (Sri Paramahansa Yogananda) wrote, 'The law of miracles is operable by any man who has realized that the essence of creation is light. A master is able to employ his divine knowledge of light phenomena to project instantly into perceptible manifestation, the ubiquitous light atoms. The actual form of projection (whatever it be: a tree, a medicine, a human body) is determined by the yogi's wish and his power of will and of **visualization.** ...... Innocent of all personal motives, and employing the creative will bestowed on him by the Creator, a yogi rearranges the light atoms of the universe to satisfy any sincere prayer of a devotee (see p. 270-271).' Thus, Sri Yogananda successfully explained the miraculous power of yogis to disappear and reappear i. e. to dematerialise and rematerialise their bodies as well as any other physical objects in one of the most scientific manner by relating it with Einstein's theory and the role of power of will and visualization in the process.

The miraculous power of yogis to make mass energy conversion by using the power of their mind or by simply making a wish or by using power of will or visualization is being practised for thousands of years although modern science has been negating it till recently. But recently, science has also taken it seriously and has started relevant research and experiments to delve deep, though with limited success. In the above examples, we see that the recent scientific research is supporting, supplementing and rationally justifying the age-old mental powers controlled by the yogis and the powers documented in old scriptures like *Patanjali's Yoga Sutras*, etc. Although, till today, modern science has only been able to prove the duality of the physical objects. It has successfully demonstrated the conversion of mass into energy by harnessing atomic energy in nuclear reactor or in the form of an atom bomb. It has yet to demonstrate practically reconversion of energy into mass, what the yogis have been doing by using their mind, wish, will, and visualization.

Similarly, there are many other miraculous powers hidden in depth of human mind which are yet to be demonstrated physically in the laboratory but they have been showing results in day-to-day life of those, who have been believing in it and using it successfully for thousands of years.

Thus, the mass-energy conversion is a very old concept and reconversion of energy (in the form of wish, desire, dream, visualization) into physical form (result or outcome or manifestation of dream, desire or visualization) does exist. It has also been explained above scientifically in context of human body as a physical quantity where mass (physical body) and energy (thought, imagination, visualization) could be converted into each other by the power of will and visualization. Thus, the principle of imagination and visualization holds ground and you must believe in its unlimited hidden potential to bring miracles in your life.

The Key to Realize Dream—Advanced Positive Visualization

In spite of having miraculous power, the process of imagination and visualization has its own shortcomings. Although every one of us is bestowed with this power, it is not limited to visualization of only the good, positive and constructive things in life, rather sometimes quite the contrary happens. Everyone in the world wants to be happy, peaceful, and successful and they desire to be so. But the screen of their mind is filled with incidents of sadness, pain, envy, conflict and fear of failure. So, the imagination and visualization of pain, envy and failure brings all despairs in their life.

Another unwanted effect of the power of imagination and visualization is the limitation set by people on themselves. Very often, after dreaming about a big goal to achieve, people lose confidence and start thinking and imagining that they have only limited capacity and so, bigger success are not made for them and since the principle of visualization, i. e. *visualization creates reality* works here also, people get constrained by their own limitations set by the power of visualization of their mind. This lack of faith and confidence, and resultantly, limitation set by them are crucial constraints on the way to their success.

If we can block the entry of this negative visualization about failure into our mind and if we can get rid of the limitation set by our own mind, then we can realise all our dreams and fulfill all our wishes.

Next question would be how to block the contrary image of pain, envy and failure from entering into our mind? How to get rid of limitations set by oneself on one's capacity, so as not to give up before trying?

The technique, I have tried successfully in my life to get rid of above hindrances and to get success, is called *Advanced Positive Visualization*. *Advanced* because it aims to give you a beautiful future, i.e. you visualize your desire getting fulfilled before it actually happens in the real world. Positive because it is necessary to visualise only about the positive aspect of life in order to materialise same in the future, i. e. good health, peace, prosperity, success, happiness, etc. and to avoid visualising the negative aspects of future, like, disease, pain, suffering, poverty, conflict, envy, failure, sorrow, etc. Visualization is simply creating an image, drawing or animation of desired future situation over the screen of mind.

Here, one important point which needs clarification is that Advanced Positive Visualization doesn't limit you to visualize positively only about your future and continue with the habit of cursing the present or recalling the bad moments of your past. Even if you focus on the negativity of on-going events of the present or recall the bad moments of your past, the screen of your mind gets occupied with the image or scene of negativity, which will appear as reality in your life in future. So you must refrain yourselves from all such activities because focusing on negativity of present and past also has immense potential to spoil your future. In fact, if you simply focus on positive visualization at all times, the purpose of Advanced Positive Visualization will be served because the main aim of *Advanced Positive Visualization* is to create a beautiful future by using the power of visualization.

Further, second important point, which needs clarification, is the extent of visualization. Upto what extent should you imagine and visualize having good health, peace, prosperity, etc. in life? The answer is –'to any extent'.

The next big question comes to mind: up to what extent should you look at only positive aspect of a person, place, thing, or job? Does it mean that even if a person is planning to murder you because of some enmity, should the matter be completely overlooked ? Well, that is not practical. Therefore, it is necessary to draw a line between practicability and idealism. The idea is to focus on the positive traits of others and avoid focusing on their negative traits to the extent that it is not causing harm to you or to society because a common man is not a veteran in using mind power to the extent that it can immediately check the ill-will of others.

Similarly, up to what extent should you avoid visualising the negative aspect of the future like disease, pain, suffering, poverty, conflict, envy, failure, sorrow, etc. ? For example, you have to pay a compulsorily visit to a place next week where dengue is an epidemic and you know that some people have died there due to this fatal disease. Is it possible that you can completely shut off your mind from evaluating the possibilities of you getting prone to dengue? Obviously, no. You must focus your mind on the signs, symptoms and source of infection in order to take necessary precautions. I don't mean that you completely shut off your mind from these negatives aspects of life and don't focus on it even for taking necessary precautions or for finding out solutions of problems caused due to these negativities in life.

You will find later in this book that I have anticipated many risks during my preparations for Everest climb and also during my actual climbing session and have taken many precautions to ensure safe and successful climb. For anticipating risks in mountaineering or any other activities in life and for taking necessary precautions, firstly, you need to visualize about those risks, so we can't close our minds away from such risks. Therefore, a short look at some negativity in life is required for a practical approach in order to take necessary precautions and ensure a smooth, safe, and happy life. But, it must not be prolonged or repeated frequently in mind in order to avoid its harmful effects in our lives and to avoid it becoming our habit.

Let's take same example of dengue spread. When you came to know that few people have already died due to dengue and you can't avoid your visit due to some compulsion, but you are scared. You start visualizing a scene where just after arriving the place, you are also infected, and consequently, hospitalized. You think your condition is deteriorating and you die. And your family is crying and blaming God for taking your life untimely. The same thought reiterates in your mind over and over again. Finally, your visualization becomes so strong that either you really cancel your visit, which might be a loss to you in some way, or you really get dengue soon after visiting the place because after all, visualization becomes reality. Such negativity must be avoided to thrive in a better way.

In fact, Advanced Positive Visualization says that the screen of our mind should always be filled with all the positivities of life, so that it would get materialised later and would make our life better. At the same time, it aims to avoid all such negativities from staying on the screen of our mind in order to ensure that it must not overcome positivities and to make sure that subconscious mind doesn't grasp the negativity and execute it to materialise in our life in future. We can argue that as long as positivity in our mind overcome negativity, we can pay attention to negativity with an objective to solve some problems in life; but just because, we are not equipped to measure with accuracy the extent of positive and negative visualization, so we must refrain ourselves from focusing on negativity to the maximum extent possible, specially the self created visualization about negativity as shown in dengue case, in order to ensure that subconscious mind doesn't catch it and materialise it in our life.

Advanced Positive Visualization has two different dimensions:

i. Advanced Positive Visualization during normal hours of day-to-day life, is practiced along with consistent positive physical effort to convince the conscious mind to pass down the image to sub-conscious mind.

ii. Advanced Positive Visualization in meditative state, is practised to bypass the filtration by conscious mind and send the image directly to sub-conscious mind.

While practising this technique in its any of the two dimensions, it is necessary to have deep faith and strong confidence within yourself that your mind have unlimited potential to make any task possible and, that you fully deserve the success you need .

But I believe, if you are successful in keeping your mind occupied with only positive visualization, then you don't need to worry about these two constraints. These will be taken care of automatically because positive visualization will ensure that your mind is safeguarded from the images of all negative things like failure, pain, frustration etc., and thus, neither will there be the fear of failure nor will you be drained of your degree of confidence to achieve the goal. People lose confidence when they are scared of failure, saying that they don't have adequate capability to achieve certain big goal.

But next question would be how to keep your mind occupied with positive visualization only and keep it free from negative ones? In fact, there is no technique to fight negative visualization. Because while you fight it, it would occupy your mind. The technique is, don't fight the evil inside you, ignore it and replace it with virtue.

As in this case, there is not any fight with any external force, you would be fighting with something in your mind, and so it will show its presence there. Hence, avoid negative visualizations but don't resist it. Don't focus on it. Don't recall it, as if it never existed in your life. Focus only on positive visualization and it would come in your life. But you may argue that in the real world, life is seldom hassle-free and so, you may have some problems going on while practicing this technique. At the same time, I am sure that you must have had many good moments in the past too. Then why should we look for problems and not reminisce the good memories? If the mind is full of virtue, there is no place for vice.

Let's take a simple example. One day, your employer, or your father, or your teacher (any authority) appreciates your good work, and the next day, he condescends you. The general human tendency is to generate consequently a degree of resentment against that person. Though your focus should ideally be on sharing better terms with him, but on the contrary, your focus will be more on negativity (act of condescension) than positivity (act of appreciation). And more you focus on such negative incidents and create its image on the screen of your mind, more you bring it in your life.

In this situation, Advanced Positive Visualization technique suggests you to recall and visualize the moments when he had appreciated your efforts and had supported you. Think over the fact that you got a chance to learn one more lesson by enquiring about the reason why did he reprimand you and improve it. The main idea is to replace the negative thoughts with good events in the past.

The next question arises, how does your visualization materialise into reality? How does it happen inside your mind? What process of transformation does it go through? To get a clear idea on these, let's have some important information on the concept of the different levels of human mind.

Conscious, Subconscious and Unconscious Mind

You might have observed that you can safely reach home as you speak over the phone completely engrossed, unaware of your surroundings. This means you are imagining about one thing and doing something completely different. This lack of alignment between imagination and action happens because the human mind doesn't work at a single level but in three different levels. These three levels of mind are the conscious, the subconscious, and the unconscious. The conscious mind is your active mind that you are aware of at the present moment; the subconscious and unconscious are below the surface of awareness.

Conscious mind is what you experience in your active life. It is your awareness about events, objects, thoughts, emotions, sensations, surroundings etc. at any particular point of time.

It includes what you are imagining and visualizing about at the present moment.

The subconscious means under or below your awareness. Subconscious describes something that is just below the surface of your awareness i. e. you are not aware of it but you can become aware of the information once you direct your attention to it and it can be recalled easily as memory. Subconscious mind is the storage point for any recent memories needed for quick recall. It also holds current information that you use everyday.

The unconscious means not conscious; lacking awareness. You are not aware of information as if you are asleep or dead. The unconscious mind contains images, memories and desires that are buried deep in mind, well below your conscious awareness and a level deeper in mind under the subconscious. Unconscious mind contains those memories and past experiences that you have simply forgotten consciously. It is possible that some of these forgotten memories may become part of the subconscious, and then, conscious. Example, a long forgotten memory of school time suddenly emerges after decades.

The conscious mind has the unique ability to focus and the ability to imagine and visualise things that are not real. It will perceive an event and store it either in the subconscious or the unconscious mind depending on the importance of the event, where it remains available to us. The subconscious mind doesn't act independently. It merely obeys the commands it receives from your conscious mind. Subconscious mind is like fertile soil and conscious mind like a farmer. Whatever farmer sow in the fertile soil, it germinates and grows; similarly whatever conscious mind commands, subconscious mind obeys. It grows either crops or weeds in the fertile soil of your life whichever you sow by mental equivalents you create using your conscious mind. Here, it is equally important to grow only crops and avoid weeds in the fertile soil i. e. to have only positive or productive things or events in your life and to avoid negative things or events; which is possible only by avoiding negative images in the conscious mind.

The subconscious mind follows the principle of gravity. The law of gravity is applicable to everything that has mass: an apple (life sustaining or constructive item), or an atom bomb (life taking or destructive item), both fall towards the earth, irrespective of whether they are constructive or destructive, whether you want them or not. Similarly, the principle of the subconscious mind applies to all types of images or visualizations. It doesn't differentiate between the positive or healthy images and negative or destructive images. Whatever image you create in your conscious mind, it passes down to the subconscious mind and the subconscious executes the images so they materialise, whether negative or positive.

An article published in 2003 by Harvard Medical School clearly proved that human brain is unable to make out the difference between something real and something imaginary. Neuroscientists at Harvard assembled a group of volunteers for a piano experiment. One group was told to play the piano actually, which is a simple five-fingered combination of piano notes, thumb, index finger, middle finger, ring finger, and the little finger. They played the notes repeatedly for two hours a day and continued the practice for five consecutive days. Another group of volunteers was told not to play the piano actually, but just to imagine playing it in their mind. So they only pictured playing it in their mind with the combination of the same fingers. But they actually held their fingers still without any actual movement. They had also practiced playing the piano, though in their mind, for two hours a day for five consecutive days.

At the end of each day's practice session, the neuroscientists carried out the examination of the brains of the volunteers by TMS (Transcranial Magnetic Stimulation) technique. The TMS data revealed that there was almost equal expansion in the region of motor cortex of brains that controls the movement of the fingers. There was little or no difference between the brains of those who played the notes with their fingers and those who simply imagined playing it. The brain areas in both groups grew significantly in size.

It happened so because the subconscious mind can't differentiate between real and imaginary. It can't identify what picture corresponds to real object in the world and what picture corresponds to a virtual one and is merely imagined. So, both the groups responded in the same way. Any repeated picture of the conscious mind is taken as real one by the subconscious, although it may be picture of merely a virtual object created by your conscious mind. Therefore, there is no limit to the capacity of the subconscious mind. It has unlimited power to make all the impossible things possible. The experiment applies to any other event in life dealing with imagination and visualization.

Subconscious mind also contains all your habits, behaviour, beliefs and attitude towards life. Whatever you learned in your lifetime exist at this level but it is from your long memories and experiences stored in unconscious mind that your beliefs, habits, behaviours and attitudes are formed. Thus, the subconscious and unconscious are directly interlinked and deal with similar things. But the unconscious is like the underground library of all your memories, habits and behaviour. Further, the unconscious mind holds the control of the basic functions of your body— breathing, heartbeat, digestion, reflexes, etc. It controls all automatic reflexive functions. But your conscious mind can influence some of these functions. So, keep a watch over the conscious mind and track its pattern of visualization as it is of utmost importance.

The conscious mind acts as a gate for filtering images that comes to your subconscious mind. Actually the conscious mind is aligned with what is already formed as attitude or belief in your subconscious mind. If the new image is in conflict with the image stored in the subconscious mind, the conscious mind tends to block that image from passing into the subconscious. This is why people resist change because they are uncomfortable to attempt anything new or different from what the subconscious is habituated to. But only the zealous and ambitious ones try to go beyond this limit. They know that complacency is great enemy of creativity and future possibilities. They go ahead with the uncomfortable feeling and try hard until it becomes a new set of pattern altogether.

Let us look at one example. You cannot swim and your brain has always registered you to be a non-swimmer. So, whenever you have yearned to swim, your thought process has always restricted you from the prior knowledge of your non-swimming past. But as you stretch yourself and try to learn letting go off the discomfort, you feel more close to developing a new hobby. In this case, you are actually practising and physically working hard to get convinced in your conscious mind and, simultaneously, passing the image to the subconscious mind.

There are techniques to bypass the filtration of your conscious mind and enter the image directly to your subconscious. For example, a suggestive image repeatedly viewed in the subconscious mind in meditative state or a sudden event with strong impact to your belief which gets stored in subconscious mind can alter the currently stored belief in the subconscious mind to a new one.

How can a sudden event change the belief in the subconscious to a new one bypassing the filtration of your conscious mind? It is well illustrated in an example given by Swami Yogananda in his book *Scientific Healing Affirmations*, where he wrote, 'A case is recorded of an emotional person who had lost his power of speech, and received it back when running out of a burning house. The sudden shock produced by the sight of fire stimulated his feeling so much that he shouted out "Fire! Fire!", not remembering that hitherto he had been unable to speak. A strong emotion overcomes the power of the subconscious mental disease habit.'

Similarly, a repeated suggestive image may be entered directly to your subconscious in a meditative state, when the conscious mind is relaxed and not active enough to take up the filtration process, during meditation or *pranayama* just before sleeping or just after you wake up, which can then lead to new belief or gradual alteration of current beliefs.

The unique process of educating Swami Niranjanananda Saraswati by Swami Satyananda Saraswati, the founder of the

Bihar School of Yoga, is one wonderful example of tapping the energy of the subconscious in its meditative state. Niranjanananda was born in Chhattisgarh in 1960 and started living with Swami Satyananda at the tender age of four at the Bihar School of Yoga, Munger, Bihar. He used to sleep in Swami Satyananda's room and Swami Satyananda taught him Yoga and Spirituality, science, scriptures and other subjects through an ancient system of *Yoga Nidra*. Thus, he gained knowledge when he was in a deep meditative state and was enriched with such deep knowledge of the universe and its power and proceedings.

The same potential of the subconscious can be tapped by anyone but the method is delicate and needs rigorous practice. But as you gain experience and do it effectively, you are saved from the physical exertions, which are required to get convinced in your conscious mind to pass the image of the object of your dream down to the subconscious, which would subsequently start working to actualize it in the physical world and thus, one day your dream comes true.

The best way to ascertain the desired result is the combination of both methods. You work hard physically to gain confidence and to convince your conscious mind to pass your desires to the subconscious without any distortion or doubt or dilemma. In addition to this, try to concentrate your conscious mind to focus only on success or positivity and not on failure or negativity during casual imagination processes, thus not leaving any room for doubt. At the same time, you start practising Advanced Positive Visualization in meditation to directly communicate with the subconscious bypassing filtration by the conscious. Both will fasten the process and you will actualize your dream in short time.

The primary role of the conscious mind is to make sure that only the best visions come to your mind, so that the subconscious will eventually manifest it in your life. So you should become diligent in monitoring and directing your mind and its working process. So it's time for you to decide to focus only on the positive images of life. Your focus on positivity, health, and peace contributes to a larger cause, positivity in the society and further, in the world. Because the reason behind happiness, sorrow, success, failure, wealth, poverty, friendship, enmity in the society and the country depends mainly on the way people imagine of a future with themselves.

Although, as mentioned earlier, the mind has been described as an expression of energy and various schools of thought have given their own descriptions regarding its forms, dimensions and manifestations. But, for all understanding and practical purpose as to how three levels of mind work, you can visualize the mind as an underground chamber. The entrance of chamber, which is located at the top is the conscious mind, where the active conscious mind acts as a guard filtering all the images, visuals, etc. entering inside. As we enter inside the underground house by moving few steps down, we enter into the space of the subconscious, where recent memories, habit, behaviour, belief and attitude are stored. As we take further steps down, we enter the vast space of the unconscious mind, where all our old and forgotten memories, images, desires, etc. are stored and it also acts as the underground library for all habits, behaviour, etc. Thus, the conscious mind acts as a filter gate for any information entering or leaving the underground chamber, i. e. between the sub-layers of mind and the outer world.

Practical Steps to Realize Dreams

Now I will take you through the practical steps to realize your dreams, so you can make possible tomorrow what until today, seemed impossible. Take a note of the following steps and you may notice some changes in your life.

1. Set specific targets on your dreams. Have faith and confidence that you can achieve. Remember that your faith plays a major role in materialising your dream to your real life. David J. Schwartz, the author of *The Magic of Thinking Big* wrote, 'Believe it can be done. When you believe something can be done, really believe, your mind will find the ways to do it. Believing a solution paves the way to solution.'

For example, if you are unemployed and want to get a job then set specific target to become a doctor with an MBBS Degree or an engineer with B. Tech degree, etc. If you are not big on money and you want to become rich then set specific target to earn a million per annum or to own a house, or a car, etc.

Once you have set your specific target, evaluate your present status with respect to the requirements for achieving the target. If you have any doubts about your capability, then read the functioning of subconscious mind given earlier and try to focus on any of your past achievements, thus avoiding doubt in the process.

2. Start working towards achieving the target with a positive attitude and complete faith that you will achieve it and make a sincere effort towards it. By *sincere effort* I mean it should be genuine, from deep within your heart. It should not be just to convince yourself or to demonstrate to others that you are making an effort. As you do this, visualize that you are moving towards the target. For example, start preparing for your medical entrance examination; make sincere efforts with complete faith that you will clear the examination with a good rank.

3. As you make sincere efforts and make progress towards the target, make positivity a major part of your everyday visualizations and don't have a single negative visualization about failure in your mind. Sometimes, in spite of hard work, you may get disheartened that you can't win because there are so many contenders and they are relatively stronger contenders than you. So, you might lose heart but don't break by getting intimidated. This doesn't work. When you visualize about a future scenario, where you visualize yourself as failed, you invite failure into your life, and then you blame your fate and bad luck. The only factor responsible for your failure is the way you imagine and visualize.

4. After making sincere effort during the day, before going to sleep at night, lie down comfortably in your bed. Then one by one relax all the muscles of your body from toe to head. After relaxing all your muscles, clear your mind of all thoughts. Try to feel like you are in a vacuum where you have no feelings or body pain. Stay in this state for some time and then try to project your consciousness outside your body and observe your body from there as if you are someone else watching your body from there. This is meditative state. Neither you are awake nor are you sleeping. Neither your conscious mind is active nor it is inactive. It has just gone dormant by shedding itself of all actions, imaginations, visualizations and thoughts. A stage just before sleep takes over you. During sleep, your conscious mind becomes inactive and other two levels of mind take over depending on stage and depth of sleep. During initial days of practice, sleep tends to take over you as you try to enter into this state but please try not to sleep in this state. As you practice, you would move towards perfection.

     In this meditative state, you are away from the distractions of the world because your conscious mind is in dormant state and you are in position to communicate directly with the subconscious mind. You may call it your subconscious mind or even God (depending on your faith), who resides deep inside you; it has immense power to make all your wishes come true if you communicate them properly with complete faith, honesty and devotion. First confess to yourself that you are making sincere effort and so deserve success and have full faith that God inside you will definitely grant you success very soon.

     To connect with the subconscious mind or God inside you, simply visualize an image or an animation about the future scenario as if your success is guaranteed. Do it in the same manner like you are in a dream. Please note that this visualization in meditative state is different than your visualization when you are active. Visualization in active state is done purely by the conscious mind on its screen but in meditative state, conscious mind is dormant and you are trying to send image, drawing or animation directly to the subconscious bypassing the filtration by the conscious mind.

As you repeat this every night, you will feel you are getting closer to success and after a few nights, you visualize your future by imagining about any scene, in which you are enjoying the fruits of success after your desire or dream has been fulfilled. You continue with this visualization during your meditative state very night, when you live a new life with the fruit of your dream in your hand. Feel as if your dream has already been accomplished and it has become a matter of past, so you are planning to have a new dream.

It is a proven fact that your imagined desires in this deep meditative state can become a reality one day if the method has been practised with full faith, confidence and devotion.

As mentioned earlier, the power of the subconscious can be tapped just before sleep and just after waking up. So you can practice this method accordingly and it will strengthen your chances of success.

During your meditative state, you can visualise your dreams and what you wish to accomplish. In above example of preparation for medical entrance examination, you can visualize that you have cleared the medical entrance examination and have become a good doctor after completing the college course. You can imagine owning a big hospital where you are providing effective treatment to the public at a lesser cost, where people are happy being treated and you are satisfied that you have become a successful doctor. Imagine this as if it is real and you are a famous doctor. For your convenience and for frequent reference, we will call the above process of imagining about your future in the meditative state as the direct suggestion to the subconscious by Advanced Positive Visualization technique in the meditative state.

5. It is possible that one night you visualise that you have already achieved success and the next day, you encounter a

big obstacle and lose hope of getting a positive result, and you give up everything. Remember to have patience and faith and continue with your efforts and positive visualization. Do not get discouraged by small problems along the way. Whenever you encounter such problems, believe that it is normal to face a few problems along the way and it will pass in some time. What is the taste of success without problems?

The crux of the matter is that you need to imbibe deeply the fact that you have no room for visualization about failure, frustration, or pain in your life and that only the visualization about your success, happiness, and health will prevail over your mind. And in no circumstance, shall you give up. Thomas Alva Edison has rightly said,'Many of life's failures are people who didn't realize how close they were to success when they gave up.' The time taken to realise your dream also depends on the way you believe, imagine and visualise. When you believe that the target is very big and you imagine that you will achieve success after a long time then it will actually take a long time. However, if you consider the same target to be small and that you could achieve it soon, then you will really achieve it relatively in shorter time.

6. Try to enjoy whatever task you have taken up.

If you do not like the work that you have taken up, it won't earn you good results. Confucius rightly said, 'Choose a job you love and you will never have to work a day in your life.' If you have a job, quite boring and tedious, try to find positivity in it and feel happy doing it. You will find out later in the book how I turned the tiring job of jogging early in the morning into a pleasurable experience.

If you follow the above steps, you will find many miracles taking place in your life. This is the technique I used to achieve success, something I have been using since my childhood as a matter of habit. Since my childhood, I was extremely imaginative. I would dream, and fantasize, and visualise. After being aware about miraculous power of visualization, I could understand its dynamics in a better way. I have the utmost faith in this hidden, unlimited reserve of power. It has helped me achieve immense success within a short span of my life.

As you read this book, you will start discovering how Advanced Positive Visualization and its overwhelming power has helped me in winning over many problems and obstructions in life and that it has brought me big success in spite of bigger difficulties in life. In this way, you can understand the dynamics of Advanced Positive Visualization in a better way and can execute it in your life easily.

With these words, I wish you all the best in life. May you always swim in the oceans of perfect health, wealth, happiness, peace and prosperity.

1

Childhood Dreams

'Man's only limitation, within reason, lies in his development and the use of his imagination. He has not yet reached the apex of development in the use of his imaginative faculty. He has merely discovered that he has an imagination, and has commenced to use it in a very elementary way.'
— *Napoleon Hill,* Think and Grow Rich

The world below the surface of the ocean is completely different from the one above it, away from earthly affairs. It is totally peaceful, miles away from the disturbance of the outside world. There is a great silence all around and no movement at all; even sea creatures cannot be seen for a long time. The only movement is the displacement of the water due to the slow movement of an airtight chamber deep into the ocean, above which are kilometres of water. Peace and tranquillity prevails all around. It is so calm and beautiful but this place has been beyond human reach until now when I am going to be the first human to reach it; the deepest point of the earth, 10. 9 kilometres below the sea.

Suddenly I was waken up by a call from my cousin. It was the summer vacation time and they were calling me to play hide and seek with them. All the kids were free from the burden of homework and so, apart from sleeping and eating, we spent most of our time playing.

When I woke up I felt like I was still dreaming; but I remembered that I was lying stomach down on my bed (a comfortable position for reading books), while I had been reading an interesting book on the journey to the Mariana Trench. Guddu *bhaiya*, my cousin, who was two grades senior to me, had given it to me. He was the one who had just called me but I was so fascinated with all the reading and the Mariana Trench itself that I didn't feel like going. I continued descending into the trench till I reached the deepest point on the Earth. It was ironic how I fancied myself plunging deep into the Mariana, even figuratively so while reading the book, whereas in fact, I had never seen the sea. All I could do, was read about it, and imagine.

Several years have passed since I read that book and I still remember this incident very well, almost like a movie. It was early 1990 when I was studying in the fourth grade and living at my maternal grandmother's home. While reading the book, I loved imagining that *I* was the first person to reach the trench, although two people have already done so in 1960. According to the book, they had been a part of the first manned expedition to the Mariana Trench that year. In my dream, I was the one playing their part and this made me ecstatic. And, thereafter, I longed to visit the sea.

My wish to visit the sea grew over the years and it took almost nine years for me to get my chance. This was when I went to Mumbai to get admission in T. S. Chanakya, a training institute for shipping, which prepares candidates for a life at sea and where one can enjoy looking out at the sea every single day.

During the days I spent at my maternal grandmother's home, I loved reading Indian comic books and would imagine scenarios where I was a superhero like Naagraj, Super Commando Dhruv, etc. I never missed the television show *Param Vir Chakra* on Doordarshan and while watching, I never imagined myself to be less than the brave gallantry, the protagonist. But unfortunately, in reality, I was a lean boy with a thin, shrill voice who had always been physically frail during childhood.

I was born and brought up in a farming family. My father was a farmer and my mother, a homemaker. I was a silent witness to the problems the farming community faced in Bihar where the price of grains would fall drastically after the harvest, as farmers did not have much contact with the government procurement facilities. The middleman was the only buyer, so he used to buy the entire harvested crop at the lowest price. In contrast to this, the price of inputs used to rise during the sowing season. I still remember how my father used to buy the fertilizer from a private shop at a higher price because the subsidized fertilizers were rarely available on time. I have seen the resultant impact of all this on my family's financial condition. I suffered from frequent dysentery and a continually-running nose but my father could never afford to take me to a good doctor given to our finances.

The first five years of my life were spent in my father's home. Then I was sent to my maternal grandmother's house for my studies, where I started my formal education at school. Both the villages are located at a distance of eight kilometres along the state highway connecting the district headquarter of my district Begusarai to the district headquarter of the adjacent district Samastipur. So the connectivity with outside was good at that time, but my maternal grandmother's village was economically and educationally much better than my father's village. The economic and educational status of maternal grandmother's family was also far better than my father's family. In spite of these, my physical weakness and frequent fevers were still a regular phenomenon even after moving there. I still remember my hatred for the quack, whom my great grandmother used to call whenever I fell sick. I recall his rough hands, how he used to pierce my buttock with his syringe and how I would writhe in severe pain.

I was the only child in my grandmother's house. The family consisted of my maternal grandmother and maternal grandfather; the later's parents, my mother's youngest sister and one servant. Although the family was big and my mother had three other sisters and two brothers, everybody except the youngest sister, had settled down in their own homes either after getting married or had a job. Everybody loved me and there was no scarcity of healthy food, but I was still scrawny and weak; this was mainly due to my meagre diet and the fact that my family was purely vegetarian. I also used to hate milk until I started understanding about nutrition and began to drink it later in my life. But everybody loved me because I was good at studies and always ranked first in class.

I continued to live there till I was in the fifth grade. There was a Hindi medium school in the village, about a one and a half kilometres walk away, which I used to go to along with all the other neighbourhood children. I wished I could study in an English medium school in the town of Begusarai, like my cousin. I expressed my wish to my father during a visit to home. He made it clear in a sentence that he could not afford such an expensive education. Such a straightforward answer at that age was disheartening to me. So were the many such instances where I used to see my other cousins at my grandmother's place wearing new clothes on several occasions but I didn't.

But I remember correctly that, it mostly motivated me to work hard to maintain my first rank in class and get a good job at the earliest. I enjoyed whatever I wished to do after that. In fact, I used to be happy just thinking that God had gifted me a good brain to use it to bring my family out of poverty and get all the credit for doing so. I felt happy thinking that I was comparatively at an advantageous position with respect to my cousins born in comparatively well-off families because even if I manage to get any job, which earned me more than the agricultural income of my father, I would be counted as a successful child. To get the same credit, my cousins would have to ensure a better job than their parents. It is said, 'If the son of a rickshaw-puller becomes a school-teacher, he would be called successful. The son of a school-teacher needs to get a higher-paying job to get the same credit, may be a college professor, and so on'.

As a child, I would feel pretty privileged that way, irrespective of the economic status of my family. Now, I can very well understand the importance and impact of that positive attitude, which taught me to count blessings in life and work for a better future rather than cribbing and weeping over things I lacked and had no control over at the past. I thank God for such a blessing, of a positive attitude throughout, which really kept me away from focusing on weakness and negativity in life and helped me in succeeding at my endeavours at such age.

In fact, the dream to study in an English medium school in town grew stronger in me and I kept visualizing and dreaming about myself staying and studying in my dream school in Begusarai like my cousin. Luckily, my dream came true when I was selected through the Navodaya Vidyalaya entrance examination. I moved to the town to study further in 1992 when I was in the sixth grade.

On shifting to Navodaya Vidyalaya, my fitness improved slightly due to regular physical training in the morning, but my overall health remained poor. On the other hand, I continued performing well in academics and mostly maintained my position as the topper of the class until my tenth grade when I shifted to Ranchi for further studies. Other than academics, I was fond of participating in speech competitions, poetry writing and skits, but not in physical activities. During my five years stay in the Navodaya Vidyalaya hostel, I had no interest in games or anything, which required physical exertion though there were facilities for almost all kinds of games and sports. I preferred to study. I never felt the need to prioritise physical activities because there was no appreciation if you excelled at games but there was tremendous appreciation if you excelled at studies. I remember how my mother's elder brother, my *Mamaji*, the only Deputy Superintendent of Police in the whole area (or DSP *Sahib* as people used to call him) used to praise my academic performance but never cautioned me to take care of my health by participating in sports.

The first time I felt that having a strong body was important was when I had a row with a classmate, Sanjay Baranwal when I was in the seventh grade. When he punched me with his closed fist, I fainted. I didn't react to this incident immediately and continued with my studies as usual. When I was in eighth grade in the next year, one of our seniors started teaching karate to a few interested juniors; I didn't miss out on this opportunity to learn. Although this only went on for three months, I did learn some basic techniques.

I was still skinny because I focused more on studying and securing a job, which were more important to me than becoming physically stronger. The social climate emphasized education more than games and sports. I observed in the surroundings of

Navodaya Vidyalaya that those who were good at their studies got good jobs and led a better life compared to those who had stronger bodies but were academically weak. This further strengthened my belief about giving my best to my studies and I made, getting a job, a priority.

Physically weak but good in academics during school days- Getting awarded by DM Begusarai (1994).

During the long summer and winter holidays from Navodaya Vidyalaya, I would come home in my native paternal village. By that time, I was grown enough to look around the village and compare it with outside world. Holidays gave me sufficient time to know the society, or know about the place where I was born and brought up and where my ancestors lived for last many generations. The village comprised of the few thousands population divided into different castes. People of the same caste generally lived together in the same locality with only a few exceptions. People of certain lower castes didn't dare to sit on the furniture at the house of people from higher castes but sat on the ground in those years. Most of the villagers did either farming and associated activities in the village, or worked outside in other states mostly Punjab, Haryana and Delhi. They worked outside mostly as labourers in factories or in agricultural fields, or as rickshaw pullers, vendors, factory workers, etc. Some of them had small shops in the village which catered to daily needs of the villagers. Very few in the village were in a government job which was also limited to the job of a school teacher or postmaster or a few group D posts in the government services.

Change in health over the years.

Most of the youngsters continued with their ancestral jobs with no further hopes or dreams of a better future. They mostly started working at a minor age to support the family's income leaving aside the school education. Even few of my cousins and later, some nephews went outside in their minor age and worked as rickshaw pullers and tea vendors to suffice the poor income from farming in the village. During my stay at home in holidays, I often heard one of my uncle, whose son worked outside as a labourer, saying, 'Agar bachche ko abhi school bhejenge, to bad me unko na to naukri mil payegi, na hi wo khet me mihnat kar payenge. Isliye achchha hai ki abhi se hi kaam karna aur paise kamana suru kar de, jis se mihnat ki adat bhi bani rahe aur ghar me kuchh paisa bhi aata rahe (If we send our children to school now, then later, neither they would get a job nor would they be able to perform physical work in the field. So it's better that they start working and earning something from now so that they would get in the habit of hard work and at the same time, the family would keep getting some financial support.).'

Such a pitiable condition prevailed in my father's village. But in spite of living in such environment of hopelessness and despair, neither I nor my father, lost hope anytime. Despite such poor economic condition of the family, he always supported my education and I continued working hard and kept my good grades up. Without being much influenced by the hopelessness of the surroundings, I continued dreaming high and living under continuous shade of fantasies. I never bothered whether I would get any of the objects of my fantasy later in my life and continued it as I enjoyed doing it.

Out of two long vacations I spent in the village every year, summer vacation was comparatively more memorable in comparison to winter vacation, mostly because summers were mango season. My father had a small mango orchard where I used to spend most of the afternoon looking after the orchard as well as enjoying fresh ripened mangoes of different varieties from trees. It was also a source of making some pocket money by selling basket full of tasty mangoes at the Sunday haat bazaar, which was organised once a week in my village to cater to the villagers' domestic needs as well as to provide a platform to sell extra produce of farmers, especially vegetables and fruits. Whenever my elder cousin would visit his mango orchard, which was just adjacent to mine, he would often tease me,'Abhi khub aam khaate jao. Jab barsat ayayega to barish me khada ho jana aur sarir me jo aam gaya hai, wo phul jayega aur tum duble se mote ho jaoge (Keep eating lots of mangoes now. When monsoon comes you should then stand in the rain and all the mangoes in your body will swell and you will turn plump from your present skinny body.).' And I actually used to believe him.

Although I never saw such miracles of change but I kept my desire of having a strong body burning. Now I think of the time when I gained a body weight of 85 kgs while preparing for civil services examination in New Delhi, I really looked like the son of a pot bellied wealthy man. People in rural areas of Bihar, where modern health consciousness of having a slim body was yet to be inculcated, believed that the fat in your body and the size of your belly is directly related to the prosperity of your family, as it ensures a nutrition-rich diet for the family members, where many people especially children were prone to malnutrition owing to the dearth of proper food.

The better memory of my holiday at home was watching my father going to the field every day and if he couldn't go for some reason, he would tell me,'Today I don't have the right to eat as I haven't worked.' His words made a great impact on my life and became a continuous source of motivation for me to work hard every day. This powerful statement is one of the most important sources of inspiration for all the success I have achieved and will continue being the most significant guiding principle for the rest of my life.

This spell of enjoying a long leave at home and staying close to my father soon came to an end. In 1997, when I secured a good score of 89% in tenth grade CBSE Board exams, I left Navodaya Vidyalaya and joined D. A. V. Jawahar Vidya Mandir in Ranchi for my eleventh and twelfth grades. I never got a chance to stay at home for more than a few days at a stretch and only twice or thrice a year after that. But my new school was a very popular one in the whole region and expensive too with respect to my father's income. So, I faced some of the toughest times of my life in those two years. It was a sudden transition from Navodaya Vidyalaya, where all my expenses were paid by the government, to my shift to Ranchi, where the entire burden fell on my father's pocket. Somehow I could secure admission in the school by paying seven thousand rupees, which could be managed on time by selling my mother's jewellery, which was gifted to her by her parents at the time of her marriage.

But later, it proved very tough for my father to manage my monthly expenditure of four hundred rupees for school fees; two hundred rupees for room rent and two hundred for IIT coaching plus some other miscellaneous expenses. I would normally receive the money late from home, and sometimes, I had to go home and wait for a few days while my father borrowed money from somebody. I still remember some of those days vividly, when I saw my father returning empty handed with his face dripping in sweat due to wandering for hours on his old bicycle in the scorching sun from door to door of few economically well-off people in the adjacent villages in his multiple attempts to arrange money while I eagerly waited at home to push off for Ranchi once the money would come in my hand. But, even in those difficult times, I would never think that my days were going to remain the same in the future. Quite frequently, while visualizing in my effort to understand the complex theories of physics given in the IIT preparation guide, my mind would often jump to my own imaginary world, where I would foresee myself as a wealthy man counting lakhs of rupees and would feel happy. Now, I can understand well that the precious time lost in positive visualization of being a wealthy man in those days of scarcities, were not really lost in vain but they paid a positive role in making me strive for what I believed in.

The new school gave me some more long lasting memories. During my initial few days in the school, the computer science teacher enquired whether any student had not seen a computer in his life, in her introductory class. Out of about fifty students present in the class, two, Anupam and I stood up confidently and confessed the truth. Obviously, both of us had to face the strange look by many other students in the class and we both were taken to computer lab and were shown how a computer looked like. From then, we both ensured that we scored well in all the computer exams and passed gracefully. Not only this, we both cleared the IIT entrance examination in our first attempt. And a few years later, while I loaded and discharged thousands of tons of dangerous cargo on ships including chemicals like sulphuric acid by pushing buttons on a very computer, my friend graduated in Computer Science from IIT Kanpur and joined Microsoft, the king of the cyber world. It is always better late than never. The important lesson in life is not to feel awkward in facing the truth even if it looks ugly for the time being, and work to meet up the shortcomings with strong confidence rather than giving the excuse to continue performing poor in life. In fact, it all depends, where you focus your mind, on your weakness and continue remaining weak or on your strength and grow stronger. Whatever you focus your mind on and visualize on the screen of your mind, you are destined to pull and bring those things in your life.

Anyway, overall impact of hard times in Ranchi was that I grew weaker than before and looked skinnier. In the first year of my stay there, I had to manage everything, from food to accommodation to my studies. There were no free meals or accommodation or education like in the Navodaya Hostel. However, in the second year, my health improved a little due to my friendship with a few locals who were pretty health conscious. But the repercussions of this were clear; I did not get a good rank in the IIT JEE entrance exam. Nor did I secure the expected marks in the twelfth board examination although I could secure a place in the selected list of candidates for the IIT JEE and got a 75 percent in the twelfth board exam.

A poor rank in the IIT JEE entrance exam could not ensure me a good stream in the IITs like I had expected and so, at last, I chose to join T S Chanakya. It is a nautical science college in Mumbai, a premier institute run by the Government of India to train seafarers. At that time, admission to this college could be gained through the IIT entrance exam.

Thus one part of my journey had come to an end; from a modest background in a village Hindi medium school to clearing the IIT entrance examination in one go, I had been able to scale educational heights in a span of twelve years. Then, I moved from Ranchi to Mumbai to be trained at T. S. Chanakya to enter the world of shipping.

A new door was opening for me which would set me through the path of another journey. I improved my health by regularly visiting the gym, learning how to swim and earning a black belt in karate in a span of three years. People began to call me a bodybuilder as I had built up my body at the gym via many physical activities during my three years at T. S. Chanakya.

Excelled in sports later - with my Sports Team during TSC training days (2001).

2

While in Shipping

Getting admission to T. S. Chanakya was the start of a new phase of my life— the shipping life. This would make me witness the sea, something I had been wishing to see ever since my childhood when I had read the book about the Mariana Trench. I believe that somehow the long cherished wish to visit the sea and my long attraction to it had brought me to this life. Other than regular academic training about different aspects of shipping, T. S. Chanakya opened the door to physical fitness for me. This was because working on a ship involves both mental and physical activities.

Gained strength - with my Karate Team during TSC training days (2001).

I trained here from 1999 to 2002, the best time when my health improved. During these three years, I earned a black belt in Ito Syu Ryu karate, won many prizes in swimming and led the winning tug of war team, which was the ultimate platform to display your physical strength. I also won a few prizes in athletics. In fact, I was considered a bodybuilder at the academy and was awarded Mr Chanakya title although this was based more on the quiz session than physical appearance. It was a great transformation. I feel that if you really want to achieve something, somehow God fulfills your wish if you actually strive for it. In school, I was not considered fit and here I was amongst the few of the strongest people in the batch.

After completing three years of training in T. S. Chanakya and getting a graduation degree in nautical science, cadets join different shipping companies of different countries, who select them in advance through campus interview, and start working on different types of merchant ships.

Merchant ships are ships that carry cargo or passengers on hire from one port to another. These are commercial ships and are different from naval ships used for defending the sea boundaries of nations and other specialised government ships used for special purposes like research, etc. The merchant ships carrying passengers are called passenger ships and those carrying cargo are called cargo ships. Cargo is any goods, materials or commodities being carried by the ship. Cargo ships have been categorised basically according to type and quantity of cargo they carry. Cargo that is dry in nature is called dry cargo, and if liquid in nature, it is called liquid cargo.

Liquid cargo is always carried in bulk or in large quantities. Ships carrying liquid cargo in tanks are called tanker ships. The main liquid cargoes are crude oil and its refined products like petrol, diesel, jet fuel, etc. or liquid chemicals like sulphuric acid, nitric acid, phosphoric acid, etc. or liquefied gases like ammonia, ethylene, methane, propane, butane, etc. Ships carrying crude oil and its refined products are called oil tankers. It has been further divided as crude oil tanker that carries crude oil and product tanker that carries refined products.

Similarly, ships carrying liquid chemicals are called chemical tankers, which has been further classified according to nature and hazards associated with chemicals. Modern chemical tankers carrying dangerous chemicals have tanks made of stainless steel and it can carry many types of chemicals at a time in its different tanks. Similarly, ships carrying liquefied or condensed gas are called gas tankers. Those carrying liquefied natural gas are called LNG carriers and those ships carrying liquefied petroleum gas i. e. propane, butane, etc. are called LPG carriers. In general, one type of tanker is not permitted to carry cargo of other type of ship in spite of being liquid in nature because of different technical requirements.

Dry cargoes are carried in bulk as well as in smaller packages or loose parcels. Ships carrying dry cargoes in bulk like in unpackaged form in large quantity are called bulk carriers. Bulk carrier generally carries cargo like coal, ore, coke, grain, fertilizer, cement, salt, sugar, etc. There are ships carrying dry cargo in loose-packaged form like furniture, machinery, garments, footwear, etc., which are called general cargo ships. Some cargoes are carried in containers the size of trucks, which are loaded and unloaded on a different type of ship called container ship.

In addition to the above, there are other categories of dry cargoes, which need special precautions during carriage. These are carried in special type of ships, which are generally meant for carriage for only that particular cargo. For example, ships carrying live animals are called live stock carriers. Ships carrying logs of timber are called timber carriers. Motor vehicles used for road transport like car, bus, truck, etc. are carried in a separate type of ship called Ro-Ro ship. Ro-Ro stands for roll-on roll-off and is thus called so because cargo is carried on wheeled container or trailers. Similarly perishable food items like meat, fish, chicken, seafood, fruit, vegetables, dairy products, etc. are carried at ambient temperature in a special class of ship where cooling facility is present. These are called reefer or refrigerated ships.

Another type of ship called the flo-flo ship or float-on float-off or semisubmersible ship, which carry very large or extremely heavy cargo like tug boats, barges, floating cranes, mooring system, oil drilling rigs, etc. These ships don't use crane to load and unload cargo because the weight of single unit of cargo may be of many thousand tons. Instead they fill and discharge sea water into its ballast tanks to lower and raise the carrying deck of ship so that the cargo floating in sea is directly picked up and discharged from water at the port of loading and destination port respectively. There are some ships, which can carry dry cargo in bulk like ore as well as liquid cargo like oil. These are combination carriers and are called OBO (ore, bulk, oil) ships.

Out of above mentioned cargoes and ships, liquid cargoes need special precautions and extra training courses and therefore, jobs on tankers ships are better paid than dry cargo ships. Working on tanker ships is also comparatively a cleaner work in terms of exposure to dust and other garbage, which are generated on dry cargo ships. But at the same time, tanker ships are equally risky due to the risk of fire and explosion and the risk of health hazards due to the exposure to vapours as well as harmful chemicals.

Other than commercial cargo carriers, there are ships used for other purposes like ships used for diving operation, drilling operation, dredging operation, and they have different construction and names depending on technical requirement of job. Similarly there are seismic vessels, hydrographic ships, oil production ships, research and survey vessels, supply vessels, feeder vessels, icebreaker ships, tug boats, barges, etc.

On the basis of quantity of cargo being carried, the size of ships vary from a few metres-long barge and supply vessel carrying a few hundred tons of load to Ultra large crude carrier (ULCC) tanker carrying more than three lakhs tonnes of cargo. The largest ship ever made was super tanker *Jahre Viking*, also renamed later as *Knock Newis* or *Mont*, but it was already scraped in 2010. It was 458 metres long, 69 metres wide and had the capacity to carry about five and a half lakhs tonnes of crude oil and the total weight of a fully-loaded ship was about six and half lakhs tonnes. Presently, the largest operational ship in the world is a container ship named *Maersk Mc-Kinney Moller*, which is 400 metres long and 59 metres wide. It was built in a South Korean shipbuilding yard in 2013.

After passing out from T S Chanakya in 2002, I started working at an Italian shipping company named Finaval spa. Some European as well as Indian personnel manned the company's ships. The Indian manning of the company was looked after by its Indian branch in Mumbai called Pentagon Marine Services under the direction of an ex-seafarer Capt. Nalin Bilochan Pandey, who was popularly known as Capt. Pandey. The company owned oil and chemical tanker ships transporting crude oil, all kinds of petroleum products and chemicals. Its ships were ranging from being 100 metres to 250 metres long, which carried cargo from twenty five thousand tonnes to one lakh and twenty five thousand tonnes. Although some gas tankers were also there in the company but they were fully manned by the Italian personnel only and so, I always worked on oil and chemical tankers.

With my Boss Capt. N. B. Pandey and Mrs. Pandey.

The operation of any ship is looked after by a group of personnel, who stay on the ship at all times. The ship runs in water day and night and continues its journey till it reaches the port of destination. These people on ship are divided broadly in two departments, depending on the nature of their job. Those who handle the technical bits, like looking after the running and maintenance of engine, machinery and equipment of ship, belong to the engine department and those who take care of the administrative, operational, and management job, like cargo operation, maintenance of the ship's structure and its fittings, maintenance of life-saving and fire-fighting appliances, safety, security, welfare of crew, navigation, hygiene and sanitation, kitchen related work, etc. belong to the deck department.

The engine department is headed by the chief engineer followed by the second engineer, the fourth engineer, engine cadet, electrician, and some technical support staff like wiper for cleaning the machinery, oiler for oiling the machinery, fitter for welding work, etc. The deck department is headed by the chief officer or the first officer, followed by the second officer, third officer, deck cadet and some support staff like a bosun (a petty officer) for maintaining the ship's structure, a pump man for operating the cargo pump, some able seamen (AB) for keeping watch, etc. The master or captain of ship is also in charge of the whole ship. He commands the ship, acts on behalf of the ship's owner and is legally responsible for day-to-day affairs of the ship. The chief engineer and the chief officer look after their respective departments and both of them report to the captain. In the absence of the master, the chief officer acts as the second-in-command of the ship.

I started working in the deck department as a deck cadet in 2002 and through promotion, worked as a third officer and second officer and finally became a chief officer in 2007, the rank I continued working intermittently till 2011. Other than routine job on board ship, I tried to keep myself in shape by regular light exercises. It's easy to make time for exercise while out at sea because the hours of duty are mostly fixed. At sea you have four hours of duty and then the next eight hours off, both during the day as well as night. The hours of duty are from 08:00 hours to 12:00 hours (day and night) for the third officer, 12:00 hours to 04:00 hours (day and night) for the second officer and 04:00 hours to 08:00 hours (day and night) for the first officer or the chief officer. I served in each position and used to manage some time out at sea to exercise. But once you enter port and cargo loading and discharging starts then the third and second officers have to do a six-hours duty. The chief officer is in charge and is completely responsible for the operation and there are other subsidiary tasks. So it is very hectic for the chief officer in port. Given all this, my exercise routine was always disrupted when we were at port but still, more or less, I managed to keep in shape, although I gained a little bit of weight because I ate heavy, wholesome food (a lot of which was non-vegetarian).

Now, I had started earning a handsome salary and was rising from poverty to affluence gradually and steadily. After one year of training on ship during which I only received a stipend, the real fun began after the on-board training was completed; I joined as a full-fledged naval officer after passing the examination to become a second mate on a foreign-going vessel. My salary kept increasing with time and promotions, and ended up at about five lakhs per month in 2010-11 (when I went sailing after writing the Civil Service mains examination in 2010) and even after the declaration of the results in 2011. My family's financial situation changed a lot from what it had been in the nineties when arranging a few thousands seemed difficult, to 2005 and afterwards when arranging even a few lakhs became very easy.

Working in shipping was one of the most exciting times of my life. In fact, every journey on a ship is an adventure in itself; small 100 or 200-metres-long ships sail thousands of metres above the seabed in the middle of the ocean, where, if something happens, there is nobody for hundreds of miles to hear you scream and come to save you. The situation becomes more thrilling when the ship encounters rough weather in the ocean or when a large wave crashes down on the main weather deck of your ship with so much power that the whole ship vibrates as the wave collides with the ship's body.

In addition to the monetary and adventurous flavour, there are many memorable instances due to other reasons as well. One such case occurred around December 2007 to January 2008 while I was working as chief officer on a tanker ship named *Isola Verde*. About fourteen years old, it was one of the oldest ships in the company. I had joined the ship hardly two months previously and it was my first job as a chief officer. It was a tanker ship 179

metre long and 28 metre wide and carried about thirty thousand
metric tons of cargo, which was mostly crude oil and fuel oil.
Within two weeks of my embarking the ship, I had come to know
that the ship had some serious problems in cargo storage and
pumping system, what was not informed by the outgoing officer
at the time of my joining. Around mid-December, an order
came from the company office in Rome that said the ship would
proceed to the United States for discharging oil.

On duty at Sea - serving as Chief Officer (2007).

The news of the ship's call to the United States port always send
an alert to all the crews on the ship because extra preparations
needed to be taken in order to prepare the ship for the United
States Port State Control Inspection, which is considered
comparatively stringent with respect to other countries. In
addition, every tanker ship visiting the US Port needs a valid
Certificate of Compliance (COC) issued by the United States
Coast Guard, which is issued after a thorough examination of
the vessel. The certificate is valid for two years and needs to be
renewed at every two years interval or at the first visit of ship to
US if ship has not last visited US for more than two years.

My ship was going to visit the US Port after more than two
years and it had to pass a thorough examination in order to
renew the certificate. Cargo operation or bunkering operation is
allowed only after ship clears the exam. As the chief officer of

the ship, I was in charge of all operations related to cargo as well as the ship's maintenance and its safety, fire-fighting, and life-saving appliances. All these areas are very crucial for the running of ship safely and I had to ensure that they were in a functional condition up to the satisfaction of the United States Coast Guard.

In the prevailing conditions on the ship with leaking cargo pipelines connecting a group of cargo tanks leading to transfer of oil from one tank to another and some other problems, it was difficult for ship to clear the examination. Over and above this, the ship had to cross the North Atlantic Ocean in winter, which was another challenge because of bad weather and rough sea conditions in winter. It was risky because the ship was going to be loaded to its maximum intake before proceeding to US in order to fill its freight or carriage charge of cargo. So most of the tanks would be loaded to its maximum capacity, which is 98 percent of volume. This is the maximum limit allowed by international regulation leaving a two percent vacant space in each tank to accommodate for cargo expansion during heating.

I was concerned if the cargo starts leaking from one tank to another due to rolling and pitching of ship at mid-Atlantic due to rough weather, then the ship may lose its stability, due to shifting of cargo from forward to aft portion of the ship or vice versa. Loosing stability in mid-Atlantic with rough sea conditions could be extremely dangerous for the safety of the ship as well as safety of the crews on board.

My ship passing over peaceful Atlantic Ocean.

Anyway, I planned the cargo loading carefully so as to minimize the risks and after the completion, I started preparing for the incoming inspection as the ship sailed from Mediterranean port for US in the third week of December, 2007. Preparations on the ship had its own limitations because Rome was not built in a day. Many pending maintenance works and technical problems couldn't be sorted out in a short period of about ten days. But my imagination and visualizations didn't know any limitations. As the tiny ship continued moving ahead with rolling and pitching over the strong waves in the vast Atlantic, so did my tiny brain, which was busy in its self created vast imaginary world of the next port in USA where I would be enjoying a smooth inspection and completing it smoothly. Many people already congratulated me for successfully clearing the ship through the US Coast Guard inspection. But the situation on ground was that even the managers in my company office in Rome were well alarmed at the ship's visit to - US and one very senior manager had already come on ship to assist during the inspection. As the ship approached the US Coast, I mentally prepared myself to manage the worst-case scenario during the inspection and was quite confident that the ship would clear the inspection.

Luckily, the ship reached the port of New Orleans on the thirty first of December, 2007 and the inspection was carried out on the first of January, 2008. Being the New Year's Day, I felt that the inspecting officers were comparatively liberal and the ship cleared the inspection without any major hindrance. I really appreciate the US Coast Guard for their practical approach to life because they focussed more on checking functionality of critical equipments on board the ship, which are related to cargo operation and emergency handing than emphasizing on going deep into paper work. Still, at many instances during the inspection, I felt that luck was in our favour because some serious lapses were either ignored by the Coast Guard representatives or my confident demeanour convinced them, who knows. Anyway, ship cleared the inspection but problems still existed, which were rectified after its return from the USA as the company was also not well aware about it at earlier instances probably due to lack of clear communication. Recalling the incident now, I feel it was the result of positive visualization, which I practiced frequently as a matter of habit during the whole passage across the Atlantic. During my job on the ship, many such incidents occurred where positive visualization helped me to handle complex situations easily, although I used it unconsciously as my natural habit.

One of the unique memories of my life at sea is my exposure to the enchanting beauty of nature. Sometimes, I definitely miss some of the beautiful evenings spent on the bridge deck outside the wheelhouse under the open sky, where I used to get lured at the sight of the reddish sun slowly setting below the horizon at one end of the limitless, peaceful blue Atlantic Ocean. The weather was calm with the ship slowly sliding over the completely uniform ocean surface, which looked like large blue unending carpet. I also cherish those beautiful moments I spent gazing at the bright stars in the fair weather night on the bridge deck when the semi spherical dark sky fully spotted with millions of twinkling gems used to allure me for hours. Nowhere except the sea or the desert, would you find such unobstructed view of the full portion of the semi-spherical sky. I used to enjoy analysing the relative position of all the major stars and the constellations. In fact, the on-board practice of taking star sight to determine the position of the ship in the vast ocean required me to have a fair idea about the stars and constellations.

The use of sun sight, moon sight and star sight to determine the position of a ship with fair accuracy have been practised since ancient times when technology was not developed enough to provide a continuous update of a ship's position electronically but thanks to modern science, it can be done now with the help of GPS. However, in order to have an alternative means of determining position of a ship in limitless ocean in case GPS fails, the above method can be quite helpful. With my own deeper interest to know about this twinkling mystery of nature, I became an expert on position and time of visibility of stars and constellations.

My ship 'M. T. Neverland' at sea.

In addition to this, some of the rare places whose beauty I witnessed and still recall, were the Strait of Magellan at the southern tip of South America, the Panama Canal, the Caribbean sea and its islands, sailing past the Bermuda Triangle in the Atlantic Ocean, the Canary Islands, Ronnskar in the upper part of the Baltic Sea, the Suez Canal, Southern Australia, New Zealand and various countries in the Mediterranean and Black Sea. The fascinating loveliness of the Magellan Strait still mesmerises me. The white snow-clad peaks just above the blue water were lovely, something I have never been able to forget. The sight was alluring because I had never been to the mountains before that and had always wanted to see what they were like.

Other than enjoying handsome salary and the beauty of nature and places, shipping also gave fair chance of socialization. Seldom did we miss any newly-released Hindi movie while staying on board, what we used to enjoy almost every evening in the smoke room (common recreational place) while sailing at sea. The Pentagon marine office in Mumbai used to frequently send all those newly released movie along with joining crews. This is the irony here that we hardly get a chance to catch up a movie in the theatre while staying in India. Further I would never forget the barbeque parties I enjoyed on the poop deck of ship in the middle of the ocean in a very good weather and the memory of delicious Italian cuisine especially crostata cake

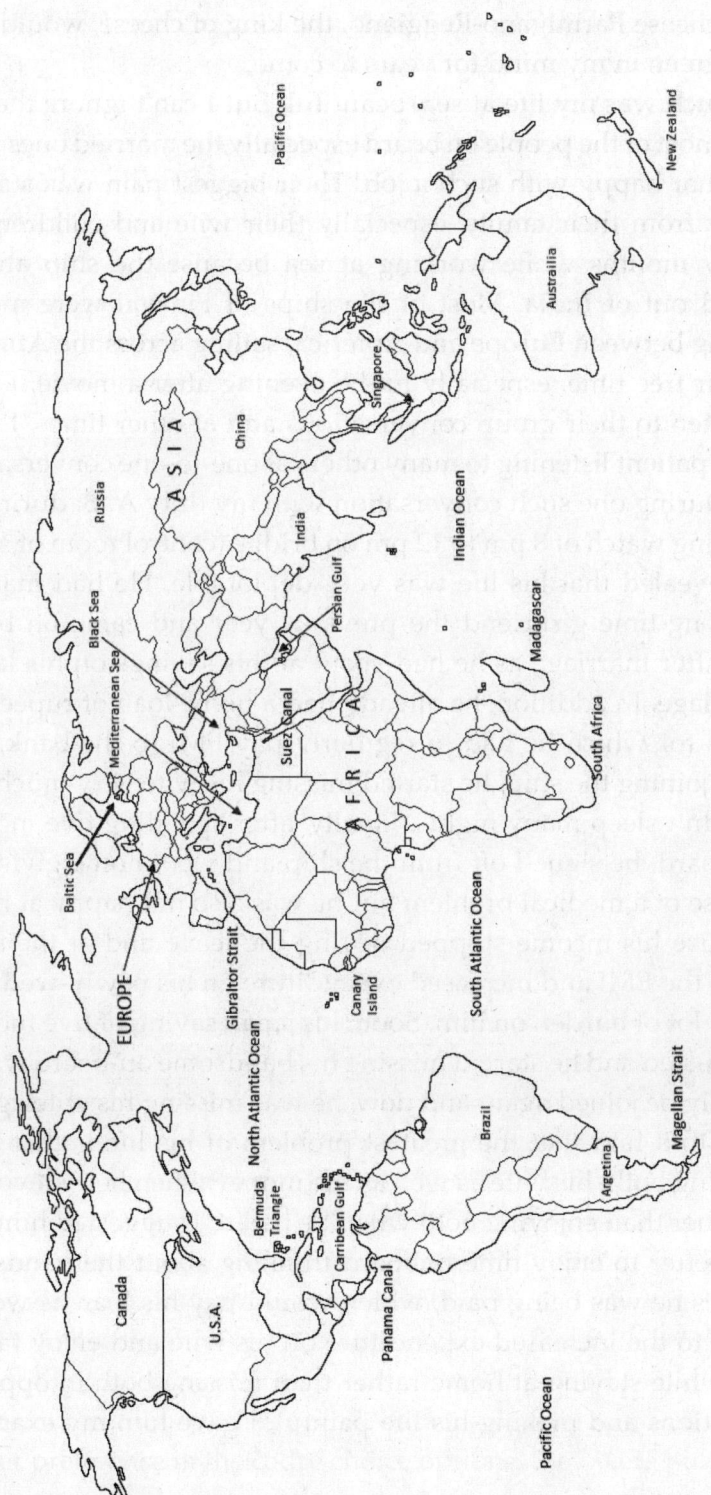

World Map marked with few places, I visited during shipping

and cheese Parmigano-Reggiano, the king of cheese, would stay evergreen in my mind for years to come.

Such was my life at sea, beautiful. But I can't ignore the fact that most of the people on board especially the married ones were not that happy with such a job. Their biggest pain was staying away from their family, especially their wife and children, for many months while working at sea because the ship always sailed out of India. Most of the ships of Finaval were mostly plying between Europe and America, sailing across the Atlantic. In our free time, especially in the evening after a movie, I used to listen to their group conversations and at other times, I even gave patient listening to many others at one-to-one conversation.

During one such conversation with my duty A. B. during an evening watch of 8 pm to 12 pm on bridge (control room of ship), he revealed that his life was very deplorable. He had married his long-time girlfriend the previous year and came on board just after marriage as he had spent all his savings on his lavish marriage. In addition, he already had a home loan of rupees ten lakhs for which he had to regularly pay EMI to the bank. Just after joining the ship, he started missing his wife very much and couldn't sleep many nights. Finally, after spending five months on board, he signed off from the ship and went home giving an excuse of a medical problem but he was also not happy at home because his income stopped during the leave and at the same time, the EMI and increased expenditure on his newly-wed wife put a lot of burden on him. Soon, his small saving of five months exhausted and he started missing his handsome on-board wages. Finally he joined again and now, he was missing his wife again.

I told him that the greatest problem of his life is that he is missing both, his wife as well as the money when he is devoid of it rather than enjoying both when he had it. I suggested him that it's better to enjoy time onboard thinking about the handsome wages he was being paid, which would pay his loan as well as cater to the increased expenditure on his wife and enjoy family life while staying at home rather than missing both in opposite situations and making his life painful. I gave him my example.

He tried it and I could observe the change in his behaviour and life within few days as he was spending four hours daily with me while on duty. Later, he also expressed his gratitude to me one day saying that his wife appreciated him that he had turned into a jolly person from a complaining person.

Thus, all conditions remained same in the life of A. B. except the shift from his habit of negative visualization towards positive visualization, and he became a happy and cheerful person. It is the irony that people focus on what they don't have rather than focusing on what they do. In this case of life in shipping, they need to stay happy on board enjoying the beauty of nature, parties, special food, and visualising about the good times they can lavishly enjoy at home during their leave with the handsome money earned.

Similarly, many other people took my suggestions seriously and their lives started improving and they could tide over all the agonies accumulated in their hearts for years and those who couldn't, continued with the prevailing pain. I believe it is applicable for every job. Even in a job on shore, it is true that most of the employees are not happy with their present jobs and keep complaining about it and in the process, make their life as well as that of their family members painful. If they can inculcate positive visualization in their life, their life would be full of happiness and turn into a blessing.

Thus, life on board kept moving slowly but happily and my bank account kept filling with every sailing and within a few years of working at sea, I bought a beautiful flat in Navi Mumbai in addition to making a new house in my native village. Thus, with new houses and a good bank balance, it seemed that I slowly moved out of my childhood memory of being a poor kid in a farmer's family, where a one room house used to accommodate the whole family. This whole journey from poverty to affluence over a period of about fifteen years was another milestone; it covered my education from first grade to graduation from T. S. Chanakya (when I had to be dependent on my parents for my expenditure), and my entry into a world of relative affluence.

My dream of emerging from poverty and having enough to enjoy whatever I liked to eat and wear or travel wherever I wanted, was now a reality.

Everybody wants to be rich but most people suppress their desires, thinking that they are not made for it because they have been living in poverty for thousands of years and nothing would change that. Thus, they are caught in the swirl of negative visualization and their conditions remain deplorable. In my case, I took it as a great opportunity to take credit because when you are born poor and you become rich through hard work, you should be commended. With this positive approach, I was absolutely confident that I would become affluent soon after completing my education. This longstanding wish came true after I began working in shipping.

Thus, firstly, it is important to develop positive visualization and focus at the positive aspect of anything, be it your job or any other thing in life and try to avoid focusing on negative aspects. Secondly, in order to fulfil your wish, it is important to focus on your wish to achieve something big, and then your belief that it is possible to achieve it, that you are completely capable of it, and it will become possible very quickly. The time it takes to realize your dream is also decided by how much you believe in it. If you feel that something is very big and takes a lot of time, then it definitely will; but if you think that it's not very significant and can be achieved quickly, then that is what will happen.

3

A Journey Through the Civil Services Examination

'For one thoroughly believes that no power in the universe can withhold from anyone anything they really deserve.'
— *Swami Vivekananda*

Joining the civil services was not a sudden decision; it had been a childhood dream. After clearing the IIT JEE, I had suddenly decided to enter T S Chanakya. This could have been a pre-destined step towards making my childhood dreams about the sea coming true after reading about the Mariana Trench journey. Or it could have been the immediate need to provide economic support to my family. I had spent a good number of years at sea as I had worked in shipping but my deep attraction towards the prestigious Superintendent of Police and District Magistrate posts was still alive in my heart. So I finally decided to discontinue my job in shipping and prepare for the civil services examination.

After long years working at a job, it was difficult to return to being a student again, especially after working at a managerial post in shipping. But the zeal to become a civil servant had brought me to Delhi. Life in shipping is isolated from the mainstream society so I knew very little about current affairs and other subjects. However, I had a lot of confidence and my inner belief in my capability that I would cover everything in due time and would clear this examination the way I had been clearing all the other examinations while I was a student as well as the promotional examinations when I worked in shipping.

This certainty had probably been developed over the years after clearing so many examinations. At that time, I had no idea about the extent of the syllabus, although I knew that civil services examination would be the toughest examination I would ever face.

As I continued gathering information about this examination, after coming to New Delhi, in November 2008, I came to know that the syllabus of this examination is very vast and seemed limitless. Also that it is the toughest competitive examination in India with very less success ratio. With only about the top one hundred and fifty selected candidates getting IAS out of more than six lakhs candidates appearing for the examination at a time, it has the least success ratio in the world. But still, my morale was not affected and I maintained the same degree of confidence with which I had arrived Delhi.

The civil services examination takes place in three stages, which spans almost one year from the first test until the result is declared. The first stage is the preliminary examination, which was conducted in the month of May when I prepared for this examination but presently, schedule has been changed to August. It consists of objective questions. The second stage is the mains examination, which is conducted in November or December every year and consists of subjective questions, the answers to which have to be in essay form. The last stage is the personality test or interview, which is conducted in March or April every year and consists of a panel of five examiners asking questions to test the overall personality of the candidates. The result is declared in the month of May every year before the preliminary examination.

In this situation, when you are preparing for an examination, which has a vast syllabus and a meagre success ratio, and especially when the examination stretches over an year, you need something more than simply dedicating an average eight to ten hours a day to study. Sometimes, you may face some unexpected obstruction, which may de-motivate you. It is equally necessary to maintain a deep belief within you and stay motivated and continue preparation with a positive notion without losing patience in due course.

I remember very well that initially I took coaching classes for general studies in a coaching centre called Khan Study Group and during the first month, one tutor mentioned the term PPP in the class a few times but I didn't know what it meant. I asked him confidently what the full form was and he was surprised that I didn't know this very basic term and was preparing for the civil services examination. He asked the same from the other students in the class and one said, it meant a public private partnership and another replied that it was the Pakistan People's Party. It looked like I was the weakest student in the class but I didn't get discouraged because of this. I just smiled and thought that it was all a matter of a few months and then I would be on par with them or even better. My confidence was not affected and I continued my focus in the class.

Few weeks after the start of the general studies coaching classes, I started my second coaching class for Public Administration with a well known tutor, Bhawani Singh. Both were going in parallel. I remember, once I came out of a coaching class of public administration. It was the month of January 2009 and many students were standing just outside class and enjoying the warmth of the afternoon winter sun. In parallel, a discussion was going on about who is targeting to clear this examination in how many attempts? Since it was my third month in Delhi since November, most of which, I had spent either inside the room for self study or in two coaching classes, general study with Khan Study Group and Public Administration with Sri Bhawani Singh. So I hardly had the extra time to interact for general discussion with other students. Eager to know about developments going on in the surrounding, I also joined in.

I guessed, the majority of participants were new and had yet to experience this examination. Varied answers were coming out. One said, he would not attempt it in that year but only the following year once all the coaching classes would be over and preparations would be completed. The next one said, 'I have always studied the humanities and so I'm not comfortable with the science part being asked in the general studies paper. So maybe it will take a minimum of two years to try for the first attempt.' The next one added, 'Let's see, UPSC allows four attempts and I will try clearing within these attempts.' And another one supported him. 'You are right, boss. You never know what the new pattern of questions UPSC would come up with. I am a B. Tech from IIT Kharagpur and an electronics engineer by profession. I have already given three attempts and also appeared for interview last year but couldn't clear. Now I have taken a year of break and will give last attempt this year.'

Then came my turn. I said politely, 'I have come back discontinuing my job at the sea with a plan that I would clear it in first attempt, like I have been clearing all other exams in the past. But let's take one more attempt as reserve because I am still unaware about the Geography syllabus, which I will start after appearing for prelims in May.' Some of them asked about my background and I said the truth including many years of job at the sea. One of them seemed like firing back to me, 'Boss, I have been preparing for the last four years and have already written mains examination last year but unluckily, couldn't clear it. I have seen so many brilliant and confident students, who gave up and returned back. This is an IAS examination, boss. Please don't compare with your tiny departmental examination and fool us by showing false confidence especially when you are not well aware about the syllabus.' And he counted the names of three IIT graduates and two MBBS doctors, who couldn't clear in their multiple attempts.

I replied politely, 'Sorry, I didn't mean to hurt your self-respect. Although I have not gone into the detailed syllabus of Geography, I have a rough idea about what Geography is all about. At sea, we use marine meteorology in our day-to-day activity. Further, I have read many success stories in *Chronicles* and *Pratiyogita Darpan*, where below average students from poor background, prepared for this examination themselves without even taking coaching classes, who also cleared the examination in their first attempts securing a good rank in the merit list.' I also counted him two success stories which I had read recently and told him that I had always taken these successful students as role models and if they can clear this examination in spite of having relatively poor academic background in the past then why can't I?

I was surprised why they were focusing more on examples of failure than focusing on success. There is no doubt that every student preparing for that examination wanted to register their name in the merit list of selected candidates but what they were actually doing was filling their minds with visualization of failure. And as stated earlier, the imagination and visualization creates reality. So the imagination and visualization of failure moved them far away from success in this tough examination.

In my case, I was in the habit of comparing myself with the weakest students who had cleared this examination in the past. This was a huge confidence booster for me. Probably, that's why very rarely, I had negative imagination about not being selected though, at that time, I was not very well versed with the miraculous effect of Advanced Positive Visualization. Now, after reading so many books on the topic and confirming the idea through these examples of my life and real life examples of many other persons, I came to understand the energy and power of Advanced Positive Visualization.

Along with positive visualization, it is also necessary to have good and helpful friends because this examination is easy to clear with cumulative efforts due to vast syllabus but too many friends also kill time in unnecessary chat. We were a group of four close friends. Two of them, Chandan Jha from Patna in Bihar, and Sudeep Velagra from West Godavari district in Andhra Pradesh were products of NIT Calicut and electrical engineers by profession, and the third one, Rakesh Ranjan from Hazipur district of Bihar was a TTE in the Indian Railways. The most positive characteristic of this group was its helpful attitude. Although all four of us were neither from the same background by profession, nor our coaching classes, optional subjects, medium of examination, and places of stay were the same, all of us were quite helpful to each other and we stayed within walking distance of one other. Whenever anyone would get any new study material in the market or new coaching notes or any recent news, which were relevant to any of us, he would pass it to the concerned by taking photocopy with his own money or by other means, like discussion or simple conversation, mostly without being asked to do so. It was indeed a wonderful group.

Here, I can't miss to mention an incident of the past, that I had witnessed during my primary school. When my final examination for the fourth grade was over, I came to know that a group of students from the sixth grade had stolen the notebooks of a probable topper of their class just before the test. One amongst those mischievous students was also the then topper of the class, who in order to maintain his rank, resorted to wrong means. Somebody has truly said, 'The trouble with the rat race is that even if you win, you are still a rat.' The way, they were competing amongst few of them using unfair means, was worse than even a rat race. I felt very bad for the hard working man, who had prepared notes over the whole year in order to use them before the examination to improve his rank and this envious group shattered his dream.

There was a stark contrast between the two groups. This can be a good example of negative and positive attitude respectively. One group had very short vision of competition within a few and they resorted to pulling a hardworking and deserving boy down in order to ensure their own success. In contrast, the other has wider vision and the members understood very well that the competition is not within a few in the group but with more than six lakhs candidates appearing for the civil services examination. They got the larger picture. That is why, they all were proactively helping each other.

We can also say that the group I encountered while in school resorted to unfair means because they were afraid of losing their present rank in the class, especially the topper. They were not aware that they were actually inviting failure in their life by their focus on failure than success because whatever is pre-dominant picture in your mind, it would turn into reality one day. May be that's why those notorious boys have been tasting failure in their life till recently when few of them have got small jobs, that too, very late. In contrast, the hard working boy got well settled much earlier with a better job.

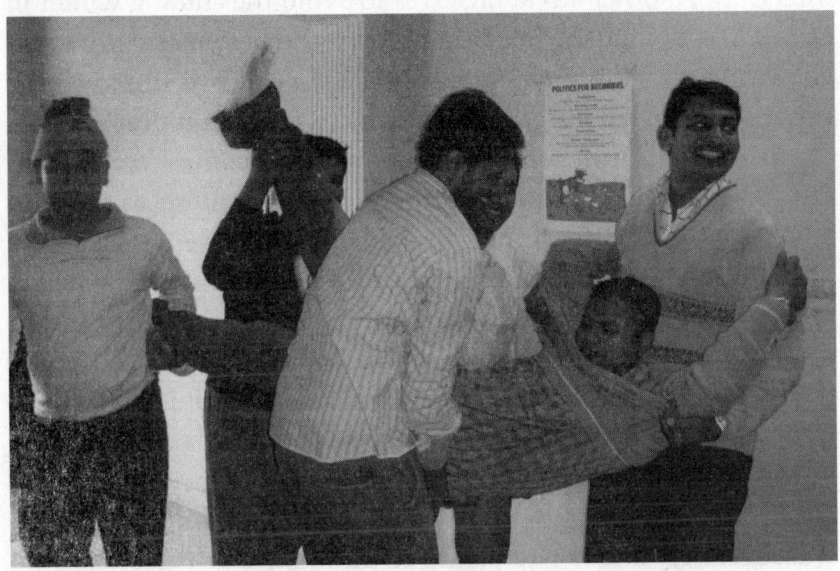

Few lighter moments with friends after hours of study during Civil Services Examination preparation days in New Delhi.

In contrast, the positive attitude of the members of our civil service preparation group definitely helped all the members of the group, including me, as it was difficult to cover everything on my own during the limited time available in hand. As stated earlier, I came to Delhi in November 2008 and had started from scratch. I appeared for the preliminary examination in May 2009 and cleared it and then moved on to the mains examination, which was to be held in November or December 2009. My subjects were such that I would be able to finish all my papers in the first five days, though the examinations would continue for about a month while different students with different subjects appeared on their due dates. So even before the examination started, I had planned to go sailing immediately after finishing. I called up my company and gave them my tentative dates of availability for joining; thus, within one week of the examination, I went back to the ship. The idea behind going back to work was to rejuvenate myself in a different environment because there is usually about a four to five months gap between mains examination and interview. Another advantage was to avoid the chilling winter in Delhi, and obviously, I couldn't ignore the large salary I would get within the short time I spent on-board, which would cover the expenses incurred in Delhi during the examination preparation.

In the shipping profession, joining and coming back from the ship depends on many factors like the location of the ship and visa availability of the country where the ship is presently located, the cost involved in the process, the availability of the reliever who would join in your place, immigration rules, etc. In my case, my signing off and returning from the ship was delayed by about a month and I could return back to Delhi in February 2010, which was good from a financial point of view but very little time remained for preparing for the interview.

In the first half of March, the result of the main examination was declared and I had made it through. But there was not sufficient time to cover the vast syllabus. My biggest mistake was that I had not carried important study material except one book on ship thinking that a period of about a month on board, as planned, would pass quickly in getting the hang of the ship's work after the interval of a long time. In fact, after returning back to Delhi, once I started revising, I realised that I had forgotten many topics of the mains syllabus as a result of lack of practice for the last three months. I was also not updated about the current affairs of the period I was at sea because of no connectivity on the ship except for important communications through satellite email or phone. There was no internet access given to crew on ships in my company during that time although some other companies had it. I tried to cover the maximum syllabus and I appeared for the final test— the personality test, but did not perform well. In spite of this, I was thinking positively.

The result was declared while I was at home in village. There was no internet in my village, so I couldn't see the result myself. After confirming the result with three friends on phone, who had internet, I still couldn't believe that I was not selected.

The next day my doubts were finally cleared when I saw the result on reaching the nearest town before finally moving to Delhi. Although I knew that my performance in the interview was not up to mark, somehow, I couldn't digest failure. It was one of the biggest shocks of my life because I had never tasted defeat before. I still remember, I felt extremely sad and broken when I was saying goodbye to my parents while returning to Delhi from home to appear for the next preliminary examination. It was an extremely bitter experience. In the past, I had cleared every examination in the first attempt whether it was the IIT entrance examination or the promotional examination in shipping, where the average student normally took two to three attempts.

Where was the confidence now? Would I be able to clear this examination? What would happen to the mental image that I have preserved over the years on my mind—my position of the District Magistrate (DM)?

My mind was filled with questions; but after thinking for a while, I decided to only focus on the forthcoming preliminary examination. I kept calm, thinking that it was a shortcoming because even I had doubted my success after observing my performance in the interview and sometimes, had even visualized not getting selected based on my performance. Further, it was better that my name wasn't in the last slot on the selection list because I would not have got my choice of service (which was either IAS or IPS). It was better to get a good rank in the next attempt so I could have my choice of service. My confidence, hence, was back and I appeared for the preliminary examination and cleared it as I was certain that I would. I appeared for the mains examination again, and, like the previous year, called up the company to return to the ship. But this time, I was extra careful and carried some books to continue studying while I worked. I also ensured that my contract was only for one month, so that I could return within two months even if there was a delay.

I returned from the ship well in advance and went over the happenings of the past two months. In the mean time, the result of mains was declared and I ended up clearing it, as expected.

The interview also went well and finally, my desire to join the IAS came true when the result came out in May 2011. Although service allocation comes later, after two attempts, I was in a position to make out who would enter what service depending on their rank in the merit list.

First IAS from village - Felicitation Ceremony organized in native village after clearing clearing Civil Services Examination.

When I was younger, I used to long to be like my maternal uncle. I was fascinated by the dignity and respect he commanded from our neighbours and the other villagers. He was a Deputy Superintendent of Police and had been selected through the Bihar Public Service Examination. He had been a meritorious student. Later, when I was studying in Navodaya Vidyalaya, the then District Magistrate, Sri Praful Ranjan Sinha, who was also the chairman of Navodaya Vidyalaya, used to be the chief guest and hoisted the flag on Independence Day and Republic Day, and then addressed us. I recalled his unique style of walking up the stage of Nadodaya Assembly Hall as he moved towards the podium and his diction and his style while he spoke. I had visualized myself in his place for the last many years as I imitated his style of walking and addressing a gathering. I used to dream of becoming like him.

With my proud father after clearing Civil Services Examination.

A lot of hard work had been involved in the process and it wasn't just the result of dreaming. My routine everyday of sitting with a book in an isolated room in the suburbs of New Delhi for eight hours on average was boring, especially after spending so many years in service. But somewhere in my mind I thought it was the result of a dream which had been in my heart for many years, and which I had been visualizing and chasing for the past two years.

Some of you might argue that getting through the civil services examination in my second attempt was merely the result of hard work, giving logic that if it was the result of long time visualization then I should have cleared the examination in my first attempt itself. I would say, firstly, if only hard work could bring success then a significant number of students preparing for this examination spending more than fifteen hours a day on study, still not getting selected, whereas some students studying a meagre amount of time were selected with good rank, wouldn't be possible. Further, on a deeper analysis, I found that the main reason, which brought failure in my first attempt, was the absence of positive visualization during the last stage. I have already stated earlier that positive visualization includes not only the visualization of success but also the renunciation of failure.

In case, a person is in dilemma whether he would succeed or not, then the idea of success and failure, both keeps coming and finally, the dominant idea will prevail and will get materialised. It is similar in the situation where two people are pulling you in opposite directions. You are in a lingo at first but are pulled by the one who proves to be stronger. The doubt had started coming up when I was delayed in signing off from the ship during the first attempt of this examination. After I came back to Delhi and started revising the optional subjects, what I had not read since completing mains examination, I found that I had forgotten a significant part of it. In that situation, if something was asked in the interview from the unrevised part then I wouldn't have been able to answer properly.

Thus, the doubt about success and probability of failure was getting stronger and I was quite concerned that if I failed to give satisfactory answer to the questions asked from optional subject, then it would create a bad impression. So, I can very well recall that I didn't face the interview board confidently, and ended up getting poor marks, which became a major factor in my non-selection. Thus, the doubt in my mind and the fear of failure was realized in the form of me not getting selected.

That's why I have emphasized upon consistent hard work in the chapter on advanced positive visualization in order to gain inner confidence about the success and sustain the image about success in my mind. In the absence of hard work, you never know when this fickle mind will ditch you by brining the image about failure and you would be drawn towards it and your chances of success will be ruined. As stated earlier, a person with perfect control over his mind and visualization (for example a yogi) can achieve the great success without any physical effort. I have already given the example of Swami Niranjanananda Saraswati previously, who gained various kinds of knowledge without any physical effort because his guru Swami Satyananda educated him with the help of Yoga Nidra. Enriching yourself with deep knowledge on various subjects is great success of life. But this is rare example and difficult for common people because this needs lot of training and control over the mind. For common people, who have no control over their mind, hard work is essential to convince the mind and to sustain positive visualization, but hard work without positive visualization doesn't guarantee success.

With kids in a remote village.

Here's an example of how hard work alone can't bring success but the combination of hard work and positive visualization can. After I cleared the examination and joined the job, one of my friends was repeatedly failing to perform well in the civil services interview and was ending up with poor marks in the interview although his mains score was good. He said to me that writing in mains examination was easy for him as he wrote on his own without any psychological pressure from any other person in the surrounding. But in the interview, he couldn't even speak well on a topic about which he was very confident, just before entering the interview room. Unluckily, for last two attempts, his performance in the interview boards was dropping. I told him to develop a positive outlook about every interview board. It was only due to his pre-conceived notion about a particular person chairing the board that he couldn't perform well.

I advised him to visualize, 'Anyone chairing an interview board is very humane at heart and fully impartial, and he awards marks fully on the aspirant's merit and not by looking at the face. Why would interviewers give lesser marks to you, if they didn't know you from before? They can't be your enemy in the first meeting itself and take revenge by awarding punishable marks. It is only the negative image about them in your mind that stops you from showing friendly gesture with them during the interview. Your inner fear is even reflected in your facial expression as well as in the way you respond to their questions, leading to poor performance and poor marks. 'I suggested him, 'Don't get puzzled even if you fall in a tough interview board. Just start visualizing in whatever time you have in your hand that your interview is going to be excellent today because people in the board will be the best people you will ever have met in your life. Feel close to them and try to develop deeper respect towards them and enter the interview room.' He practised it for a few weeks before the interview in the following year and performed excellently in one of board with what, he was not previously comfortable with.

Thus, you can make out the degree of impact of positive visualization on your success.

4

LBSNAA: The Wonderland

'Do not train a child to learn by force or harshness; but direct them to it by what amuses their minds, so that you may be better able to discover with accuracy the peculiar bent of the genius of each.'

— Plato

Life at the IAS Academy in Mussoorie was wonderful. It seemed as if I had returned to hostel life. The daily schedules at the IAS Academy almost like my earlier hostel life in T. S. Chanakya or Navodaya. The only difference was that Navodaya Vidyalaya was in a plain area in the Begusarai district of Bihar, or T. S. Chanakya which had also been in Navi Mumbai near the sea. But the IAS Academy was built on the slopes of the hills of Mussoorie and walking on the slopes was exhausting. Physical training is easier in plains than on slopes. During my training period in LBSNAA, we had to walk about one kilometre down to the playground for our morning physical training sessions.

Our training instructor was Mr Rawat, who had been a physical training instructor at C. R. P. F. Recruits Training Centre at Neemuch (M.P.) and Chennai; and had later joined IPS Training Academy, N. P. A. Hyderabad after which he had come to IAS Academy, Mussoorie. He was very strict and demanded a high level of fitness from probationers. So training was exhausting, because most of the trainees had been bookworms since their childhood and were not used to hard physical exercises. After our physical training, we had to climb about one kilometre to return to our hostel. This was tougher than the actual physical training. After getting ready for the day, we had to climb up steep slope again to reach the dining hall and most of the trainee officers panted along the way. There were weekend treks for all the trainees in and around the Mussoorie hills, which were an additional bonus for us to get into shape.

Tug of War during training in LBSNAA.

I used to exercise seriously because I had to get back into shape. To my surprise, I reduced from 85 kgs to 72 kgs within three months of joining the academy. In fact, I managed to win a prize in a five-kilometres race during the athletic meet in the academy and also secured the best PT award for maximum push ups, sit ups, and crunches within a minute. I was happy that my arms were strong because I used to do regular push ups when I was working on the ship and this caused me to be able to do eighty push ups within one minute during the test for the PT Award.

The academy gave me a golden opportunity to learn and participate in many other extreme sports, something I will cherish for a lifelong . The memory of the thrill of bungee jumping, scuba diving, skin-diving, horse riding, parasailing, river rafting, shooting, etc. can never be forgotten. The IAS academy was where I did the first trek of my life and I, later, continued with this new hobby in Sikkim during district training.

During Horse Riding Show in LBSNAA (2012).

Other than physical fitness and adventurous activities, the academy has a well-developed and well-planned schedule for the trainees. Teaching class starts after physical training and breakfast in the morning. Theory classes were scheduled before lunch. During these, trainees were taught about the practical aspects of law, economics, public administration, management, and history. Modern teaching methods are used in classes and they are not limited to typical unidirectional lectures by the lecturer but involve group discussions, role-play, etc. Faculty members, who visit the academy from different parts of India and who are experts in their own fields cover the major part of the syllabus. Some of them are very famous personalities in India, whom we have seen only on the television screen before coming to the IAS academy.

Among many eminent personalities, who made long lasting impact on our memories by their interactive and interesting classes, one is Sri J. Radhakrishnan, an IAS officer of 1992 batch of Tamil Nadu cadre. As a district collector, his active participation and managerial skills during the relief operations in post-tsunami in the two worst hit districts of Tamil Nadu really put a long lasting impression in our minds. During such big disasters, causing death and destruction everywhere, his proactive role provided quick relief to the people. Many countries outside India and the United Nations as well, applauded him for his great contribution to humanity. Another impressive class was taken by Sri K. Vijay Kumar, an IPS officer of 1975 batch, who took a lead role in killing the forest brigand Veerappan (also known as the Sandalwood smuggler) in 2004. He headed Operation Cocoon as the chief of Special Task Force that killed the notorious bandit, who was active for many years in the forest covering large areas of three states of India, namely, Karnataka, Kerala, and Tamil Nadu.

Their unique and practical, achievements and experiences shared during the class definitely gave us a wide exposure to different aspects of administration. Post lunch sessions are kept for lighter classes like computers, languages and hobby classes which include music, photography, public speaking, painting, cooking, dance, etc. Other than this, activities like horse riding, badminton and karate classes are also organized.

Cultural Mixing - Fashion Show in LBSNAA.

The trainees are kept busy in the evening as well, in different pursuits like cultural programmes organized by the academy. Renowned artists from different parts of India come to entertain and familiarize the trainees with their art by performing as well as explaining the history and significance. Our batch had the opportunity to see Pandit Birju Maharaj and many other famous artists, dancers, painters, and more who were rare figures to be seen in India. A wider exposure to different cultural activities and different renowned personalities of India opened up our minds and gave trainees a wider perspective, moulding them into officers who could run districts smoothly.

The trainees themselves use many evenings to put on show their cultural knowledge and talent. The trainees are divided into four zones: North, East, South, and West covering the states to which they belong and they perform according to their respective zones. In this manner, they are kept busy with activities the whole day and also most of the evenings, which trains one well in managing one's busy life during district posting.

IAS Trainees organising feast in Dining Hall of LBSNAA on India Day Celebration.

Other than this daily schedule, extracurricular activities are organized like ten-day treks in the hills of Uttarakhand, a one-week village visit to the neighbouring states, athletic meets, two-day jungle safaris, and adventure sports at weekends. And we cannot forget the India Day celebration, where trainees from each zone put on cultural shows on floats in the morning. This is followed by cultural shows by trainees from two zones in the day and a lavish lunch by trainees of the other two zones. In the evening there is also a colourful cultural program followed by dinner organised by the trainees of the other zones that participated in the cultural show in the morning. The trainees wear their traditional clothes, arrange dishes from their regions during lunch and dinner and also showcase their local culture during the cultural show.

Festival Time in LBSNAA-Trainees and Faculties enjoying together on India Day Celebration.

There is a society system to take up such activities organised by the trainees regularly. More than fifteen societies cover different kinds of activities like social services, games and sports, mess, movies and entertainment, magazines, etc. These societies consist of a chairman (who is generally a faculty member), a president, and trainees who are members. Different clubs and societies organize their own schedule of activities in addition to the academy's regular routine and thus, keep the overall schedule of the trainees quite busy. Being in charge of the social service society, I used to organize weekly medical camps for the poor in the surrounding areas and organized many blood donation camps and large-scale health check-up camps for children (including check-ups for Hepatitis B). I also organized a fete, or a fair, where all the trainees were divided into smaller groups who then put up stalls for food and games in the playground. Trainees and outsiders participated in this fair and the earnings were donated to the social service society to be used for the welfare of the poor people in the surrounding areas. In fact, so many activities take place in the academy at once that it is extremely difficult for one trainee to participate in all of them.

Additionally, the schedule is so busy that trainees can feel relaxed only when they are sleeping in the hostel at night and while sitting in class. In fact, after the exhausting morning exercises and climbing steep slopes of the hilly path, most of the trainees feel tired and after a healthy breakfast, the classroom becomes a good place to relax. The classroom became a wonderful place to sleep for some of the trainees, who stayed up late at night, indulging in entertaining pastimes. As a result the first few periods were funny. The trainees had become experts at finding different ways of sleeping in the class to avoid being caught by the faculty. Some took serious positions, looking down with their books open on the desk, others leaned against the wall and some tried to sleep with their eyes half open. But some also fell sound asleep until the classmate sitting next to them shook them silently. The sight during classes in the Sardar Patel Hall was especially funny with many of the trainees sleeping peacefully in the hall during lectures and many monkeys silently sitting at the glass windows all around, calmly listening to the lectures. We used to say that after listening to so many lectures, the monkeys in the IAS Academy had become more intelligent than the IAS trainee officers.

And so, time spent at the IAS Academy was memorable in spite of the busy and tiring schedule because it was a combination of hard work and fun. It becomes special for every trainee present there because these 100 days of foundation course is the only period in the whole life, when the candidates of all three top services selected through civil services examination i. e. IAS, IPS, and Indian Foreign Services (IFS) are brought together at one place for a considerable period of time. This is the period when they get familiarised, they get to mingle and understand each other well. This bonding developed during those 100 days helps a lot later during their job in their respective services when inter services liaison and cooperation is required for smoother and more successful completion of some important projects of the Government. Although the trainees of different services do get sufficient time to know the people of their own services later in their respective training academies where they are sent for service related specialised training on completion of foundation course in IAS Academy, it helps in developing personal relationship within their own service people and not inter-services personal relationship.

Memorable moments with friends in LBSNAA.

I remember when the foundation course started on August 29 and all of the brilliant brains from different parts of India assembled at LBSNAA. There were excitements everywhere. After all, they had come to the premier training institute of India and it was an assembly of the best brains of India. Apart from people belongings to three different services to which they were allotted after getting selected through the civil services examination, they belong to different backgrounds as well. Out of total 264 candidates of IAS, IPS, and IFS assembled at LBSNAA, there were 92 engineers, including products of IIT Kanpur, 26 doctors, including graduates of AIIMS, 15 management graduates, some from IIM Ahmedabad, 2 from shipping, and remaining from other backgrounds. Out of these, 33 percent were from rural background. 18 percent of the students were female. Everybody looked like a winner and in fact, they were winner because they were few selected lots out of several lakhs of people who appeared for this examination.

Spirit De Corp -Joint Trek with fellow trainees from Indian Revenue Service (IT).

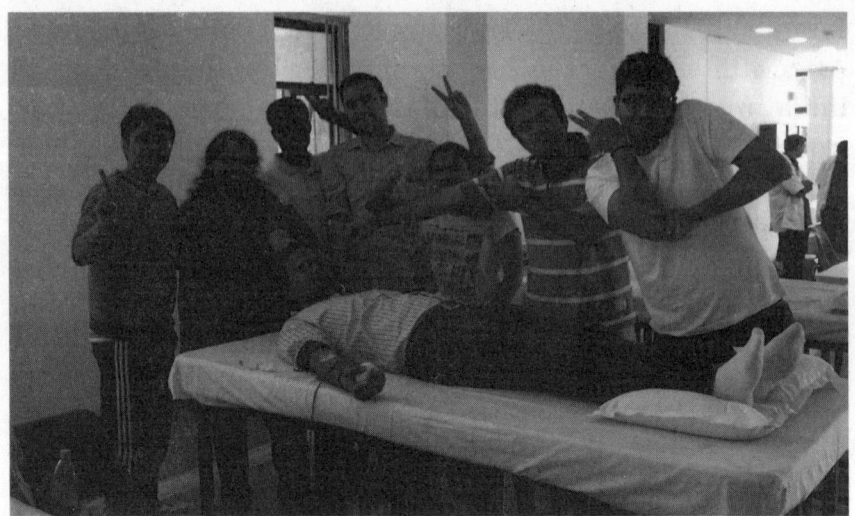

Social Work - Blood Donation Camp in LBSNAA.

As the time passed and we started getting to know each other, we came to know about their extra-curricular talents as well, when they started revealing it during cultural programs, athletics and adventure activities, social services, etc. But there were grey areas as well. I interacted deeply with some trainees from all three services. I discovered that some of them were still under severe hidden inner pain and not at all satisfied in life although everyone looked happy from outside because they didn't share their grievances initially during the first few conversations. Other than few personal and family problems, the main reason was due to high but unfulfilled ambition.

There were other reasons too. One of my close friends in IFS revealed his agony one day. He liked one IPS girl very much but she probably wasn't interested in him. According to him, if he had been an IAS then there would not have been such dearth of girl from All India Services in his life. Same was the concern of some officers in IAS, also especially those who were expecting North East Cadre.

The dissatisfaction due to not getting services of choice was more in IFS than IPS because IPS could reappear for civil services examination even after joining their services and that's why a good chunk of them actually re-appeared for the examination and so, didn't come for foundation course. IFS and IAS can't reappear for this examination after joining their services unless they resign from service and appear again. I heard of a few examples where an IFS officer resigned from his job and appeared again and got IAS but this involves a great risk. This is where the role of confidence and power of Positive Advanced Visualization becomes crucial.

With all my IAS batchmates alongwith faculties in LBSNAA 2012.

I believe, the ability to gain expertise in positive visualization and to stay content, and at the same time, work with peaceful mind for fulfilling your desires is the greatest achievement of life. This is the only achievement, which can ensure you everlasting happiness in life in continuation with enjoying the materialistic comforts of the world unless you decide to give up all material happiness, renounce the social world and become a yogi and stay away from the society. In the above examples, you have just now seen that the ability to inculcate the habit of positive visualization and stay happy with everlasting peace of mind didn't come even to one of the most successful group of people.

Thus, it is evident that if you can achieve the ability to visualize only the positive aspect of something by sufficiently training your mind, then you can fulfil all the dreams of your life and stay ever happy and peaceful in life. But, even if you achieve one of the biggest dreams of your life by hard work and determination but lack positive visualization in life, like looking at drawbacks in life and you continue to focus on negativity then you will be devoid of peace and happiness in life. So, it's high time you practice and inculcate positive visualization in life because it is not only limited to give you great success, but it's also more important for inner peace and happiness in life, which, I feel, is the ultimate aim of every human being.

5

An Idea in the Making

'When you are inspired by some great purpose, some extraordinary project, all your thoughts break their bounds. Your mind transcends limitations, your consciousness expands in every direction and you find yourself in a new,
great and wonderful world. Dormant forces, faculties and talents become alive, and you discover yourself to be a greater person by far than you ever dreamed yourself to be.'
— Maharishi Patanjali

While working at sea, I had developed an interest in the mountains. The memory of the fascinating beauty of the snowy peaks above blue waters of the Magellan Strait still attracts me. I used to imagine having a small house in the midst of the greenery on top of a small mountain, where I would like to stay someday. I imagined myself sitting on a ridge and looking at the green mountain slope opposite me and the valley below. Deep in my heart, I had developed a powerful longing to go from blue waters all around me in the middle of the ocean to the greenery on the slopes of mountains. I believe that this profound attraction and this idea later brought me to the mountains.

It is said that everything exists first in the mind and then becomes a reality. Anything in this world, whether an invention or any other project first enters our mind as a thought or idea and then we start executing it and make it a reality. I feel that my shift from the sea to the mountains is not an exception. Somewhere, in a dormant corner of my mind, a deep-seated longing was created and was coming true; I wanted to spend some time on the mountain slopes and so, when I had a chance to choose my cadre, while filling the civil services mains examination form (an option to choose different Indian states to serve in after clearing the civil services examination, which are divided into twenty four cadres), I picked hilly states over plains. In my first attempt (which was unsuccessful), my wish was so strong that I had chosen hilly states like Uttarakhand and Himachal Pradesh as first and second options and my home state Bihar, the last option, out of the twenty four options available. But, in the second attempt (when I was selected), my two choices were my home state and Jharkhand and I followed them up with a few hilly states. Sikkim was my fifth option in the IPS and eighth option in the IAS.

After the final results for civil service examination were declared in May 2011, all the selected candidates were called to begin their training in different designated institutes throughout India. As stated earlier, the trainee officers of IAS, IPS and IFS were called to the training academy at Mussoorie, Uttarakhand. The Lal Bahadur Shastri National Academy of Administration in Mussoorie is where the Indian Administrative Service officers are fully trained and where the Indian Police Service and Indian Foreign Service officers are trained only for their foundation course. I reported there at the end of August 2011 for a training of 100 days for our foundation course. During this course, the trainee officers made many calculations and predictions as we discussed the cadre allocation. After completing the foundation course, the IPS and IFS trainees went to their respective training academies and the IAS trainees remained at Mussoorie academy.

After the foundation course, phase one of the training starts and this is exclusively for IAS trainees. One week after the phase one of the course starts, trainees are taken for a two months long Bharat Darshan. The declaration of cadres was in January 2012 during this Bharat Darshan. Darshan is an official tour to some parts of India during which the trainees are taken to different places ranging from the extreme north to the extreme south of India and are attached with different sectors like government enterprises, defence (army, navy and air force), NGOs, and private sectors which have excelled in their fields. In this way, trainees can learn the best practices followed in such organizations and apply them in their respective areas after they are posted to their districts. It is a wonderful way to disseminate the best practices being followed in one part of India to all the other parts. For the sake of convenience, all the trainees are divided into smaller groups with separate tour plans, in order to manage travel and stay arrangements. The day when cadres were declared, our Bharat Darshan group was in Goa. We celebrated this by having a great time on the Calangute Beach.

Bharat Darshan Group at Porbandar, Gujarat

Like past years, some of my batch mates were happy and some were disappointed with their cadres. Unhappy were mostly those, who landed up in so called less popular cadres like Jammu and Kashmir and North Eastern Indian States. I got one of the north eastern states, Sikkim, as my cadre. Some of my friends and batch mates were not happy and surprised that Sikkim was my cadre. When I revealed that I got Sikkim as my preferred cadre choice and not as one of remaining cadres from the neglected pool of cadres, which nobody has opted, because I had given Sikkim as higher preference in the cadre choice options, they were puzzled.

When some close friends talked in such manner as if I had done some blunder by choosing Sikkim as higher preferred option, then as a human being, I was also forced to think twice on my decision whether I had really been wrong in my choice. On analysing all pros and cons, I came to the conclusion that whatever decision I had taken, I was perfectly right because positive visualization is an inherent or inculcated habit of human being. People in the habit of pointing out shortcomings in cadre will not be happy in any cadre because every cadre has some pros and some cons. I knew that so called mainstream cadres had its own complexities in terms of high political interference in administrative works, frequent politically motivated transfers, etc. At least, Sikkim is free of these extra headaches and there are many other positive attributes, which needs to be focussed upon to get advantage of the same.

Opportunities are everywhere, we need to explore and exploit them. Now I started ignoring such conversations and started looking for opportunities by reading more and more about Sikkim. In this process, I learned that there had been a big earthquake in Sikkim on September 18, 2011, which had taken many lives. Roads had been broken in some places and blocked at other due to a landslide that had resulted from the earthquake. Other modes of communication had been disrupted, so immediate help could not reach the public. In addition to a rescue team of army from outside the state, some local mountaineers were called to reach disconnected and isolated areas to offer immediate relief to the victims. This was a turning point as I got an idea: to learn mountaineering, which could be used in an emergency to reach the people in times of need. In this manner, I would gather support from the service fraternity as well as the Government.

The mere thought of rescuing people in an emergency was a satisfying thought and I started dreaming of different rescue scenarios where I saved many injured people and brought them to hospitals. I imagined checking up on their health after they had been admitted and seeing the smiles on their faces after their recovery, which would give me immense satisfaction. Days passed after the declaration of our cadres and a few of my batchmates used to joke that I would climb Kanchendzonga, the highest peak in Sikkim, because by that time, people knew me as a strong and tough person. This gave me more incentive to think that it could be done once I learned mountaineering and I started practicing it seriously. Later the idea evolved; if I could learn mountaineering and climb Kanchendzonga, with a little more effort, I could climb the highest peak in the world, the mighty Mount Everest. All these developments took place within two weeks of the declaration of our cadres. I really fancied the idea of climbing Mount Everest.

The idea was slowly growing in my mind especially as till now, no one from my service had gone to Mount Everest although one IPS officer had, a few years ago, in 2008. So I decided to undertake this as soon as possible to prove to myself that I had done nothing wrong by choosing Sikkim as a higher preferred option and I couldn't be called foolish based on this decision. As the thought took root, I started jogging long routes in the morning, whenever I got the time. Jogging had a dual benefit during the Bharat Darshan; first I could closely observe the place we were visiting and its culture, and secondly, it is a fitness training. By the time we completed our Bharat Darshan in the second week of February 2012, I had decided to climb the Everest.

I have always been grateful to God for giving me so much confidence that I was sure that I would be able to climb the highest peak in the world without thinking about the difficulties involved. I didn't know anything about mountaineering at that time but I had decided to do it. And anyway, who could stop me from imagining and fantasizing being on the top of the world? As I started reading and looking through photos of Mount Everest on the internet, I picture myself standing atop the peak. Sometimes, there would be a shift from dream to reality, as I would ask myself how to execute this idea. And then I would seriously analyze all the pros and cons. When I was deep in thought, the only difficulty that I could think of was whether I could get the opportunity to do it while in the service and how to plan it so that I would encounter the least resistance from the Government for a long leave for training to climb.

I searched the internet and found that there were a few good institutes like the Nehru Institute of Mountaineering, Uttarkashi and Himalayan Mountaineering Institute, Darjeeling, which provide mountaineering training. Now my next step was picking when to do it.

The nature of our service is such that workload increases with seniority. By this time, I had seen a few documentaries about the Everest and was aware of the preparation it would demand. I thought I would give it my best and would try to get an opportunity during my district training between June 2012 and June 2013. This period is meant for training and it is not compulsory to hold an independent charge, which would restrict my leave as well as the time to prepare for climbing the Everest (although most of the trainees do get an independent charge during some part of the training). Still, I was not sure whether I would get time to do it during my district training. So when we returned to the training academy in Mussoorie immediately after the Bharat Darshan, I met my counsellor, Shri Dushyant Nariala.

One faculty member for each cadre counsels the trainees who are allotted that particular cadre. The counsellor gives information about the cadre, solves any problem, etc. Shri Dushyant Nariala was the cadre counsellor for West Bengal and Sikkim and so I told him about my plan to climb Mount Everest during my district training period. He was very supportive of my idea and he immediately called Mr Rana, who was the physical training instructor in the academy and had been there for many years. Mr Rana had been a good climber in his days. Now, he was retired from physical training but still trained our seniors who came to the Mussoorie academy for in-service training. He met me at Dushyant Nariala's office. He seemed over fifty years old but still very fit.

We discussed the training required, the training academy and the opportunities that were available to climb Mount Everest.

I learned for the first time that climbing Mount Everest was very expensive and required lakhs of rupees and a sponsor, whether a Government sponsor or a private sponsor. Till now, I had been happy with the meagre training fee of four thousand rupees for a twenty-eight day basic mountaineering course at the Himalayan Mountaineering Institute Darjeeling. I didn't worry about the money aspect because I thought that the cost of climbing Everest would be one lakh, at the most, which I could easily afford from my earnings from my shipping job.

Mr. Rana advised me to read mountaineering books from the library and watch videos while I was developing my stamina with activities such as long jogs to strengthen my leg muscles, push ups to strengthen my arms, yoga to keep my mind peaceful, etc. He suggested that Nehru Institute of Mountaineering, Uttarkashi would be better for training.

I followed his instructions and started with a book from the library called On the Top of the World: The Indian Everest Saga, written by Capt. Kohli who had led the first successful Indian expedition to Mount Everest in 1965. I also watched *Surviving Everest*. In the meantime, I gathered information about the training schedule at the mountaineering training institute and found that their training period was from March to May and then September to December. They don't train during the monsoon or during the extreme winter of January and February. I wanted to get into the pre-monsoon training period from March to May; but it was not possible because Mussoorie Academy would never let me go for such a long duration during the IAS training. We were scheduled to graduate from the academy in the second week of June and had to move to our cadres for one year of district training. So I planned to do the basic mountaineering training course in September-October and then the advanced training batch in October-November.

Thus, Sikkim proved to be a blessing in disguise for me to accomplish this wonderful feat of climbing the highest peak of the world. I should really thank God for bestowing me the ability to look positively on anything and the ability to positively explore opportunities everywhere and reshape my destiny. That's why His Holiness Dalai Lama correctly said, 'with realisation of one's own potential and self confidence in one's ability, one can build a better world.'

Examining from another angle, if I had agreed to the views of others that Sikkim is one of least preferred cadre because there is not much opportunities in comparison to mainstream cadres and if I had accepted that the decision to choose Sikkim as my preferred cadre was big mistake of my life, then my life would also had been full of pain and suffering like others.

But my focus on the positive aspect of Sikkim and refraining myself from focusing on its shortcomings made a big impact on my life, and my life continued with peace and happiness as usual. I am sure, this ability to focus on only positivity and ignore negativity can be applied in every walk of life.

6

The Struggle over Sikkim

'Human Spirit is the ability to face the uncertainty of the future with curiosity and optimism. It is the belief that problems can be solved, differences
resolved. It is a type of confidence. And it is fragile. It can be blackened by fear and superstition.'

—Bernard Beckett

Due to a busy schedule, time passes fast in the IAS training academy. Before, I realised it, we were close to the end of the first phase of our training. In the coming week we would be at the academy for almost nine months. The first week of May 2012 was examination week; the end of phase one. Once the examination was over, the trainees were relaxed and began preparing to join their respective cadre states for a year-long district training.

Another interesting incident occurred at this time. Two weeks before passing from the IAS training academy in Mussoorie, I got a copy of the letter from the Government of Sikkim, which had been sent to our training academy. The letter stated that they had rejected my service to the state saying that they didn't need any IAS officers that year. They had sent a copy to the Department of Personnel and Training (DoPT), Delhi a few months ago but not receiving a reply from the Department, they had sent a reminder to DoPT copying to the IAS training academy, Mussoorie.

This was not good news for me because it was not clear where I had to report after graduating from the academy. I couldn't go to Sikkim as they had rejected my service and couldn't join anywhere else. Nor could I stay in the academy because a batch would come in for phase two of training immediately after we graduate. Still, I was calm because the Government had to send me *somewhere*. In the meantime, suggestions were coming from everywhere regarding the different options I had. Somebody was telling me to take it seriously and clear up the matter before leaving LBSNAA. At the same time, others advised me to try to get a good cadre, as this was a very good chance to get out of the Sikkim cadre.

The matter was brought to the notice of the director of the IAS Training academy. With the efforts of the director, Sri Padamveer Singh and a faculty member, Shri Tejveer Singh, the Department of Personnel and Training (DoPT), Government of India, New Delhi, was requested to expedite the decision and I was told to go to Guwahati for the training. The discussion regarding this matter was in progress amongst the LBSNAA (Mussoorie), DoPT (New Delhi) and the Government of Sikkim (Gangtok), when the phase one of training in LBSNAA came to an end and I came home for a week. Although I was quite calm on the cadre matter because it was the work of the Government to secure me a cadre, yet obviously, my active contribution would expedite the matter. I thought to push the matter forward so as to catch up with my district training just after completion of training at Guwahati as well as North East Darshan. Otherwise, I might have to wait for cadre clearance even after returning from Guwahati and the precious time for district training would not be utilized for district training. In addition, my mountaineering plans might also be affected adversely in case of undue delay in cadre clearance. So I didn't rest at home and I spent some time in Patna meeting some officers and one ex-minister, then came to Delhi to meet an officer in the DoPT, who didn't help much. One of my old friends took me to a minister regarding the same issue and I also met the DoPT Minister of State.

By this time, my leave was over and I had to report to the Administrative Training Institute, Guwahati for a three-week training, which was for all the probationers of the North Eastern Cadre States as well as the AGMUT cadre (comprising Arunachal Pradesh, Goa, Mizoram and all seven of India's Union Territories). So I came to Guwahati for the training and my personal efforts related to the cadre clearance came to a halt. A few times, I called up the District Magistrate of the East District, Sikkim, with whom my immediate senior was attached for district training and with whom, I was also expected to be attached. I informed him of the matter and he assured me that he would pursue it.

Leaving the cadre matter at the back of my mind, I focussed on my Guwahati training. We enjoyed ourselves a lot during the three week training. It included classroom teaching as well as a visit to the other North Eastern States like Meghalaya, Nagaland, Tripura, and Mizoram. Although a few of my friends showed some signs of worry and advised me to pursue the matter seriously, I took it lightly because it was very clear that the Government would allocate me a cadre if the Government of Sikkim did not accept me; so I continued to enjoy the Darshan of the North East. This didn't mean that I was not concerned about the issue but I didn't like worrying about the matter if I couldn't solve the problem. I had learnt to work to find solutions to life's problems with a cool head. I thought I would do my part by informing all the concerned people, remind them sometimes and wait for their orders.

Understanding Tribal Lifestyle In a Tribal Village near Kohima, Nagaland during North East Darshan

In fact, I guessed that the Sikkim government would accept me after some discussion between all the stakeholders as a senior had informed me that no state could reject an officer on a whim until the cadre was at full allocated strength. In Sikkim's case, there were a few seats left before the cadre could be at full allocated strength and that gave me the confidence to remain calm regarding the matter. I continued with my morning jogs as part of my preparation for the Everest. I still remember my early morning jogs outside Ginger Hotel in Guwahati on a small stretch of road, making multiple rounds from one end to the traffic point.

Finally, after our North East training was over, I headed towards Sikkim though the state hadn't confirmed my candidature yet. However, my DM had told me to come to Gangtok; he had arranged for a room in the circuit house and I went to stay there. Thanks to him I was given a vehicle with a driver, at my disposal, which my immediate senior had been using while he had been a probationer. In the meantime, one of my friends advised me to take a letter from the state government stating that they had not accepted me as a probationer saying he would then try for a good cadre for me through a judge from the High Court. I reported to my DM the next working day and then called on the Chief Secretary of Sikkim to find out the status. The moment I met him, he said that he had already cleared my file; with this, it was clear that the Sikkim cadre officially accepted me. I was happy to join district training on time as I formally joined on July 15, 2012.

With this formal joining, I officially became part of Sikkim cadre and I felt a sense of belongingness with the state. It is one of the twenty-nine states of India and is located in North Eastern India, north of West Bengal state. Three countries from three sides border it. Nepal shares the international boundary on its west side, China's Tibet Autonomous Region on north side and Bhutan on east side. It is the smallest state in India by population and second smallest by area with only about six and a quarter lakhs people scattered over an area of about seven thousand and one hundred square kilometres. So, the state seems tiny in comparison to the overall size of India with one hundred and twenty five crores people living over thirty two lakhs eighty seven thousands and five hundred square kilometres. In fact, many districts in the rest of India are much bigger than this state in terms of population as well as area. But still, the state of Sikkim enjoys a respectful status of a full state from politico-administrative point of view as well as a separate cadre from All India Services point of view because of its uniqueness in terms of its history, strategic location, and many other features.

Historically, Sikkim was a separate kingdom being administered by a king called Chogyal and it became a part of India in 1975. Located in the lap of the Himalayas, the state is bestowed with mesmerising natural beauty. The locals are inherently peace-loving and God-fearing in nature. In fact, it would probably be the most peaceful and beautiful state of India. People of Nepali origin make the major chunk of the state's population and follow Hinduism but its original inhabitants are the tribal community of Lepcha and Bhutia, who follow tantric Buddhism and tribal culture. Thus, its natural beauty, peace and tranquillity as well as unique culture and tradition also give the state a special significance on the map of India.

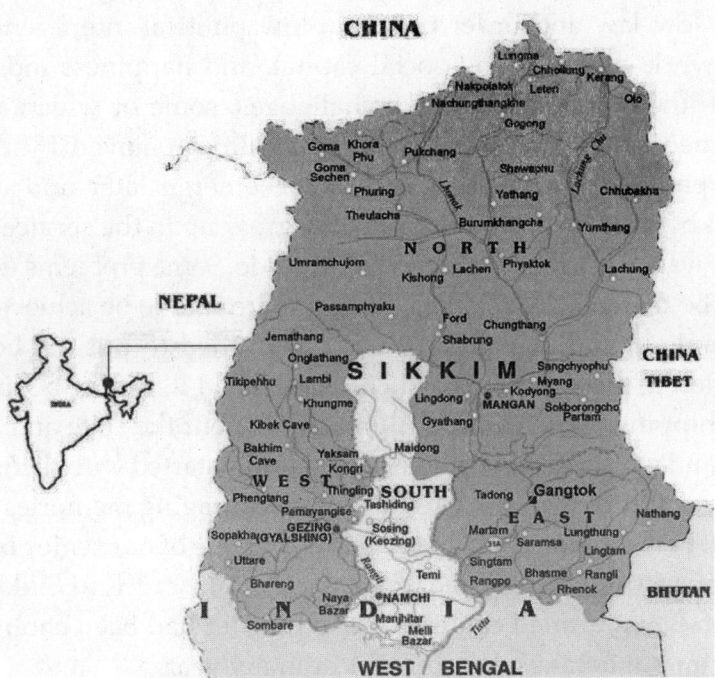

Map Of Sikkim Showing Its Four Districts

The state is politically represented in Indian parliament by one member out of five hundred and forty three members in Lok Sabha (House of People) and one member out of two hundred and fifty members in Rajya Sabha (Council of states). Similarly, the allocated strength in the state for All India Services officers are also much lesser than the most states of India. For the All India Services officers especially IAS and IPS officers, the state provides a different environment than rest of India because administration by All India Services is new to the state and came here only after its merger into India in 1975. Unlike most other states of India, where there was system of ICS (Indian Civil Service) officers and IP (Indian Imperial Police) officers from the British era, the system as well as the mindset of people towards this system is pre-established. Although, a lot of changes have taken place since 1975 but still, working environment is different than the rest of India. I was informed by service seniors that I would have to built up my own image here unlike my batchmates posted in most other states where there is pre-set image of an IAS officer. There are some unique advantages of serving here due to very low law and order problem, low political interference, liberal work culture, good social capital, and happiness index, etc. But, there are some unique challenges, some of which are felt immediately, especially the basic facilities enjoyed by my counterparts in other states and, some emerge later and are realized by officers posted here as they grow up in the service.

Anyway, I felt there is always the flip side. Some problems will always be there because ideal conditions are rare to be achieved. Even sunlight comes with a shadow. I decided to put my best dedication to the service for which I had joined it leaving behind job in shipping, which would ultimately benefit the state and its people and would gain me inner satisfaction. I started with district training with full vigour forgetting all discouraging memories of the past. Few days later, I came to know that one of our senior IAS officers had been transferred from the Tripura cadre to Sikkim last year. Being a small cadre, this one transfer had been enough for Sikkim not to take one more officer in my year.

Later, on analysing the whole incident, I was happy that I stayed calm during the whole period, tried to expedite the matter with a peaceful mind and later, fully enjoyed my time in Guwahati and other North eastern states during the tour. In any way, my worry was not going to help in the matter. In fact, unnecessary worry would definitely have diluted the degree of my enjoyment in the North Eastern states during the tour. In fact, while my stay in Guwahati, many a time I had visualized that I was going to Gangtok to join and start my district training soon after Guwahati episode would be over and the same thing actually happened. Not a single time, the scene of myself waiting for cadre clearance, after completion of Guwahati training, came to my mind. Thus, I believe that it was another evidence proving how positive visualization creates reality, and this was one evidence where the whole development took place over a short period of about a month only.

7

Jogging Amidst Nature

*'A pessimist sees the difficulty in every opportunity,
An optimist sees the opportunity in every difficulty.'*
— *Winston S. Churchill*

It was exactly 5 am., and was dark outside, but the streetlight illuminated the road. A few hundred metres ahead, dogs were barking and it was cold. Dressed in my LBSNAA tracksuit and sports shoes, I opened the main door of my quarters and disappeared into the semi-darkness, away from the brightness of my residence. I started jogging slowly, ignoring my surroundings; this was my regular routine in Gangtok. I knew that it would be dawn in the next thirty minutes or so and by that time I would be mid-way to Gangtok's M. G. Marg area. I was not concerned about the barking because dogs ran away from me when I approached them; I thought that Sikkim dogs were as peaceful as the people of Sikkim and they wouldn't harm me if I didn't upset them.

While jogging along an upward slope I would begin panting after a few hundred metres and after some time, sweat would trickle down my face. But I was used to this. I knew that panting would start reducing in about the next twenty or twenty five minutes and my breathing would return to normal after about forty to forty five minutes of slow jogging. It was better to continue inspite of the panting, though the initial panting and sweating would sometimes discourage me. I used a trick to avoid this trap and would think of a quote that is frequently referred to, 'The more you sweat in peace, the less you bleed in the battle.'

Merely by remembering this quote, I would feel happy about the sweating because I would become more confident about climbing the steep slopes of the Everest.

Thus, I slowly became used to panting and sweating and the feeling of uneasiness started decreasing as days went on, but I was still somehow not satisfied. I used to often question myself, why do I start panting so quickly? Is there any way to avoid it and thus avoid the feeling of discomfort? After thinking about it deeply, I found that when I began jogging, all my focus was on my body and destination. I would count every kilometre as it used to pass and also focus on my breathing, my legs, my ankles, etc. Thus, all my focus was on the process of jogging and panting and I could tell that the fault was in my thinking. The American writer Peter McWilliams said,'Our thoughts create our reality. Where focus is the direction we tend to go.' Now the next question was how I could avoid it. American television host Brian Tracy said, 'The key to success is to focus our conscious mind on things we desire, not things we fear.'

So I decided to avoid thinking about running and my focus was on something more interesting, which would also help in diverting my attention. One way was to try focusing on daydreaming and thinking of some other places, things, or events. I tried this for a few days but it didn't work. Suddenly, I had the idea of focusing on the natural beauty all around me, and that was the solution. Now there was a glint in my eye and I was sure to successfully control the panting to a good extent. I experimented with this and it worked well. I started feeling good about jogging and began enjoying the whole process, although my speed was reduced to some extent as I focused on the surroundings.

Now, while jogging, my main focus was enjoying the freshness of morning, breathing crisp air and enjoying the beautiful surroundings. I used to be lured by the enchanting greenery of the opposite valley, the tens of flowerpots kept on the parapet of houses. I would also catch sight of people sweeping the road, people coming out of their houses with garbage bins in their hands and garbage vehicles collecting the trash. It was no surprise that Sikkim was so clean and beautiful. The overall effect in changing my focus and thinking was that I started enjoying the whole process and my panting was reduced to a minimum. Although this was a new conclusion I had just tried, it was not new for the rest of the world. Later, when I read Chinese philosopher Confucius, I realised the same. He said, 'Choose the job you love and you will never have to work a day in your life'. After that, I started enjoying the process and jogging was not tedious any more. Upon changing my thought process and my focus, jogging seemed to be a new experience and I would have wanted to do it even if I was not preparing to climb the Everest. There were also additional benefits. It made me feel great during the daytime and my body seemed to be lighter and my movements would be easy after sweating it out in the morning.

I felt fresh when I jogged; it was like enjoying a slow morning walking except for the times when any vehicle passed or crossed, releasing smoke on the road. But it was still much better than the dust and pollution in New Delhi or Mumbai. An early morning jog on the road was better for me to avoid the dirty smoke from vehicles in the absence of a big stadium. But I preferred to jog on sloping paths even if it was at the cost of inhaling a little bit of smoke because it gave me a real feel for mountain terrain which would help me in climbing the Everest. This was why I preferred jogging along the road rather than visiting gyms or running on the flat surface of a playground.

Life had been happy and peaceful in Sikkim since I had joined, around mid-July. I continued jogging in the morning. In fact, now I slowly started increasing the duration in order to improve my stamina. It was obviously due to my motivation to scale the Everest. There was nobody to guide me or discipline me to do the same on time and hit a certain target within a time limit. I was my own boss. On an average, my weekday morning routine was to wake up at 4:30 am, freshen up and get ready by 5 am. I would jog from 5 am to 7 am, during which I would jog an average of 15 kilometres to 25 kilometres and then stretch, rope climb, etc. for another hour. So, my morning routine was over by 8 am or 8:30 am. Next, I would listen to the national news update on TV; this was a time for relaxation after the morning grind. Then I would get ready for the office and leave at 9:30 or 9:45 am. Normally, I would spend the evening on other activities apart from exercise. On the weekends, I would trek in the surrounding areas, which was on an average from 5 am to 1 pm with a rucksack weighing more than 15 kilograms on my back. I would normally cover a distance between 25 to 35 kilometres.

Among all these activities, the only hard part was getting out of bed on cold mornings and getting ready. I used to be strict with myself about this but, after all, the main rule of life is to live happily and this would remind me to relax. Sometimes I would excuse myself from daily drills of jogging and would join the Lumsey Loyal morning walk group to accompany some of the health conscious senior officers or sometimes would even excuse myself fully from all morning physical activities by waking only after the sun was up, with a relaxed smile on my face. I still miss those pleasant moments of walking in the lap of greeneries from Lumsey colony to the rivulet side and the wonderful company of Vineet Vinayak Sir, A. K. Yadav Sir, K. Sreenivasulu Sir, A. K. Singh Sir, and Manoj Tiwari Sir in the process. Those memories would remain evergreen in my mind as we all are separated presently due to being posted at different places.

Jogging in a state like Sikkim is a very pleasant experience. My normal route was the road from my place to Gangtok Bazar area, which was free of traffic early in the morning. I would slowly jog upwards for about seven to eight kilometres (an exhausting task) and my T-shirt would become thoroughly soaked in the cold weather by the time I reached the highest spot. The jog down used to be easy and relaxing. To avoid taking the same route every day, which was boring, I had selected four different routes of different distances in different areas.

But jogging and weekend trek itself were not sufficient for training myself to climb a peak like Mount Everest and it was essential that I should get some technical training to develop my climbing skills. I had earlier planned to do mountaineering courses from the Himalayan Mountaineering Institute in Darjeeling, but I could only attend them if I got leave to do so. My next challenge was to convince my district collector to grant me leave and simultaneously, arrange for sponsorship for the expensive Everest Expedition or become part of a government sponsored team.

Meditating and relaxing the body after long jogging in Gangtok.

I was being trained in Gangtok, the capital of Sikkim, as well as the district headquarters of the East District. I was given government quarters in the All India Services Colony where many senior officers from IAS, IPS, and Indian Forest Service stayed. I used to accompany a very senior officer from the 1980's batch, Shri Alok Srivastava, for morning walks when I wanted to take a break from long-distance jogging. I shared my Everest plan with him, which proved to be a boon. He had worked as the Secretary in the Tourism and Civil Aviation Department and had known a few mountaineers in his times. He told me to come to his office and when I went, he had called a mountaineer, Mr G. T. Bhutia, the Director of Indian Himalayan Centre for Adventure and Ecotourism (IHCAE), a training institute for mountaineering and other adventure sports, a platform to promote eco-tourism, that is located at Chemchey, South Sikkim. The Director of IHCAE was popularly known as Director Chemchey.

He proved to be very supportive. He revealed that one such expedition was in the process of being approved by the Government of Sikkim and if approved, he assured me that I could be a member of the team. He said that the expedition would be the first Everest expedition fully sponsored by the Government of Sikkim that was to go the following year. Headed that I was lucky it would be during my time and because I was young and looked very energetic, he was quite confident that I would be able to make it to the top. He told me that Mr Atul Karwal, the first IPS officer to reach the Everest, had also climbed under his leadership at the age of forty plus. I was much younger and looked stronger, so I would be able to make it. On asking about the training courses required, he explained that if I did basic mountaineering course from HMI Darjeeling, it would be better. Even if I didn't do it, he assured me he would give basic and advance training to each member of the government sponsored team during the Pre-Everest training camp and that would be enough. This was a ray of hope and therefore, I did not worry about the matter much further.

However, I still wanted to do the basic mountaineering course so I would be better equipped with the professional skills as I had heard that HMI Darjeeling was the best institute for mountaineering training in the area. I needed four weeks leave to do the course because that is how long it was. My training officer who was also my boss was Shri D. Anandan, an IAS officer of 2000 batch, who was considered very strict, disciplined, and hard working. As I had recently joined district training under him, so I sought to enquire about his nature and whether he granted leaves to trainees, etc. I enquired with my immediate senior Shri Kapil Meena (who had also been trained under the same collector as I had), who told me that the district collector was very strict and went by the rules. The previous year, the former had hardly got any leave during one year stay but I was determined that I would go for the training at any cost.

Now I had to devise a way to get leave for it. I thought that it would be foolish to ask the district collector directly for leave so soon after joining district training because my request would be rejected if he was not persuaded. So I tried to think of other ways to first update him about my seriousness and high degree of commitment to scale the Everest through third parties, conveying that I was preparing hard and was looking forward to his support and had even started long-distance joggings in Gangtok as part of my training. Because I was staying in the All India Services Colony where many other senior officers lived, who served at prominent posts in Government of Sikkim once, I would meet them often. I started sharing my plans about Mount Everest with them and all of them were supportive of it. Feedback was also going to my district collector. At the same time, I was taking my formal district training very seriously and was trying to cover as many areas as possible in the shortest possible time so I could compensate for my leave period. This was probably sending a good message to my district collector. Around mid-August in 2012, I booked my basic mountaineering course, which was scheduled from 15th September to 12th October, 2012.

Finally, in the last week of August, I asked my district collector for leave so I could take the basic mountaineering course, citing my plans to climb Mount Everest as the reason. Luckily he turned out to be very supportive of the idea and even suggested that I should take earned leave and go for the training, because if I tried for on-duty training it was possible that I wouldn't get leave on time. I took earned leave and went. Although I also wanted to take leave for the advance mountaineering course, it was not the right time to ask for anything else.

8

The Toughest Training: My Experience at HMI

On September 14, 2012, I reached HMI Darjeeling in my official vehicle. I knew that for the next four weeks, I had to forget that I had cleared the Civil Services Examination and had become an IAS officer because even thinking about my profession would be a major obstruction in completing the training. So, I came out of my vehicle and went to the registration office straight away. Luckily, there was no one in line and the person at the registration desk ticked my name off. I completed the joining formalities and was allotted a room meant for eight people; it had four bunk beds. The other seven roommates were: a physical training instructor in paramilitary, a soldier in the Indian army, a software engineer who was posted in a foreign country, a management professional from Delhi, a NCC cadet from South India, and two students from Nehru Yuva Kendra, Bihar. Together, we had good fun.

The course was partly a training module at the HMI campus in Darjeeling and partly in the mountains in West Sikkim. The first training session of ten days took place at Darjeeling and consisted basically of morning exercises, then theory classes and rock climbing practice at a nearby spot where we practiced on different types of rocks, artificial and real. Short treks to different places were also organized, to understand the capacity of the trainees. Those were good days, with my performance satisfactory and I enjoyed the training.

After the warm-up training at the HMI Campus, trainees are sent for field training to Chowrikiang in West Sikkim, which is located near the Nepal-Sikkim border around the Kanchendzonga Base Camp area. It is the Base Camp of Mt. Kabru, the second highest peak of Sikkim after Kanchendzonga. It is situated at 14000 feet above the sea level and it can be reached from Darjeeling after a day's drive followed by three days of trekking.

Climbing Artifical Rock Wall in HMI Darjeeling.

The first day, we drove to Yuksom and stayed there overnight. It was monsoon and the trainees were asked to stay inside in a building that was under construction; it had no doors or windows and was surrounded by thick woods. The location was not the problem but the leeches that were coming in, were certainly a problem. All the HMI staff and instructors stayed in the tourist hut, which HMI had been renting for many years. We had to go there for dinner and then return to our building through the jungle. The route was full of leeches. It was a horrible night and I couldn't sleep. There was a trek to Bakhim the next day. My rucksack was very heavy but I took this as a challenge. With a few breaks on the way, as the instructors decided, we reached Bakhim, where the trainees stayed in the Bakhim Hut belonging to the Forest Department of the Government of Sikkim. I was quite exhausted but a mustard oil massage gave me some relief and I continued on the journey with the group till we reached the Base Camp after three days of trekking and one extra day of rest on the way to acclimatise.

Climbing natural rock.

The trek was alright except for the intense exhaustion. However after arriving at the Base Camp, I felt like I had a fever and a headache. This was probably because it was my first time being at this altitude for more than an hour. Although I had trekked till about 5000 metres in the past during a ten-day trek in Uttarakhand while my stay in the IAS training academy, I hadn't remained there for over an hour. Additionally, there was a rash on my right leg, which hurt me to walk, whereas training on the glacier required hours of uphill climb just to reach the spot. While analysing the situation I considered quitting the course and returning like a few other trainees because I couldn't participate in any training activities in such bad health.

Camp Site at Dzongri during Trekking

It was very difficult to give up at this stage; I thought of the situation in Gangtok and with how much difficulty I had got leave. Quitting at this stage meant the end of my Everest dream. I thought of the poster in my room in Delhi where I had prepared for the civil services examination. It said, *I will try before saying no.* So I changed my mind and decided to try for a couple of more days, keeping an eye on my health. I met the HMI doctor, took medicine, and tried to focus on training rather than on health-related issues. Soon, I found that the problem disappeared and used to resurface only when I would come back to Base Camp to rest. Slowly this also disappeared. Gradually, I started enjoying the training and my performance started improving.

**Trainees of Basic Mountaineering Course of HMI practising
Ice-climbing in Rathong Glacier.**

This is strange that although the problem in my leg was the same throughout the day whether I was in training or resting at the Base Camp, I felt it only when my attention went to it. I never felt it while training in the glacier. You might have also experienced the similar thing in your life. For example, you were suffering from some health problem like frequent dry cough, which seemed very uncomfortable to you but once you got busy with some important work then you completely forgot about your cough and also you stopped coughing during that duration until you remembered it again, once free from work. Thus, it is not the extent of problem that becomes obstruction in your progress but always, how you focus on it.

I recalled one incident. During my training at Rathong Glacier, we had to climb very steep ice wall with the help of two ice axes without any support of fixed rope, and just below the wall, there was a long but narrow crevasse. The situation was such that if somebody didn't pick his ice axe or his crampon properly into the ice and slipped down then he or she would fall into the crevasse. I saw one trainee, who was repeatedly failing to climb more than a few steps and was slipping down, although the instructor had told us to reach till the top of wall and then descend down in the same manner. I observed that he was piercing the front point of his crampon as well as the ice axe perfectly into the ice but for only few steps and then he was losing balance and slipping down. I asked why he couldn't continue his perfect step forward till the top and he said, he was afraid if he went higher and slipped, then he would fall in the crevasse. He could only imagine himself falling into the crevasse after slipping. I told him to take a deep breath, and first, to forget that any such crevasse existed. I asked him to look and focus only on the slope just ahead of him and climb comfortably. After few trials, he successfully climbed till top of the wall and also descended down safely. Such is the power of visualization. Negative visualization becomes an obstruction to your progress and positive visualization paves the way to your success.

Training on Rescue in Glacier Area.

We stayed at the Base Camp for about twelve days, which we spent getting trained in snow-craft (ice-wall climbing and descending and walking on the glacier), rock climbing, rappelling (descending from the tops of rocks with the help of a rope and other mountaineering equipment), rescue techniques, traversing water bodies or big pits or crevasses with the help of a rope (which we call suspension traverse and taro line traverse). Our day would start at five in the morning and after freshening up and breakfast, everybody had to assemble and stand in a queue at exactly 6 am in accordance with his group. We had to be dressed and rigged with mountaineering equipments and rucksacks on our backs before the assembly. After a head count and some other short formalities, the group would depart towards the Rathong glacier.

Ice Climbing practice session during Basic Mountaineering Course.

We would reach the glacier after one and a half hours of walking uphill. Glacier training started with a basic walk on the glacier on the first day to get a feel of it; many of us had never experienced walking over a glacier before this. We also learned to climb the alpine style with two ice axes, and rescue techniques, route fixing, etc. We would return at around one in the afternoon when lunch would be ready. After lunch, there were demonstrations by the instructors where they showed us various techniques. This was at the Base Camp itself and was comparatively relaxed with respect to the morning schedule. After this, people were free to go to their rooms to change but nobody was allowed to sleep during the day. In the evening before dinner, we used to watch movies about mountaineering and after dinner, people were free to rest and recover for the next day. Near the end of field training, trainees were taken to climb the Renok Peak, which is about 15,500 feet high.

Two unique things about life at HMI Base Camp will always be memorable. The first is the stinking socks in the huts. There were two big huts for students at the Base Camp. Our batch consisted of eighty five students and we were put into these two huts. There was such a lack of space that our foam sleeping mats would overlap. The Base Camp was very cold and trainees carried a limited number of socks. Reusing the same socks caused a foul smell in both the huts. It was very difficult to adjust at first; but slowly, when we focused more on the tough time on the glacier, this issue bothered us less.

Another memory is the freezing cold during night, and after our hot dinner, when it was time to wash our mess tins with our bare hands. The moment we put cold water in the mess tins, the oil would turn solid and we could not clean them until we had added soap. But using our bare hands for cleaning was uncomfortable. The shortcut was to rinse the tins with some warm drinking water without using hands, or be satisfied with cleaning them once a day, and just keep away the mess tins without cleaning for the remaining time after our meal. Sometimes, on using our bare hands for cleaning tins in the morning or night, the fingers were so numb that we thought we would lose them, as they felt dead. But after some time, they would recover.

Trainee's Over-Crowded Hut At HMI Base Camp at Chowkrikiang

Sometimes, I used to feel that life was very difficult there even though I was only there for one trip. I wondered how hard it was for the staff and the instructors who came there regularly with every batch of trainees, and I really admired their determination. I used to remember the hard working nature and will power of my favourite action icon, the legendary Kung-Fu master, Bruce Lee, whose dedication had always motivated me to work harder. I had always been fond of watching his movies and would be spellbound by the perfection with which he fought, ever since I had begun learning karate as a student. Later, I went on to earn a black belt in Itosu Ryu Karate during my training in T. S. Chanakya. Bruce Lee had once said, 'Do not pray for an easy life, pray for the strength to endure a difficult one.' These words motivate many willing mountaineers in the making to happily accept the quality of life at the Base Camp and take it positively. Otherwise, everybody wanted to take a break from this tough life and wanted comfort, but mountaineering requires endurance and perseverance. This training would definitely help us when we would take an expedition to a peak in the future.

Finally, it was time to depart from the Base Camp and we began our journey downwards. But the memory of the twelve-day training and the bodyache would stay for a long time. This would be specially true for me because of the fever and the weakness I had felt on the first day, which had made participating in daily activities difficult. On the second day after my arrival, I had thought of giving up because of bad health, the difficulty of training, lack of hygiene, and the stinking socks. I decided that mountaineering was not my cup of tea, as I couldn't live in such harsh conditions. But I thought my senior officers had high hopes from me, and, I changed my mind. I continued, saying myself that I simply couldn't give up. I adjusted to the conditions within the first few days and in my free time started enjoying the environment, especially the beautiful mountains and the surrounding clouds. Gradually, I started sharing my plan about Mount Everest with the instructors and finally decided to go for the advanced mountaineering course, which would start one week after the current course. I thought that it would make me more confident because climbing the Everest takes almost two months as you have to get from Kathmandu to the peak, and then back to Kathmandu. If I could bear these two courses well (which lasted for a total of two months), I could be confident enough to survive for two months during the Everest journey.

After returning from the field training, there was an artificial rock climbing competition and a race. I participated in both and although I didn't win a prize, I did make a mark by being among the first ten in both. On finishing this, trainees are given different grades. I got an A. This meant I had performed well during the training and thus was recommended for the advanced mountaineering course. It was now the right time to call my district collector and ask for further leave so that I could pursue the course. I called him and shared that I had got an A and he congratulated me. But I added that the HMI instructors had suggested that I should go for the advanced course because the Everest expedition is life-threatening. I said I had also made a personal request to the principal of HMI Darjeeling to allow me to join the incoming advanced course. These courses were generally booked well in advance, so getting a seat was difficult. Luckily, the principal had allowed me to join the advanced course. When I requested my district collector for further leave, he agreed even though there were upcoming Panchayat elections in Sikkim.

After finishing the course, I came back to Gangtok to resume my duties and contributed to the preparation of the incoming Panchayat elections in Sikkim, scheduled to be held on November 3, 2012. In spite of the elections, my district collector let me attend the mountaineering course; I will always be grateful to him for this.

So, I returned to HMI Darjeeling for the advanced mountaineering course scheduled from October 19 to November 15, 2012. Exhausted from the basic course, it was a challenge for me to complete another twenty eight days of the advanced course. But the new thrill during this course was that I found new friends, some of whom were very warm and energetic. In contrast to my mental image of the advance course, the course was not as tough as the basic one. Most of the trainings were repeated with some additions. After training for a few days at the Base Camp at Chowrikiang (at an altitude of 14,000 feet), we went to the advanced Base Camp, (located at an altitude of about 15,500 feet) and stayed there in a tent. We went up till 18,000 feet, which was where the advanced Base Camp of Kabru Dome peak was located. The camp is located near a glacial lake named Bhale Pokhri, which was formed by the receding of the Rathong Glacier and is considered as a sacred lake. Many visitors from Nepal and Sikkim come here to pay their worship. It is believed that wishes come true here.

Trainees Enjoying Hot Tea During Trekking On The Way to HMI Base Camp

Unlike the Base Camp, where the natural water supply from the glacier was available on a 24x7 basis (unless pipe got chocked due to freezing of water in extreme cold conditions, especially during night) through a rubber pipe laid from the foot of glacier until the Base Camp; the water supply system at the advanced Base Camp was different. Water had to be carried manually in plastic containers from the sacred lake till our camp up to a distance of about 150 metres, where water was stored in two big plastic drums kept for domestic use. Every evening after the day's work, all the trainees were queued up starting from the lake till the camp at an interval of one- to two-metres distance and the containers would be passed from one trainee to the next in the queue till it reached the storage drum. The empty containers were returned to the lake through the same process. About twenty containers were used in the process involving about forty four trainees including boys and girls. It was a half-an-hour to forty-five-minutes job to fill both the storage drums. We were not allowed to use the water directly from the lake either to wash mess tins, or for that matter, for any other purposes. It was deliberately done to maintain the sanctity of the lake.

During the stay at the advanced Base Camp, I had a chance to have a fairly long conversation with Sri Kushang Sherpa, one of the most senior instructors of HMI Darjeeling and one of the few climbers, who had successfully climbed Mt. Everest via its Kangshung Face. He successfully summited Everest via the most dangerous and challenging route of Kangshung Face in 1999 along with two other Indian climbers, Sri Sangay Sherpa and Sri Amar Prakash. I asked him eagerly why very few people have climbed via the Kangshung face. He said that it was tough mainly due to overhang, where climbing was required, which was an extremely exhaustive process. This was why many tough and experienced climbers also gave up. I asked him whether he felt scared climbing overhang at such a great height. He replied, 'Don't look down. Look up and focus on the route above. Looking down would obviously scare you.'

What I learnt from his answer was, he didn't mean that you keep your eyes closed from any of the dangers prevailing down. He meant to avoid watching deep down, so as to avoid a scary view of the extremely dangerous location you are in and thus, avoid focusing your mind on the dangerous location where there is no hold for miles down. It would seriously put you in dilemma and threaten you. You would be preoccupied in thinking the consequences if you might slip and that would force you to give up.

Thus, it is extremely necessary to train the mind to avoid all such negative visualizations. It is not only applicable in mountaineering, but also in all other facets of life. It is essential to focus on only those things in life, which would bring success and happiness.

On completion of our stay at the advanced camp, all the trainees came down to the Base Camp and after a few days of stay there, we returned back to Darjeeling. But we had a memorable time spent during the advanced course. On the completion of course, here too, I secured an A.

With few Course mates in HMI Darjeeling.

On completion of these two consecutive mountaineering training courses stretched over a duration of approximately two months, I felt that one stage of my rehearsal for the Everest Expedition was over because during the actual climb, climbers spend roughly two months at the Everest Base Camps or other camps. As I had spent these two months comfortably during the HMI mountaineering training, I was confident and my mind was fully convinced that my body would sustain a two-month stay at the altitude of 17,600 feet at the Everest Base Camp comfortably.

This is very important because the body gets weaker as people stay for more time at higher altitude in thin oxygen. In the absence of such actual stay for such longer duration in mountains during these two trainings, your mind will doubt, whether you can really sustain such a long stay in the Everest region, especially when you are going to do this for first time in life.

It is quite natural that if you are going to do some work for the first time in life, there will always be some degree of anxiety and uncertainty. So, you must rehearse well before embarking on the unknown path. That's why the practice of training is followed. Otherwise, in absence of such rehearsal to overcome the dilemma or fear, fills you with doubt, which, in turn, results in failure. This happens because while you visualize about the probability of the failure in your conscious mind, your subconscious picks up the images of failure from your conscious and acts to turn it into reality. Thus, your visualization becomes the reality.

This is the reason I had planned to have a first-hand experience at some of the major obstructions on the way to Everest by practising the similar situations before actually going there. It would definitely strengthen my confidence and pave the way towards success. In addition to two months stay at a high altitude, there were few more obstacles on the way to fulfilling my dream of reaching the summit.

One such obstacle was a week of very hard and continuous uphill trekking practice, so that I would be able to sustain myself during the final journey, which takes about a week to climb to the peak and descend down to the Base Camp. It takes about five days to reach the peak and about two or three days to descend down depending on the health and stamina of the climbers, and weather conditions prevailing in the area.

Next obstacle was the rehearsal of the final stretch of climb on the Everest, which starts from the south col to the peak of Everest and which takes about twelve hours to reach the top, and about five hours to descend down. The journey starts in the evening and climbers reach the top in the morning and after short break on the peak, they start descending down.

The next obstacle was the practice of climbing during dark hours because I had read that some dangerous stretch of Everest is covered during night times.

Thus, merely completing two mountaineering courses wasn't sufficient for climbing the Everest. I had a lot of homework to complete before leaving for it. This was, obviously in addition to, securing my name in some expedition team. But presently, securing sponsorship, i. e. enlisting my name with an expedition team seemed as the top priority.

9

Staying Motivated

'The key to success is to focus our conscious mind on things we desire not
things we fear.'

— *Brian Tracy*

I returned from HMI Darjeeling after completing the advance mountaineering course in mid-November, 2012. Along with resuming my official duties, the first thing I did was to meet Director Chemchey, who had promised to take me as a member of the Sikkim Government-sponsored expedition to the Everest, once it gets approved by the Government of Sikkim. He told me that the expedition was approved on paper but there was a lack of funds, though he was trying to have them released. He asked me to keep in touch saying he would update me about the progress. He also suggested that I should talk to senior IAS officers and ask for their help in getting the funds released. The advantage of living in the All India Services colony was that I was in touch with senior officers who I would often meet during my morning jog. They would ask about the progress of the expedition and I would update them. One of the senior officers told me that he would talk to the finance secretary regarding the arrangement of funds and I updated Director Chemchey about it.

In the first week of December 2012, it seemed that the money would be arranged through contributions from different departments like finance and revenue expenditure department, tourism, and civil aviation department, and the department of development and planning, economic reforms, and NECA. But one day, Director Chemchey told me that since the list of the members for the expedition had been approved by the Government of Sikkim, especiallythe Chief Minister of Sikkim, I had to get a written approval from the Government and only then would he be able to include my name on the list. I thought this made sense and the very next day I talked to my district collector, who moved a file on December 5, so I could obtain permission to be part of the expedition.

Although the file was moved so I could be a member of the team, the uncertainty of funds and the delays were causing me some degree of worry because everything should have been fixed up by this time. But I was still struggling to get my name with any team. Over the years, while working in shipping, I had learnt to deal with such situations logically and with a cool head, understanding that worry wouldn't solve the problem. I started focusing on alternative ways. Sometimes I thought about trying for a private sponsorship and I started looking to see if I could get some. I looked on internet and prepared a list of companies who were sponsoring mountaineering expeditions. But finally, I decided not to contact them because of the complexities that could arise later if an IAS officer received sponsorship from private parties without apprising the government.

I preferred to contact the IAS association, Delhi, after getting the email addresses of their prominent members from the IAS association page on Facebook. To my surprise, they didn't even reply except for one, and I didn't receive any help. I felt the pressure building up but would not focus on these issues and continued with my physical preparations, considering these were normal difficulties. I had taken up a task, which was unusual for an IAS officer, so they might not have believed that I was pursuing the Everest expedition very seriously. Perhaps that is why they didn't respond. I would assure myself not to worry, and that they would soon realize the degree of my seriousness when they would hear that an IAS officer actually climbed the Everest. I was so inspired and motivated that there was no room for doubt that I wouldn't climb Everest. I had grown much stronger and confident by reading a book, which spoke about the struggle of a person, who survived in the mountains only due to his undefeated hope and positive visualization in life.

The book, *Touching the Void*, written by Joe Simpson, a British mountaneer, was based on his life, when he, along with his climbing partner Simon Yates had gone to climb a peak in South America. The book depicted a rare example of hope, courage, and positive outlook towards life, which is worth inspiring millions of people to never ever give up in life. In 1985, the two young British mountaineers in their twenties went for their first ascent of the previously unclimbed west face of Siula Grande about 21,800 feet high, and located in Peruvian Andes. For support, they had kept only one person as stand by at the Base Camp.

They climbed the peak successfully but while descending, Simpson fell through a cornice and broke his right leg and heel, when they still had to descend about 3000 feet. His partner Joe, then joined two ropes to lower Simpson in turn. He would lower his injured partner 300 feet at a time and then would descend down to him to lower him further. While doing it in a hurry in the dark hours of night in bad weather, he lowered him over a cliff and Simpson was hanging on the rope over a deep crevasse, as the rope was not long enough to reach the bottom. Waiting high on the mountain, Joe couldn't see or hear Simpson shouting for help. After waiting for some time, Joe had no option but to cut the rope. Simpson fell down into the deep crevasse but luckily landed on a small ledge after about 150 feet fall, and became unconscious.

Joe descended down the mountain alone thinking that Simpson died. Later, Simpson gained consciousness in the crevasse but he was severely injured and frostbitten and it was impossible for him to climb up to the entrance of the crevasse. With no hope of any help from outside, he himself had to save his life if he could do so. He didn't give up. Instead of dying there by losing all his hopes, he took a strong and optimistic decision to lower himself deeper into the darkness of the crevasse in a blind hope to find some way out. His hope brought positive result when he got another small entrance in the lower part of the crevasse and he managed to come out on the glacier. Further, he continued crawling and hopping over the glacier and moraines for next three days without food and almost no water to reach the Base Camp and met his climbing partner.

This book immensely inspired me not to lose hope and never to give up even in the worst circumstances and always to look forward with optimism and positive visualization in every moment of life. I felt stronger than before and was determined to face and jump over any obstruction in my way to Everest. So I left all this uncertainty of sponsorship to God and decided to continue with my physical preparations. I decided to take a break from this web and go on a trek from Gangtok (where I was posted) to Mangan which was the district headquarters of the north district of Sikkim, 68 kms from the zero point of Gangtok and 76 kms from where I was staying in the All India Services colony in Lumsey.

Around mid-December there was a three-days holiday in Sikkim for a local festival, Losoong. This was a good opportunity for the trek. The following morning, I woke up and packed my things into a rucksack (including warm clothes, water, dry fruits, a few chocolates, Chyawanprash, etc.). The rucksack weighed more than 15 kgs. I started my journey at 6 am and at about 10 am I called Prabhakar Verma Sir (IAS), Additional District Magistrate of Mangan and told him that I was coming to visit. He invited me to come for lunch. I replied that I would only reach by the evening, so could not be there for lunch. After some time, he called again to confirm why I couldn't reach by lunchtime because normally it takes two to two and a half hours from Gangtok to Mangan. He asked whether I was coming on foot and I confirmed that I was. He said that whenever I got tired, to tell him and he would send a vehicle. I replied I would cover whatever distance I could until 4 pm then I would call him.

I walked till 4 in the evening but I still had 20 kilometres to cover, which would not be possible before sunset; so I caught a public taxi that was coming from Gangtok. I took it to Mangan thinking that it would not be good to trouble Prabhakar Verma

Sir to send a vehicle over, I would call him just before reaching Mangan, which I did. So for the first time in my life, I had covered about 55 kms in a day as I trekked continuously for ten hours with more than 15 kgs on my back. This gave me a lot of confidence but it wasn't an easy journey. When I reached Prabhakar Sir's residence in Mangan and took off my shoes, I had a big swelling near the ankle due to the uneven finishing in the shoe although it was new. What could I do? I had planned to return on foot. I had wanted to start back early next morning and reach Gangtok by the evening, covering 68 kms in a day by trekking continuously for twelve hours but this was extremely difficult with the swelling.

I spent the night at his place and enjoyed the delicious chicken he had cooked. I finally decided not to change my plan of returning on foot due to the swelling. So just before going to sleep, I punctured the swelling with a needle. It was full of pus and I massaged it with mustard oil and slept. The next day, I decided to rest so the soreness would settle down. Prabhakar Sir had arranged for a local fish, Trout. I cooked it and it was delicious. We both ate so much that neither of us was feeling too hungry in the evening, but Prabhakar Sir advised me to eat a little because I had to walk the whole of the next day. I ate a little unwillingly and slept early.

I woke up at 3:30 am and was ready at 4 but it was very dark outside and many dogs were barking. Prabhakar Sir was also fast asleep. I waited for some time and when it was about 4:40 am, I couldn't wait any more as I had to reach Gangtok by the evening. I decided to let the dogs bark; they couldn't stop me. I woke Prabhakar Sir and, after saying good-bye, I disappeared into the darkness with a small headlamp attached to my forehead. I passed by the barking dogs, who couldn't stop me. They kept barking. This time, I was going through Pangthang unlike the last time when I had come via Phodong.

I walked without taking a break from 4:45 am to about 11 am. My watch showed 11:05 am when I was en route from Dickchu to Pangthang. This is a continuous upward trek at a distance of about 22 kilometres. It was a sunny day and I was famished because I had started on an empty stomach. I took a fifteen-minute break during which I hungrily ate a few slices of bread that I had been carrying from Gangtok and drank a lot of water. On the way, I asked the local people about the way, wherever two roads caused me any confusion. They wanted to know who I was and why I was on foot. They informed me there were shared taxis, which I could use because my destination was very far. I smiled and moved ahead wordlessly at this.

Finally, at about 4 pm that evening, I passed Pangthang and then walked for one more hour. Gangtok was still 10 kms ahead and it was going to be dark soon. Fearing that I would not get a taxi after this, I took a lift in a private vehicle around 5 pm and reached Gangtok. It had been a very good day. I had covered almost 58 kms in about twelve hours but the day's trek had been even more tiring than the one I had undertaken the day before the previous day. This had been because of a long, continuous 22-kms upward trek in the sun. But I was quite satisfied because I had been planning this long trek for a long time just to assess my stamina and to see whether I could trek continuously for a full day or not. I had read that the last stretch of the Everest climb is extremely difficult and the trekker has to climb the whole night to reach the top and again for about 5 hours to descend to the last camp.

So this trek gave me a lot of confidence about my stamina, although the low altitude conditions in Sikkim were quite different from those on the Everest, but I had trekked with sufficient weight at the back covering many kilometres in a sunny afternoon. So it convinced me very well that I was in a good position to cover the final stretch of the Everest as I gained practical exposure of twelve hours of continuous walk up and down with weight at the back. I felt relaxed that from then onwards, I could stick to sustainable positive visualization about that particular stretch of Everest, which is considered the toughest part of whole journey, without any chance of any image of failure creeping in my mind. William Jennings Bryan, a famous American lawyer and nineteenth century orator had truly said,

'The way to develop self-confidence is to do the thing you fear and get a record of successful experiences behind you.'

Thus, I felt that it had really been a productive three days holiday. Life continued as usual in Sikkim. I went on preparing myself physically for the Everest in the morning, continuing my regular government duties during office hours and trying for sponsorship over the phone and through internet, in the evening. In the second half of December, the Government of India sent two officers (a joint secretary and additional secretary) as its representatives to Sikkim to enquire about the progress made with regard to the preparation for launching the Direct Cash Transfer scheme as a pilot scheme in two districts of Sikkim. The two Government representatives, my district collector, and a few more All India Services officers assembled for a dinner. My district collector took me along with him. During the conversation, the additional secretary introduced me to the joint secretary and briefed him about my plan to climb the Everest. My district collector, who added that I was very hard working and determined to scale the mountain, supported this. On hearing this, the joint secretary started discouraging my district collector, wondering how he could give me such a long leave during the probation period, which was the training period for an IAS trainee officer. If something happened to me then my district collector would be responsible. But the latter was well versed in all the rules and regulations and he defended himself smartly. However, he was obviously discouraged.

Although I also felt strange on the disheartening behaviour of such a senior officer but I completely ignored it thinking that he must be right in his own opinion depending on his past experiences. I guessed that he might had come across some cases in the past, where some probationer would have taken a long leave giving any such excuse. So, I should not complain and curse him. Unnecessary anger on strange behaviour of that officer was going to harm me rather than making any impact on him.

Owing to this incident, my district collector suggested me very next day that I should take a no-objection certificate from the IAS training academy in Mussoorie. I contacted Dushyant Nariala Sir (a senior IAS officer who was our counsellor in LBSNAA) and mentioned what had happened. Dushyant Nariala Sir consoled me, telling me not to worry. He said that he would send me a no-objection certificate. He added that he was on leave and asked me to send him an email enclosing necessary supporting documents and asking for the certificate the following week and he would get it done immediately after returning. After one week, I sent the email along with all the related documents to ensure the release of NOC so I could participate in the Everest expedition 2013. To my surprise I received the certificate from the academy within a week. I mentally saluted my counsellor's management and the academy management for the certificate's speedy release. I showed it to my district collector the next day and he was overjoyed.

10

The Struggle for Sponsorship

'The Secret of change is to focus all of your energy, not fighting the old, but on building the new.'

—*Socrates*

2013 brought with it, lots of hopes and expectations. As the day of the expedition was getting closer, my preparation was speeding up. At the same time, my concerns for securing a sponsorship were growing slowly. However, I consoled myself by saying that worrying wouldn't help, so I was not worried in the true sense. I continued preparing myself physically and went on with my work but on analysing the issue practically, I realised that the matter was always in the back of my mind. In fact, my eagerness to climb the Everest had grown so strong that I didn't like to take any chances and started exploring my alternate options. The first North East Everest Expedition, which was planned to scale Mt. Everest the same year, was in my mind for the previous few weeks and so, the very next day, I talked to my district collector and told him about my wish to be a member of the first North East Everest expedition as the future of the Sikkim government sponsored expedition was not bright. He agreed and so I wrote a membership application (on January 7, 2013) for the same. He moved another file that very day, asking permission from the Sikkim government.

While my two applications (one written on December 5 for membership in the Sikkim government-sponsored Everest expedition and the other written on January 5 for a membership in the first North East Everest expedition) were going back and forth among the departments of the Sikkim government, I was in touch with Director Chemchey for updates, although I was not very hopeful about my prospects due to actual situation on the ground.

A few days later, I came to know from a secretary level officer that there were no funds for the expedition in the departments as the available funds were already exhausted because the end of financial year was coming closer, so it was not very likely that the funds would be released. This supported my plan to be a member of the first North-East Everest Expedition. I went to the secretariat office building to trace the status of the file for this expedition. I came to know that the file had been approved by the honourable chief minister of Sikkim as well as the chief secretary and the other senior secretary concerned. They would write to the chief secretary of the Government of Manipur, who was the chief patron of the said expedition.

On January 23, I received the approval letter from the Sikkim government confirming my membership to their Everest expedition under Director Chemchey's guidance. But by this time, my hope in the prospect of the Sikkim Government Expedition had gone down because it was not certain that the funds would be released. However, I had learnt to be optimistic. Without thinking about it any further, I met Director Chemchey and gave him the letter confirming that I would participate in the expedition he was leading.

While these recent developments regarding my Everest dream were going on, I thought I would go on a trek to higher altitudes to regain confidence in my stamina as well as to acclimatise myself to the altitude. After I had returned from the training at HMI Darjeeling, I had mainly been absorbed in securing my name with the above mentioned expedition teams. I was not doing anything other than my daily morning jogs in Gangtok and small weekend treks in the surrounding area. This was because I also had to cover the formal training schedule as per the IAS training academy guidelines (which was my main job as a trainee) and send all the assignments to them. I also had to attend duty from 10 am to 5 pm in the district collector's office in Gangtok. Although I had been thinking about the trek for the previous couple of days, there had been no holiday around the last week of January and I had already taken a lot of leave from my district collector to attend the mountaineering training, so I was hesitant to ask him again and was looking for a good chance to do so.

As usual, on January 26, 2013, Republic Day was celebrated in the Palzor Stadium in Gangtok, in the presence of the Chief Minister, the Governor, and all the top bureaucrats of the Government of Sikkim. I also attended the celebration and was invited (along with some seniors) to come to a party organized by a few seniors in the IPS Guest House after the event.

In the evening, as planned, everybody assembled at the IPS Guest House for a bonfire under the open sky in the Gangtok winter. My district collector was also there and I thought that it was the right time to ask him what I had to because everybody was in a lighter mood. Anyway, I was not asking for leave to enjoy a holiday but for a genuine cause. So I told him my plan to trek from Gangtok to Gurudongmar Lake in North Sikkim. It is located near the Indo-China border and is about a 200-kilometres journey one way. I got a week's time to go around and then come back.

It was a good development and I came back and packed my rucksack for the next week. It included normal clothes, warm clothes, dry fruits, one bottle of Chyawanprash, a one-litre water bottle, a rain coat, basic medicines, a head lamp, chocolates, a small diary, and a pen, a book, etc. I always carry enough t-shirts, socks and handkerchiefs, which I need to change daily as t-shirts get soaked with sweat every day during a trek; I am very particular about hygiene. After packing the rucksack it weighed over 15 kgs. Once the packing was done, I was relaxed for the next morning. After setting the alarm, I slept peacefully.

The next morning, I woke up at 5 am. After getting ready, I left my residence in Lumsey, an hour later. With the uphill walk, it took an hour and half to reach the Gangtok Burtuk area after covering about 10 kms. I still had to cover about 65 kms more to reach Mangan. Although I had taken permission for a week, while walking I was also calculating the time it would take to get to Gurudongmar and come back. After many permutations and combinations, I was sure that it was not possible to cover Gurudongmar and come back within a week; there were very few places to stop along the way and there was also the acclimatisation factor with the increase in altitude of about 11,500 feet from Gangtok to Gurudongmar. These factors were very important, in addition to the one-way distance of 200 kilometres. So I decided to avoid trekking from Gangtok to Mangan and cover the distance by vehicle and then trek to Chungthang from Mangan. It was about 8 am and I called up Prabhakar Sir thinking that he could be on the way back to Mangan,as he had to come for the party in the IPS guest house the day before.

Luckily, he had just started from Gangtok and I took a lift in his vehicle. Now it was comparatively easier because I had to cover only 125 kms from Mangan to Gurudongmar. We reached Mangan together in his vehicle at 10.30 am the same day where I got a pass for entering the prohibited area of North Sikkim. I began marching alone from Mangan on foot at 11 am with about 15 kgs on my back. Chungthang is 28 kms from Mangan. The increase in altitude is about 1700 feet. Initially, for more than half of the route, the road goes a little upwards and downwards with an overall altitude that is almost the same as Mangan's. But after crossing Toong police check post the slope becomes steeper. The area beyond the Toong check post is restricted and you require a pass to enter. This is issued by the district administration. Chungthang was 10 kms ahead of the Toong check post. Even though I was a member of All India Services and was posted in the same state, I needed a pass to enter the area. After showing it, I moved ahead on a dusty road going upwards, where I inhaled a lot of dust from every passing vehicle, but I kept moving and reached Chungthang at 4:45 pm. I covered the distance within five hours and 45 minutes at an average speed of about 5 km per hour.

That evening at Chungthang was pretty good as I attended a party with the local Sub-Divisional Magistrate, Raj Kumar Sir, of the 2009 IAS-batch. As usual, the next morning I commenced my journey when it was dark outside and a few dogs were barking. But by then, I was used to all of this, although I was visiting a totally new area. I was going to explore the wonderful natural beauty for the next 25 kms along the gentle sloping route, and then would climb 3000 feet because the next destination, Chatten, was situated at about 8700 feet, whereas Chungthang was 5700 feet above sea level. The route was almost parallel to Teesta River with a lush green forest on opposite slope of the valley. The area is sparsely populated with some locals and army establishments in some places along the way. Enjoying the natural beauty and taking photos, I reached Chatten at around 10:30 am, after a five-hour journey, and took shelter in the Indian Army transit camp. The Indian Army has its own wonderful set up and they are very warm and helpful during these kinds of ventures.

The next day was a day to rest as a part of the acclimatisation process because I had already climbed more than 3000 feet with respect to Gangtok, which is situated at 5400 feet above sea level. There was also a lunch party at the army camp and top officers from the district administration were also invited.

The next day was January 30 and it was going to be a relatively tougher day for me as I had to reach Thangu, which was situated at about 12,700 feet and it was 35 kms ahead of Chatten. After dinner, I retired to bed a little early. The next morning, I woke up at 3:15 am. After freshening up, donning my trekking suit and finally packing up my rucksack, I was ready to move at 4 am. But as I peeped outside, I saw it was pitch dark and so, thought I would wait for sometime as it was too early.

After half an hour of waiting impatiently for it to become less dark outside, I finally left my room (room no. 1) at the transit camp 235 at 4:30 am, although it remained dark. I was wearing the headlamp with my rucksack (which weighed about 15 kgs) on my back. I silently closed the door and moved towards the main entrance where the guards were on duty. Silently, I opened the small grill in the big door not to disturb the guard who I expected to be asleep. But to my surprise, he lit his flashlight and I confidently said I was leaving room no. 1. I moved ahead, thinking how sincerely the Indian Army men take their duty.

As I came out of the transit camp and crossed the village beyond it, I encountered pitch-black darkness. I was entering an area, which was totally uninhabited for about the next 2 kms. There was jungle on both sides of the road. I was entering the area for the first time and was alone in such darkness. Although, I had enquired about the probability of finding wild animals in this area, and was sure that I would probably not come across leopards and other similar dangerous animals, but there were fair chances of encountering snakes. I just focused on walking, cutting through the darkness with my tiny head lamp. I was determined that nothing could stop me from reaching Thangu that day. I mentally accepted some light comments by a senior army officer during lunch party, the previous day, about my capability of reaching Thangu in a day, which is 35 kms and at an altitude of 4000 feet, from Chatten.

As I moved ahead through the dark, the noises of night beetles and other insects coming from all around sounded like an eerie orchestra and I felt like a character in a horror movie trapped in the jungle with ghostly spirits all around. Fear engulfed me. But I tried shrugging it off. Over the years, I had developed the ability to look at my situation from an onlooker's perspective and carefully watch the changes taking place inside myself whenever negative emotions attempted to overwhelm me. I tried focusing my mind on the road ahead and started imagining the beautiful snow, which might be around, on the route in Thangu. Then I realised that I was no longer that afraid. After about twenty minutes of walking along the lonely road, I saw something shiny across the road. *What was it?* I continued walking to find out. When I went nearer, I could see a small stream passing over the road, there was a small structure near it. It looked like a mosque. *But a mosque in this lonely place?* I continued walking towards it and found a small wooden bridge to cross the stream.

I found that there were two stones on both sides with about a metre's gap in between for the stream to pass. I wanted to jump over it. I put one leg on one stone and jumped so my right foot would land on the stone on the other side. But I slipped and landed in the water and both my shoes got wet. Then I realized that there was a thin layer of ice on the stone. *What could I do now?* The mere touch of the ice-cold water on my leg warned me that it was extremely cold and there was a good chance of getting frostbite if I didn't take off my shoes and wet socks and warm up my leg.

I was standing and thinking whether to return or to continue. Obviously, I couldn't go on in this condition because I couldn't take up the risk of getting a frostbite at this early stage. At the same time, I couldn't simply give up. If I gave up where the threat was not really major, then what would happen in the Himalayas where there would be an immediate threat to life even during minor incidents? I had decided to climb the Everest and would definitely do it. There was no question of giving up. I was lost in the battle inside my head. I remembered the words of Eric Thomas, an American writer and motivational speaker, who in one of his books said,'When you want to succeed, as bad as you want to breathe, you will be successful.'

With this passionate thought in mind, I felt completely energized, without giving the matter any further thought, I came out of the water, went to the bridge, sat down, took off my shoes, and tried to pour out as much water as I could by shaking them back and forth. Then I took off my undershirt, the only one I was carrying and put it into one shoe and then into the other so it would soak up as much water from the wet shoes as possible. In the meantime, I took out three pairs of socks. I always carried extra pairs of socks and this time I had seven. Two of them were already wet, so keeping two to spare, I put on all three, one over another, and then put on my shoe, ready to go on. But the stiff shoelace alerted me as the water had frozen in a few minutes and the lace had become stiff. I lost almost ten minutes doing all this and restarted at 5 am.

Again I carried on along the lonely, dark road. After some time, I started seeing houses and I could make out that this was Lachen village. I was relieved that now I was among people although they were probably sleeping in their houses, it was still dark outside. But there were some streetlights. My thoughts were interrupted by a sudden sound of many dogs barking. The sound was coming from a far off corner of the village. I continued and as the sound seemed to grow more distinct, I found that most of the dogs were far away from the main road, but a few of them seemed to be on it. I saw one big dog standing on the road about 50 metres ahead and.

I slowed down. *What could I do?* I stopped and waited for a few minutes. I told myself that I couldn't go back, and I started walking towards the barking dog thinking that dog might leave my path, as I had no intension to harm it. I was just on my way ahead without any intension of intervening in its jurisdiction. I was absolutely determined not to stop even if the dog was haughty enough to confront me because there would be many more challenges ahead. If I turned back on this minor obstruction like barking of one dog, then I would probably need to further develop some more strength to even think about a project like climbing the Everest. As I was moving ahead lost in thought, the dog went inside a house when I was almost 10 metres away from it. I felt relieved and went on. About half an hour later, the darkness seemed to be reducing and light coming in, and at about 6:15 am I had enough light to see the road ahead clearly. I switched off my headlamp and continued my journey.

As I moved ahead, I thought was it justified to be so stubborn to take so much of risk. Since my departure from the army camp at Chatten this morning, I had first encountered the lonely forest, then the stream where I nearly escaped frostbite and then the dog— all alone during the dark hours in my first visit to the unknown area. *What if the dog hadn't cleared my way and bitten me?* I became aware of negative thought taking over my mind. I told myself that there was risk everywhere. If I got scared of these tiny challenges coming up now, then how would I face the mighty mountain, for which I had been dreaming for the last many months? It was fully justified to fight my fear residing inside me and conquer it, so that fear won't dare to raise its head again while I would be on my way to the summit of the Everest.

I recalled the life of Reinhold Messner, the famous mountaineer and the first climber to scale all the fourteen eight-thousanders, while he completed his solo ascent of the Everest in 1980 without any aid of supplemental oxygen. He described the journey in his book *The Crystal Horizon: Everest – The First Solo Ascent*, which I had only read recently. In this book, he beautifully described his close interactions with nature, while he climbed alone. It was just him and the mountain and nobody else in the surroundings.

Walking alone since early morning with nobody else except the silent nature and me, on this lonely route of North Sikkim, I felt a similarity in both situations, although the degree of challenge he had taken, could no way be compared with my journey, I thought. But obviously, this journey gave me an opportunity to discover myself against the fear encountered along a lonely route. And that gave some similarity between two journeys as he revealed in his book, 'In us all the longing remains for the primitive condition in which we can match ourselves against nature, have the chance to have it out with her and thereby discover ourselves. And this is the real reason that for me, there is no more fascinating challenge than this; one man and one mountain.'

He further goes on in this book to say, 'The notion of climbing the mountain again, and this time alone, was for a long time mere fantasy. Only when the day-dreams – stirred up by all that I had read about Rongbuk – outgrew fancy, did there begin an exciting year in my life.' This is why I have a strong belief in the power of fantasy and day-dreams, a form of wild imagination, which can be carefully channelled to get materialised by the way of positive visualization. Until then, I have found that almost all great and successful people have dedicated their success directly or indirectly to something that lies inside them. They have called it by different names—daydreams, fantasy, imagination, or visualization, or mere thought. They all meant the same, the magical power of mind when you bring something repeatedly on its screen, i.e. it is the power of Advanced Positive Visualization.

Busy in my own world, I kept moving ahead following the road and kept turning left and right while moving uphill. In contrast to the darkness a few hours ago, it was beautiful this time. I was walking along the gentle road with the deep gorges of Teesta on my right, taking a very steep slope from the edge of the road and near a vertical face of rocky mountain on my left. It was clear that this narrow road was cut into this vertical ridge, the gift of modern technology. But anyway, this road didn't attract me and I kept moving ahead watching the amazing greenery on the opposite valley. The lush green forest covered the opposite valley from top of the hill till the bottom near the bank of Teesta and looked magnificent. I kept moving ahead enjoying the enchanting beauty to my full satisfaction.

I carried on till 10 am when I reached TCP, where people on duty were already waiting for me. They had received a message from Chatten army camp yesterday saying that I would be arriving there. They took me inside where they had prepared *roti* and *sabji* (cooked vegetables) and requested me to have breakfast. After about five hours of continuous walking up and down the hills, I was famished. I had my breakfast and tea and then after thanking them, I started again at 10:30 am and reached Thangu camp at 12:00 pm.

There, I was greeted by the Army personnel at the 225 army transit camp and enjoyed a comfortable stay with warm water to sooth my aching legs. As planned, I wanted to go up till Gurudongmar Lake but I was informed that the route ahead was blocked due to heavy snowfall and it was not at all safe to travel alone. Although, he agreed to have one person accompanying me, I was not carrying ice boots and additionally had already spent four of my seven leave days. I could not talk to my district collector either, because there was no mobile signal in that area. So I made a logical decision and decided to abandon going to Gurudongmar. After spending the night at the transit camp in

Thangu, the next day, I returned to Chatten after a five-hour journey and halted at the same army transit camp in Chatten for the night. As the night ended into the dawn of January, I was thinking of what could be happening at Gangtok and the status of the file I had moved before coming for the trek.

As usual, I commenced my return early in the morning about at 5 am but it was still dark outside and hence, I expected to hear dogs barking while passing through Chatten but it didn't bother me at all. I felt as if they had identified me as their friends in a day. The downward journey was comparatively easier and I reached Chungthang around 10 am. After a short break (during which I ate two oranges and a few almonds) I continued my journey towards Mangan. Although I was feeling tired during the second half of the Chungthang-Mangan journey, I didn't stop and reached Mangan at about 3:30 pm. I took shelter in a guest house that had been arranged by the Additional District Magistrate of Mangan, Raj Kumar Sir who had been promoted and transferred to Mangan while I was on the trek. Although I was tired and felt that my legs needed some rest, I was happy that I had covered 53 kms in about ten and a half hours.

The next day was February 2, the seventh day and a Monday. I thought I would report to the district collector and pursue my file in the secretariat. Although I had started this trek about a week back thinking that I would trek continuously for a week and go to Gurudongmar Lake and come back, but I had to return from Thangu. Still, I was happy that I could complete a hard trek of 176 kms in six days from January 27 to February 1 with an average of 29 kms every day. Thus, I could roughly complete the long planned rehearsal for the final journey to the peak of Everest, which takes about one week to reach the peak from its Base Camp and then to descend down. Thus, I had mentally cleared one more obstruction for realising my dream of climbing the Everest. Further, there would be no more doubt or fear in my mind whether my body can sustain the journey.

So, the next day morning, I took a vehicle to Gangtok and reported to the district collector at 11 am. With his due permission I went to the secretariat to track the status of my file for my membership in the North East Everest expedition. Luckily, progress was going well and a letter was sent that very day from the Chief Secretary of Government of Sikkim to the Chief Secretary of Government of Manipur. I also called Director Chemchey for an update on the progress of the Sikkim state-sponsored expedition. I informed him about my solo trek in the North of Sikkim. After returning from the trek, I continued my schedule of morning jogging in Gangtok.

In the meantime, while the file for my membership in the North East Everest expedition was in progress, I was trying all possible means and contacting different senior officers to find a link to the Government of Manipur. I was also pushing through the Government of Sikkim's Everest expedition. One of the Sikkim cadre seniors, who were posted in New Delhi, told me during a telephonic conversation that he knew the chief secretary of Manipur very well and would talk to him if I could send him an application and a bio-data with the details of my adventure activities. In those days, I was so overwhelmed by the idea of climbing the Everest that I stayed awake till 3 am preparing all the documents and emailing some. But I didn't receive any reply from him.

A few days later, another senior posted in Sikkim told me that he had received a call from the senior whom I had sent email, who had told him to guide me to focus on my district training and not to go beyond a certain point in trying for the Everest. The senior posted in Delhi also told him that I had sent him an application to contact the Chief Secretary of Manipur and it was difficult for him do so as he had met him only once at some seminar.

Although I was annoyed at this kind of response, it was not the right time to express the annoyance. I simply justified that I had only sent my details because the same senior had asked me to do the same, saying that he knew the Chief Secretary of Manipur very well and that he would talk to him on this matter. Although this was disappointing, I decided not to use up any further energy with regard to it and move on, ignoring the matter. His Holiness Dalai Lama says, 'Do not let the behaviour of others destroy your inner peace.'

God was probably testing my patience and tolerance before giving me the big reward with the chance to climb the Everest and that's probably why nothing seemed to be working out. Thinking back about it now, I think that whatever had been happening was somehow for the good because I had to go through this trial time to realise what true happiness meant after returning from the Everest. Sometimes people, who achieve success easily, don't really understand its true essence. God probably wanted me to understand it and that's why he had been putting me through this difficult time. Our ex-president, A. P. J. Abdul Kalam had correctly said, 'Man needs his difficulties because they are necessary to enjoy success.' A few days later, I received a call from the office of the Chief Secretary of Government of Manipur. They said that it was too late, that everything had been finalised and it was not possible for them to take me that time. I requested them to convey the same to the office of the chief secretary of Government of Sikkim and it was done. A call from the latter office confirmed the same to me.

Now, my hopes were completely on the release of funds for the Sikkim government-sponsored expedition. On hearing about the latest development, few senior officers living in All India Services Colony, as Lumsey consoled me, would try and talk to the officers in the concerned departments, especially the finance secretary to somehow arrange for the funds for this expedition. Luckily, on February 8, Director Chemchey came to the district collector with a formal letter of invitation for the pre-Everest training at Chemchey, which would then continue in West Sikkim. I felt as if my dream had come true. I was happy about this development and shared this news with my seniors in Lumsey colony where I was living.

After this development, one night, around 10 pm, I was accompanying a senior on a post-dinner walk and we were chatting about things in general. He had probably been drunk that night. Suddenly, he said, "Ravindra, you shouldn't go to the mountains." I was surprised but calmly asked him, "Why Sir?" He replied that a senior had predicted that I would die if I went to the mountains. He continued that that senior hadn't told me himself when he had examined my palm the previous week, but had later told the companion I was walking with. I am not superstitious but obviously, if somebody was talking like this, it caused a doubt. For a moment, I was slightly unsure, but acted as if I had completely disregarded his statement and would continue preparing for the expedition. But within a minute, I decided not to entertain such a statement. I told myself to ignore such conjectures. But I didn't believe in it merely due to a faith or superstition, but as a science. I had also read a few books and even knew a palmist from the neighbouring district from Bihar.

I thought I should meet him to confirm whether there would be any such risk involved and decided to visit home before leaving for the mountains. In any case, I had planned to go home and meet everybody and get some homemade food before leaving for the mountains. Now, both the purpose could be served at one go.

I was taking this precautionary measure of meeting another palmist to ensure full inner confidence in me. It never swayed my decision for a moment. I was fully determined to continue my journey despite any prediction by the palmist. But at the same time, I was visualizing positively hoping that my palmist would speak positively and I could go peacefully. I never imagined anything to the contrary. Probably, positivity had become part of my habit over the years.

I fixed up a plan to visit home just after finishing my training at IHCAE, Chemchey. While going for the pre-Everest Expedition at IHCAE, I planned to take enough clothes to visit home without returning to Gangtok as it was a shorter distance.

11

The Chemchey Chapter

'Life's battles don't always go to the stronger or faster man. But sooner or later, the man who wins is the man who thinks he can.'
— *Vince Lombardi*

The pre-Everest training for the seven team members of the government sponsored expedition was planned from Feb 14 to March 11. One day before the start of training, I reported to IHCAE or the Indian Himalayan Centre for Adventure and Eco-tourism at Chemchey in South Sikkim. It is popularly called the Chemchey Institute.

IHCAE is located in a beautiful place at the top of the ridge of a hill near Chemchey village in South Sikkim. It is at an altitude of 6582 feet covering an area of twenty one acres. Green valleys on three sides surround the institute. The fourth side opens towards the North with a road running along the ridge connecting it to the outside world and going up to the nearest small market, Damthang, which is 15 kms from the town of Namchi. Around the institute, there are some tourist huts facing the valley; this comes under the tourism department of Government of Sikkim and is the ideal location to spend some peaceful time away from busy city life.

Our trainer at the Chemchey Institute was Kazi Sherpa, an Everest summiteer from Sikkim who was also going to the Everest for the second time. He would be a member of the first North-East Everest expedition and was with us for one week. He is very hard working, skilled and humble.

Our training started on Feb 14, 2012. The training schedule was something like this: we woke up at 5 am, freshened up, and assembled together at 6 am. From 6 am to 7 am, there would be physical training, which consisted of jogging and stretching. From 7 am we were free until we had to assemble together again at 8 am. During this time, we had to have breakfast and then change into down suits with all our climbing gears. From 8 am to 12 am, we were taken for field training which consisted of different activities on different days like rock climbing, jumaring, rappelling, rope coiling, commando crawling along a horizontal rope, monkey crossing, etc.

IHCAE Campus In the Lap of Nature

We also practiced night walking. There would be a sudden whistle at 1:50 am and we would be ordered to assemble immediately with all our gears. At 2 am, we would start for an 8-kms-long night trek through the jungle with headlamps on our head. Once the whole team (including the leader) lost its way and it took about ten minutes to find the right way. One day, we were taken to the nearby Tendong Hill for a trek. It was located at an altitude of 8800 feet. That day, we trekked for 16 kms and climbed from 6582 feet to 8800 feet, which meant the altitude gain of about

2200 feet. The afternoons were for the theory classes about the climbing, equipments, the dangers in the Himalayas, etc.

After one week of training at the institute, we were taken to West Sikkim for field training as well as acclimatisation. Two trainers were called from outside to train us as our only trainer, Kazi Sherpa, had left after one week to join his team, the first North East Everest expedition, 2013. The team members and the trainer wanted to go up to about 20,000 feet height for a better acclimatisation but due to heavy snowfall and the expected danger during the trek, Director Chemchey, (who had also come with us) decided to limit the journey to 13,000 feet (3950 metres) at Dzongri and thus, we camped there in a tourist hut.

There, at Dzongri, our routine was to wake up at 6 am, breakfast at 7 am, and assemble at 8 am in full gear (rucksacks, crampons, ice-boots, gaiters, wind cheaters, ice-axes, harness, ascenders, karabiners, descenders etc.) and carry on to field training in the surrounding area. From 8 am to 1 pm, there would be field training during which we would cover different activities on different days like trekking on fresh snow (which was exhausting with boots weighing 2kgs and crampons on each leg), jumaring and rappelling on ice-faces and rock faces, trekking to the Black Kabur slope to a height of 15,500 feet and more. After returning from the day's practice with hungry stomach, lunch would taste like a delicacy. The time after lunch was comparatively relaxed, and was kept aside either for lighter activities inside the hall in the tourist hut, or just outside it. Some of our days were completely free after lunch and then I would hear loud laughter from adjacent room, where other trainees would tell jokes in Nepali followed by loud laughter.

Evenings were for music as almost all the trainees and instructors would assemble in the dining hall. A few were singers, few were dancers, and the rest used to contribute to the music, using their plates, palms, etc. Some lovely singing and dancing sessions were organized. Everybody except me was either from Sikkim or Darjeeling and so had been born and brought up in culture where women would sing and dance freely with men without any hesitation; this is missing in the mainstream Indian culture. So you could witness perfect team spirit during the cultural evenings. Nobody could dance so well as that old man, Director Chemchey, who was over 60 years old. But while dancing, he was more active than the teenagers. His swift movements during the Bhutia tribal dance would make him the centre of attention.

After the dance, we would ask him about his youth period then he would tell us that it had been very colourful and that girls were crazy for him and some, still date him. At this, he would smile and everybody else would clap. The evening event shifted to dinner at the same place whenever the food was ready. After this, everybody would retire to their rooms except for a good number of trainees, who were staying in the dining hall and who would spread their foam mats and sleeping bags after clearing away food waste. So the evenings at Dzongri were as lively as they were in the plains. The night was mostly for rest except one, when we went for a night walk in the snow with our headlights on.

Overall, the training was enjoyable and memorable. We returned to Chemchey on March 2, and were free from next morning. Thus, our training at the Chemchey Institute came to an end. I was happy that I was able to refresh my memory of climbing skills learnt at HMI Darjeeling and also improved physical stamina during this training conducted by IHCAE. But I was much happier that I had practised night walk on snow, fully rigged with all the climbing equipments and the headlamp on my forehead. Now, I was confident of doing same in the Everest where some stretch of journey is also covered during dark.

Thus, I had mentally cleared the last obstruction on my way to Everest with the practice of trekking in forest and walking over the snow during night time. Previously, I had already completed a rehearsal of two-months at the Everest Base Camp from a training of two months at HMI Darjeeling. One week of continuous movement during the final journey for the Everest peak, by one week of hard trek in North Sikkim, and twelve hours of continuous climb during the final stretch of the Everest from south col to the peak by twelve hours of continuous trek from Mangan to Gangtok. Although we can't compare the atmospheric conditions between Everest and Sikkim-Darjeeling, but these practical exposures for a longer duration gave me a better confidence that I could very well sustain my body for a longer period during the Everest climb.

I felt relaxed, with my mind devoid of negativity and the heart brimming with confidence. I believed the fact that I would sustain positive visualization about scaling the highest peak of the world without letting anything bring me down.

12

Nobody Has Seen Tomorrow

After finishing our training at Chemchey, I went home (with the district collector's permission) to meet my near and dear ones before leaving for Nepal for the expedition. I had planned to meet as many relatives as possible over a few days of leave because when you are going on such kind of life-threatening adventure, you never know what might happen to you. I always pictured myself climbing the Everest to pay homage to Mother Chomolungma and returning happily. But being a rational person, I couldn't keep my mind and eyes totally closed to the risk associated with mountaineering. This seemed true especially after watching so many movies and reading so many write-ups about mountaineering (and the Everest journey in particular), and also hearing from many mountaineers over the last one year that one couldn't be sure if they would return alive from the mountains. I had already read and seen accounts of many people meeting with unexpected death. In fact, nobody who died while climbing the Everest knew that they were going to lose their lives; otherwise they wouldn't have tried at all. So, long ago, I had decided to prepare for the worst and hope for the best.

After leaving Sikkim, I first came to Patna, where a meeting with the palmist was arranged at my cousin's hostel in Nalanda Medical College and Hospital (NMCH). I look at palmistry more as a science than its prophetic value and don't intend to spread any superstition. I believe that it is a systematic study of the structure of hand and it's lines' formation, ridges, and creases on the fingers and palms, formation of nails, skin texture, and colour, flexibility of hand, etc. I believe some palmists read the various characteristics of palms and hands and come to the conclusion based on certain calculations.

Although modern science has not taken it seriously and has considered palmistry as a pseudoscientific or superstitious belief, here, I will try to explain you how my belief in palmistry deepened, based on scientific research and findings, by giving brief information on the matter.

Our body consists of organ systems, organs, tissues, cells, molecules and atoms, which are the building blocks of our body. Although an atom is the smallest possible piece of an element that retains all the properties of that element (For example, an oxygen atom reacts the same as a bottle full of oxygen), a cell is the smallest unit of our body that performs many important functions and so, is called the fundamental unit of life. The nucleus of each cell in our body contains DNAs, which carry the genetic information and which are tightly packed into structure called chromosomes, which consist of long chains of DNA and associated proteins.

DNA (or deoxyribonucleic acid) is the molecule, which consists of long chains of nucleotides. Gene is basic unit of hereditary information. It consists of a specific sequence of nucleotides at a given position on a given chromosome that codes for a specific protein. Each nucleotide consists of three components, a nitrogenous base, a five-carbon sugar molecule and a phosphate molecule. Nitrogenous base, basically, contains nitrogen atoms. A sugar molecule contains carbon, hydrogen and oxygen atoms. A phosphate contains phosphorus atom and oxygen atoms. Thus, we see that DNA as well as gene consists of nitrogen, carbon, hydrogen, oxygen, phosphorus atoms etc.

The major elements present in our body by mass are Oxygen (65%), Carbon (18. 5%), Hydrogen (9. 5%) and Nitrogen (3. 2%).

Almost 99% of the mass of human body is made up of six elements: oxygen, carbon, hydrogen, nitrogen, calcium and phosphorus. Thus, the prime constituent of whole body is same as constituent of DNA carrying hereditary information.

Similarly, the planets and stars, which are used for planetary calculations in astrology, are also comprised primarily of the combination of few of these important elements. For example, Earth and Mars consist of central core of metallic iron and nickel, mantle of silicon and oxygen and lesser dense crust of lighter materials. Similar to Earth, the atmosphere surrounding Mars consists of carbon dioxide, nitrogen, oxygen etc. but, unlike Earth's atmosphere, atmosphere of mars contains mainly carbon dioxide with some nitrogen and less than 1% oxygen.

My palmist explained to me that astrologers believe that the gravitational force exerted by planets and stars as well as the rays coming from these heavenly bodies affect the development of a child in womb. He said that the gravitational force exerted by the other heavenly bodies on Earth is not the overall force exerted on Earth as one unit, but this force influences each and every element on Earth including the development of DNA and gene in the mother's womb. Thus, the different constituents of the planets in terms of different elements and its varying distance from Earth have great impact on the development of DNA and the gene, while the embryo develops into full-grown baby during nine months in the womb. The whole life of a person is coded in a DNA, which develops during the gestation period. Also that palm of the hand reflects the DNA formation in a particular person.

We are well aware of gravitational forces. I could make out the concept of rays coming from planets also because Paramahansa Yogananda mentioned in his book, *Autobiography of a Yogi*, 'A radio microscope, devised in 1939, revealed a new world of hitherto unknown rays. Man himself as well as all kinds of supposedly inert matter constantly emits the rays that this instrument sees. " The existence of such rays coming from man and all living things has been suspected by scientists for many years...

'The discovery shows that every atom and every molecule in nature is a continuous radio-broadcasting station (see p. 151).'

My palmist explained that a good astrologer can decode the DNA formation or 'codon' based on the planetary positions at the time of birth and they can accurately predict the whole life of a person. Similarly, a palmist can decode that DNA formation or codon by reading the palm of the person and can predict future.

For example, if a person has to die due to cancer in his forties then the Cancer gene is placed in the chromosome of that person during his growth in mother's womb only but it will be active after four decades. Such a gene becomes a part of the DNA formation or codon, which is decoded by an astrologer or a palmist depending on their knowledge and practice.

I also knew that many studies and researches had been carried out by the scientists at the University of Southampton, UK and the National University of Singapore to determine how much a baby's development in the womb was determined by the genes inherited from the parents, as compared with the prenatal environment like mother's nutrition, mental health and lifestyle. The research provided new evidence that most of the variation between babies arises from the interactions between the environment experienced in the womb and the genetic information inherited from the parents. This study is done under Epigenetics, which is a branch of the Genetics studying the external modification to DNA caused by external environmental factors without changing underlying DNA sequence. External modification to DNA causes heritable changes in gene expression, i.e. it turns the genes active or inactive and affects how cells read genes.

So, we can make out the impact of environment on the development of embryo in the womb. Although these researches have not accepted the impact of planetary position as one of the environment, astrologers do believe in it. Thus, we can make out the impact of planetary position on lives of people based on scientific research on Epigenetics.

Leaving behind above scientific explanation also, over the years, I have learnt to look at the positive aspect of anything and get benefited without focusing too much on its flipside. In case of palmistry too, I look at it from the point of view that if people believe in palmistry then whatever a palmist tells, they would believe it and probably would imagine happening the same in future. They would create some definite image about their future in their conscious mind and subsequently, the conscious mind will send the image to the subconscious and the subconscious would start working to materialise the image in real life and the image would be materialised in life if properly transmitted to the subconscious mind. Here is the benefit. And if people don't believe, then this question doesn't arise.

You may question that what would happen if palmist forecasts negatively. Paramahansa Yogananda mentioned in his book *Autobiography of a Yogi*, 'The message boldly blazoned across the havens at the moment of birth is not meant to emphasize fate- the result of past good and evil— but to arouse man's will to escape from his universal thraldom. What he has done, he can undo. None other than himself was the instigator of the cause of whatever effects are now prevalent in his life (see p. 162).' Thus, it is always possible to nullify the negative forecast by astrologers or palmists by our continuous positive visualization.

Furthermore, we can't ignore the fact that, in the yogic and acupressure methods of healing, different parts of palms and hands are pressed at prescribed intervals to cure some of the serious diseases of human body like cancer, kidney failure, eye sight failure, etc., which were considered incurable by modern medical science until recently. Many researches have been carried out on the hands and palms, which have considered it something more than merely normal parts of the body.

Over the last decade, research has found the hand and palm as an instrument to gauge health, innate abilities, personality traits and even sexuality. The hand has been viewed as a map of psychological development in human in the uterus much like the rings inside a tree mark its growth. One of the most fascinating facts discovered about palm is the ratio between fourth (ring) and second (index) fingers and its link to levels of testosterone and oestrogen. The fourth fingers length is positively correlated to testosterone, while the second finger with oestrogen. Men tend to have longer fourth (ring) fingers compared to their index finger, while women have longer index fingers. Similarly, Diabetes is often accompanied with Terry's nails (half white and half pink nails), blue fingernails indicate poor circulation, lung or heart problems. Even certain swirl patterns of the lines on our palms are known to be associated with certain genetic disorders. These few aforesaid facts indicate that there are many things, which are yet to be discovered about palms and hands, and thus, leave a room for further research on the matter.

This time, my only focus was my safety during the climb. The Everest was famous for taking the lives of climbers in different ways. I just asked the palmist for a risk analysis for the next three months telling him my plan of climbing the Everest and the prediction one of my seniors had made. He read my palm and said very confidently,'You won't get even a scratch for the next one year.' I looked very relieved as I had always trusted his readings and predictions. But still, as both the predictions from here and the previous one were completely opposite to each other, I had a little doubt. But I squished them in time. I said to myself that nothing was going to happen to me and that I would return with full confidence and good health.

This thought boosted my morale a lot and the same day, I came home to Begusarai.

During this visit home I deliberately met most of my relatives living in my district Begusarai and some in the adjacent district, Samastipur. I had not visited Samastipur over many years, they had been living there. I did not tell them that I was going to the mountains as there might have been a lot of negative speculations. Even at home, I was not very clear about my mountain climbing plans and the risk associated with it. I just told my father that I would be going to Nepal for two months and so, they would not be able to reach to me over my phone. I knew that if I told them the truth, it would had been a problem. They would had been worried about my safety, which would disturb me. Although I didn't want to waste my energy convincing other people and had decided to give them a vague picture about my Nepal visit except for my *Mamaji*, who I had considered a wise person and he did understand the matter well. I had told him mostly everything, except the death cases at Everest.

After having a good time at home and collecting the necessary eatables, I came back to Sikkim.

13

Trough of the Tide

'Things don't go wrong and break your heart so you can become bitter and give up. They happen to break you down and build you up so you can be all that you were intended to be.'

—*Charles Jones.*

When I came back after the few days' visit to my home, the whole team was expected (as Director Chemchey had planned) to meet the honourable Chief Minister on March 12 before the formal flag-off scheduled on March 16. But it wasn't possible as he was unavailable.

After I returned to Gangtok, I joined my office and thus resumed district training. But a new development was taking place in town. I heard that a few local groups in Sikkim (TAAS, SAATO, SMA, SAMA) united against Director Chemchey and submitted a petition to the secretary of Tourism and Civil Aviation Department, under whose umbrella the Chemchey Institute as well as the Everest Expedition were covered. They complained against Director Chemchey for lack of transparency in the selection procedure in picking team members for the Everest expedition. On March 14, they issued a press release talking about the irregularity in the selection procedure and demanded the expedition to be postponed till fair selection was done.

The next day, March 16, most of the local newspapers covered the news but Director Chemchey and other members were unaware about this development. The Director called up all the members of the expedition in morning and told them to assemble at Samman Bhawan (the Chief Minister's office) at 9:30 am the next day for the flag-off ceremony. We were also issued the official outfits for the same. But he called again in the evening to inform us that the flag off had been cancelled because of a protest by a group of people about the selection procedure. There were allegations against him that he had kept everything as secret and the selection of the team had not been transparent. They wanted fair treatment for whoever was interested in joining the expedition.

I got a call from a mountaineer from the Sonam Gyatso Mountaineering Institute who told me that a few days before releasing the statement to the media, one of the groups had met Director Chemchey and demanded that their members should also be given a fair chance. But the Director had told them that the expedition was actually being organized for the training instructors of the Chemchey Institute, so he had not made an open advertisement for the selection of the team. As far as the inclusion of an IAS officer in the team was concerned, the Director explained them that it was done only after approval from the Government of Sikkim, and the honourable Chief Minister, in particular.

For the next two weeks, there were many discussions and negotiations between Director Chemchey and the representatives of TAAS, SAATO, SMA, and SAMA. Some of these were informal and some formal, held in the office of the tourism secretary. The question of my membership on the team was a hot topic of discussion. The Director would tell me that a group of people were objecting to my presence in the team, questioning how some non-Sikkimese could be in the team. People from the opposite group would tell me that whenever they had told the Director that the selection procedure had not been transparent and that he had selected a team at his own discretion, he had always answered that it was not by his discretion but that my name had been approved by the Government of Sikkim, the honourable chief minister in particular, so he couldn't do anything.

When I learned that my membership was unsure even after Government's approval, I started trying to ensure that my name would remain on the list. I started contacting senior officers and would tell them, 'I want my name in the list, not because I am a member of the premier service but because I am fully eligible to be in it. In fact, only a fool would go to the Himalayas to die without being absolutely prepared. So, it is not a question of being an IAS officer or Sikkimese. After all, I was serving people of Sikkim and so, shouldn't be debarred from being in the team, just because I ethnically didn't belong with them. To make it fully transparent and completely impartial, there should be an open competition and whoever s selected, should get a chance to be a member of the team.'

By then, I was quite confident and determined that nobody could stop me from securing a position in the seven-member team even if the selection was by open competition, because I had evaluated my performance during the basic and advanced mountaineering courses in HMI where most of the participants were from the defence or adventure backgrounds, or from the hilly areas. Even during the three week pre-Everest training in Chemchey, my performance was the best according to the trainers. In the worst-case scenario, I would be in the top three anyways. Sometimes, I would even openly challenge those who were asking for transparency, to compete in an open competition. But I think that my destiny lay elsewhere.

During that time, my morning schedule of physical training was sometimes hampered as, sometimes, I was engaged on telephonic calls since early in the morning. I was not fighting alone and some bureaucrats from the All India Services as well as the Sikkim Civil Services also supported my case.

After many rounds of negotiations between Director Chemchey and the representatives from the opposing groups, they finally came to the conclusion that some members of the present team would be replaced by members from their groups. They decided that my name and that of two more people (one Bhutia girl from Yuksom, and a Limboo boy from Sombaria, who was a trainee constable in IRB) would be replaced by four of their members. So in spite of the efforts of many senior officers, my name was cancelled.

While writing down my experiences now, I wonder whether in spite of so many senior officers' efforts, my name was really cancelled from the list, though I was completely eligible and the Government itself had approved my name. Sometimes, I wondered whether everybody genuinely supported me or if it had been just a unwilling gesture. It is difficult to say but I am happy that they at least supported me even that much. Some of them held prominent posts in the Sikkim Government. Some locals commented, 'Bureaucrats are effective when it comes to official matters. When it is a matter of vote politics then the public becomes more important and stronger. With the elections (both Lok Sabha and assembly elections) due next year, nobody would take a chance when the representatives of the TAAS, SAATO etc., were demanding something as they control thousands of votes. So even though the Chief Minister himself had approved your name for the expedition, the same Chief Minister probably had to bow down to public demand.'

Those two weeks were an extremely turbulent period for me. Some of my near and dear ones advised that I already had a good job which many were still dreaming of, so, even if I didn't get a chance to go, nothing was going to affect my career. But, by this time, there was not the slightest chance that I would give up my dream, not after coming this far. I was determined to climb without thinking much about how to secure sponsorship. Whenever I tried to logically think about any other alternative, I noticed that signs of worry would begin to surface. However, I always tried to subdue the rising wave of worry with a statement that the young Dalai Lama had made in the movie *Seven Years in Tibet*, a movie that was partly about mountaineering. When Brad Pitt's character went to meet the young Dalai Lama in the movie, the latter told him, "If a problem can be solved there is no use worrying about it. If it can't be solved, worrying will do no good. " So I was keeping calm and remaining normal by reminding myself of this statement. I kept noting these developments as a key lesson in my life. I would tell myself that my fate probably lay somewhere else, instead of this expedition.

At that time, the Everest expedition was a hot topic for the local newspapers due to the tussle between Director Chemchey and other local groups. Anyone following the newspapers and with a little interest in the topic was aware of the developments. So all the seniors at Lumsey were well aware of these developments and some of them seemed genuinely concerned about me. However, I had learned to be calm when the situation was not under my control. I stayed very calm and it was reflected from my body language. I looked so indifferent that once during my morning walk in the All India Services Colony in Lumsey (where I was staying), a senior officer asked me whether I would really be able to climb. I answered immediately that there was no doubt about the fact that I would climb and return successfully. I would have to return only if all the other climbers attempting to scale Everest returned without climbing due to bad weather conditions. A good weather is one of the most important factors for climbing mountains, especially for this one, which is affected by the Jet Stream wind round the year (blowing at a speed of over 100 miles per hour).

By the morning of March 30, while talking to one of the secretaries, it was confirmed that my name was no longer on the list of the new expedition team and the file containing the names of the final members would be taken to the Chief Minister for his approval that day. It was a crucial day for me. It was close to the time I should have started my journey for Nepal but all my dreams seemed to have been shattered in absence of sponsorship. I really missed helpful service senior like Vishal Chauhan Sir, who had told me many months earlier that he would make financial arrangements provided I make it to the summit. But he was not serving anymore in Sikkim and had gone to his native state Uttar Pradesh on deputation. However, I was determined not to give up then, after one year of extreme hard work.

So I consulted a few seniors and planned to meet the Chief Minister that day along with an application. My plan was to request him to include my name on the list, or grant me permission to go through a private agency. After meeting two supportive secretaries, (local Sikkim civil service officers) around 10 am, I went to Samman Bhawan, the chief minister's office, at 10.30 am. I planned to meet the Principal Secretary to the Chief Minister and ask for permission to meet the chief minister but the former was very busy himself, so I couldn't meet him. Finally, I met the PRO or the Public Relation Officer to the Chief Minister and gave him the application telling him about both options. Still hoping to meet him, I waited at the Samman Bhawan till 4 pm. As I waited, I was continuously updating my new district collector Aunjaneya Kumar Singh (A K Singh) Sir and the Superintendent of police Manoj Tiwari Sir about the developments. They were equally concerned about my case. At 4 pm, I got a call from one senior officer asking me to come back. He said that one very senior officer had met the Chief Minister that afternoon and had already talked about my case and the honourable chief minister had nodded his head in agreement.

The next day, March 31, was a Sunday and I accompanied my district collector for protocol duty to the Chief Minister in the morning as he was visiting the ex-Chief Secretary's residence. It was the funeral of the latter's father. This was deliberately done to show to the Chief Minister my presence so that he would get reminded of my case. In a small state like Sikkim, the Chief Minister knew almost all the officers in the state. There, I had a chance to meet him for a moment but this was not the right time and the right place to discuss a personal issue. Later, I continued on with the protocol duty to the Chief Minister as he was going to attend a program somewhere else (Chintan Bhawan) about women's empowerment, and it continued till 4 pm. I came back home. Later, in the evening, I got a call from one of the members of the team saying, that day was supposed to be the flag-off day for the new Everest team but the expedition had been postponed to the next year by the government. Some new group had raised objections and the message had finally reached the Chief Minister, who had postponed the expedition.

This put a stop to all my efforts for the Sikkim government-sponsored expedition and once again, I did not know what to do. The evening seemed very dark. It was beyond my understanding and I blamed it all on myself, thinking that I was not prepared enough to arrange my sponsorship even after nine-months long efforts (since July 2012) when I first came to Sikkim. I felt that the service conduct rules have constrained me more than helping me for a genuine cause. If I had been in my previous job in shipping, the salary of four to five months would have been sufficient to support the total expenditure of the Everest expedition and there was also no need of running behind files for getting the government's permission because it was a private job in a foreign company. In the flow of thoughts, sometimes I felt to just move ahead towards Nepal without depleting any further energy on matters like permission from the government, etc. and if any disciplinary action was taken on account of violation of conduct rules, there a was always an option of my previous job which I could join again. If I couldn't fulfil a worthy dream, being in this service, it's not worth continuing this service.

But the next moment, I would control my emotions and would remind myself that it was only after joining the civil service that the idea of climbing the Everest came to my mind and additionally, there was full support from many of my service seniors, who really wanted me to go. I recalled a very motivating statement of Mahatma Gandhi, who had said, 'God sometimes does try to the uttermost those whom he wishes to bless.' I felt that the same was happening with me. Although, I was going through these tough times, there was no doubt in any corner of my mind that I would not be able to climb. Something inside me was not ready to accept that I wouldn't climb the Everest that year after so much of turbulence since the last year.

The recall of Mahatma Gandhi's tough times during his fight against the British and consequently, the inflow of positive visualization brought a new ray of hope in me and I tried to bring myself back to normalcy. I tried to live with the silent evening, which seemed to grow brighter, peaceful, and charming. I remembered these beautiful lines:

'O God, when I lose hope
because my plans have come to nothing…
Then help me to remember that,
Your love is always greater than
my disappointment and your plans
for my life are always better than
my dreams.'

With this mere change of thought, I left everything to God and surrendered myself to the night retiring from the tiring day. The next morning was probably going to be a new dawn for me.

Thinking about those moments now, when I am documenting my journey, I believe, that phase was the toughest phase of my whole Everest Journey, including the climbing part. In fact, I get more emotional now when recalling the series of de-motivating events I had gone through than what I actually felt during that period. I can observe now only that, whenever I encountered any tough time during that period, God always gave me an alternative positive path to overlook the obstruction and move ahead. That's why, I was able to tide over all those problems and could maintain my inner faith of reaching the top of Everest even if all the options seemed exhausted. Somebody has correctly said, 'Strength is when you have so much to cry for but you smile instead.' I am really grateful to God for bestowing me so much inner strength and positive visualization in life that I could survive through it without being emotionally broken.

At the same time, in spite of this tough phase, I could really materialise my long-time visualisation of climbing the Everest by actually climbing it later that year, which really deepened my faith in the miraculous power of Advanced Positive Visualization.

But sometimes, I think I should not have restricted myself to visualizing only the image of myself climbing the slope of Everest and standing on the top, but also, I should have visualized a scenery, where I was going as the member of a well organized expedition, where everything was executed in a pre-planned and smooth manner and even the flag off was done by some high dignitary. Definitely, I missed all these in my pursuit of the Everest climb without an Advanced Positive Visualization. And hard part is that, in absence of such visualization, my journey passed through a lot of uncertainty and hardships, what you witnessed previously in the last few chapters. But I feel, it probably happened because my will to reach the top of the highest peak was so strong that it ruled my mind most of the time and never gave me a chance to think of the other less important aspects of the whole journey.

14

The New Dawn

Next morning (Monday, April 1), I updated my district collector and the Superintendent of police about the latest development during the morning walk. They said to collect the application for permission to participate through a private agency from the Chief Minister's office and to prepare to participate through any private agency. They told me not to lose hope and assured me that I *would* be going for the expedition. This really seemed like a new break for me. Just after my return from the morning walk, I got ready and reached office a little before 10 am. First, I collected the signed application from the Chief Minister's office during the first hour of the office. Now I had the permission to go through a private company.

The next challenge was to collect funds and contact a private agency. To fix the agency, I enquired and learned that by this time, most of the private agencies would probably had formed teams with the members who had applied to their company or consulted another agency to form a team of a minimum of seven members to lower the Nepal Government's permit charge. It is very expensive for individual members to get a permit to climb the Everest and costs 25,000 USD. But the total permit charge comes to 70,000 USD for a seven-member team, which is 10,000 USD per head. So, all the private agencies try to put a minimum of seven members, either on their own or from other agencies. In this way, they can apply for a permit to reduce their competitive price for the customer.

It was too late and very difficult for me to arrange for seven members. Suddenly I had an idea and I contacted Kushang Sherpa from HMI Darjeeling. He was a renowned mountaineer. He held the world record for climbing the Everest from three sides including from the Kangshung face which was the most dangerous one and which very few people had done. He had been a senior instructor during my training at HMI Darjeeling. He had told me that one of his relatives ran a company in Nepal, which organised expeditions to Mt. Everest. On my request, he contacted Nepal and this proved fruitful. I got a call from Seven Summit Treks Pvt. Ltd., which, later, turned out to be a very reputed company in Nepal in terms of standards of safety as well as the services it provides. The company's boss, Mingma Sherpa, was a renowned mountaineer and had been the first in Nepal to summit the world's all the fourteen eight-thousanders. They were ready to take me without charging extra for being late, and I agreed happily. The day was very fruitful and everything seemed to be moving at a faster pace and more smoothly than earlier.

Now the next challenge was to arrange for the expedition expenditure, which needed a big chunk of money, about twenty lakh rupees, out of which sixteen lakhs was to be paid to the agency in Nepal before my departure for Nepal, and the remaining four lakhs would be used for extra warm clothes, extra climbing equipments, climbing bonus for the Sherpa guide, emergency rescue services, etc. But, after struggling so much and coming so far on the way to my pursuit for climbing Everest, I couldn't be stopped here on account of lack of funds. By the grace of God and active support of a few old friends in my previous job in shipping, family members, especially my younger brother who was also working in shipping, seniors in All India Services in Sikkim, especially my district collector and Superintendent of police, and other friends and well wishers, all the money was arranged over the next few days, which included some private borrowings, some contributions and a loan of rupees five lakhs from bank. By the evening of April 4, it was also paid to the agency in Nepal, Seven Summit Treks.

The next day, April 5, I went to the local monastery, the Inche Monastery, in the morning to offer *pooja* to God and receive some blessings. This monastery is located on a high ridge of a hill above Gangtok city along Gangtok-Nathula road and is more than a hundred years old. The local people believe that powerful deities like the mountain God of Kanchendzonga reside there, who fulfil their wishes. A local Everest Summiteer, who advised me with regard to the local traditions, accompanied me during my visit to the Monastery. Later, I went to the Sonam Gyatso Mountaineering Institute (SGMI) to meet its Deputy Director, Principal, and some other Everest Summiteers. The Deputy Director Rajiv Ahir, an IPS Officer posted here on deputation, met me warmly. He also assisted me by lending me some personal climbing equipments from the Institute, which proved very handy during the climb. The Principal, Sri D. D. Bhutia, with whom I was in communication for more than six months to gain inputs regarding the climb, had become a very good friend. I often heard him talking about the 3Ls and 3Ms of mountaineering, whenever I met him.

3Ls stand for Limb, Lung and Luck.
3Ms stand for Money, Muscle, and Mind.

He often emphasized on the importance of luck and money in mountaineering. By then, I had understood the importance of money involved with mountaineering very well. The Everest expedition costs, in total, about twenty lakh INR and thus, money becomes a big factor and so, it is not everyone's cup of tea, even if someone is perfectly fit physically and mentally to do it.

Sri D. D. Bhutia along with some of his colleagues wished me luck by offering me *khadas*, and he gave me some rice as *prasaad*, kept in a plastic pocket. He told me to keep it always with me during my stay in the Himalayas and while passing through an avalanche-prone zone, I had taken out a few grains of rice and had spread them outside. I kept that *prasaad* with me all the while and it is still with me, at home.

In the evening, I finally finished packing, something that I had been doing for the last few days, carefully ticked off every item off my list. I was ready to leave for Kathmandu the next morning, April 6, 2013.

Next morning, my phone woke me up to soft music. It was exactly 4:00 am and as usual, I wanted to freshen up at my normal, comfortable speed and go out for my scheduled jog. But it wasn't any other day. I was well aware that it was April 6 and I had to catch a flight for Kathmandu from Kakarvitta in Nepal near the India-Nepal border in West Bengal. I also had to travel by road for about six to seven hours to reach the airport. So I was very alert and active but was in no hurry because everything was going as planned. I knew that a vehicle was expected to arrive at 5 am and I had to be ready and ensure that all the essential items were packed. Reaching the Everest Base Camp without essential items could shatter my entire dream. I was well aware that expeditions had failed in the past just because the team had forgotten to take a matchbox. So, maintaining my composure as if this could be the case when I would be on my final climb to the peak, I checked the list again. Money had already been transferred to Seven Summit. Plus, I had taken extra that I could use. I was careful to have only hundred-rupee notes in my bag and no five-hundred or thousand rupee bills, because they were not allowed in Nepal (although Indian rupees were quite accepted).

At 4:45 am, I gave a wake-up call to my help, Mr Chandra who was living in the servant's room outside the main door. At the same time, the car, which was expected to arrive at 5, arrived fifteen minutes before time. I hurried to get ready finally as I didn't like to be late at this initial stage. In the mountains, timing is very important and I was assuming that my actual mountaineering would start from the moment I would step out of my residence for my journey to Kathmandu. At 5 am sharp, when I opened the door, I saw Aishvarya Singh Ma'am, the Additional District

Magistrate of East District and her husband Chetan Chauhan Sir, waiting to wish me luck and bid adieu. At the same time, Manoj Tiwari Sir, the Superintendent of Police of East District, had also arrived for his morning walk. We took a group photo in front of the car, which was already stuffed with all my luggage and was ready to go. Manoj Sir advised me to take the last morning walk of the season with him before leaving. As we were approaching the main road, we met a few more well-wishers, who were also on their morning walk. They too wished me luck. I bid all of them a temporary farewell and headed for Siliguri at about 6 am.

I felt relaxed in the car. I sent a goodbye SMS to my District Magistrate A K Singh Sir. He called back to say that he had assumed that I had already left at 5 as scheduled and thought he had missed conveying his best wishes to me, although he had been awake at around 5:30 am. I thanked him from all my heart for his support and regards, and resumed my relaxed state in the car. I mentally went through everything I had packed in my bag again just to ensure that I hadn't forgotten anything. Even if I had forgotten something important, there was still enough time to procure the same in Siliguri or Kathmandu. I was satisfied that I didn't miss anything important. It was almost like scaling one big Everest, overcoming all those obstacles I had faced during the last one year.

I had been taking every hindrance like bad weather. And as I recollected how all such hindrances passed, I felt very happy and relaxed. I came to the conclusion that it had all been possible because of Mother Chomolungma's blessings; she is the mother goddess of Everest and had been calling me, hence, despite those many obstacles I was able to be there, right then, on my journey to the summit of the world. From there it was all smooth. I thought of myself climbing the slope of Everest, reaching the peak, offering a *khada* and paying respects to Mother Chomolungma. Lost in deep thought, which was sometimes interrupted by the beauty of green valley on the other side of Teesta River, I didn't realize how fast I reached Siliguri. When the car entered the town and heavy traffic sirens woke me up from my meditation, it was 9:30 am.

I remembered that I had to go to Mandeep Tuli Sir in Siliguri and to have breakfast with him before travelling to Kakarvitta. Mandeep Singh Tuli Sir was posted as the Deputy Inspector General Range in Sikkim and had also helped me in getting a loan for this expedition from the bank. He had come to Siliguri that day. He had called me to have breakfast with him. I enjoyed a healthy breakfast with him and his two beautiful kids. I finally departed for Kakarvitta at about 11 am. I checked in to the airport after paying for extra luggage I was carrying.

When I arrived at Kathmandu airport, someone was waiting with a placard with my name on it. This immediately reminded me of my job in shipping, when one person would be sent by the agent to the international airport. The former would receive me and drop me to the hotel to wait till the ship arrived at port.

The thin man at the airport introduced himself as Passang Sherpa, cousin of Mingma Sherpa, the chief of Seven Summit Treks. He said that he had been on Mount Everest six times. He welcomed me with a big and beautiful *Khada*, a ceremonial scarf, and then took me to Hotel Yak and Yeti, Kathmandu. He left me there to relax, saying that Mingma Sherpa had organized a dinner in the evening for the group of climbers. I was very much impressed by the fact that Mingma Sherpa, the owner of Seven Summit was a renowned mountaineer and the first person from Nepal to climb all the eight-thousander mountains, since I came to know about his background a few weeks earlier.

There are a total of fourteen peaks in the world, which are above 8000 metres in altitude and are thus called the eight thousanders. Mingma has climbed all of them. Earlier, I had only talked to him over the phone. I used to get frequent calls as well as prompt replies to my emails till I confirmed my Everest plan with his company after which part of the money was transferred to the company's bank account. So, I expected that he would meet me once I reached Kathmandu. But when I enquired about him after arriving I understood how important he was. The person who dropped me to the hotel said that Mingma Dai would come to the party in the evening as he was very busy organizing everything for the climbers coming from different countries.

Team of Lawrence School Sanawar at Hotel Yak & yeti in Kathmandu (before leaving for Everest Expedition).

In the evening, we went to the restaurant where dinner was organized. The venue was lovely with a pleasant atmosphere. Nepali folk singers and folk dancers entertained the guests and finally, Mingma Sherpa arrived.

After exchanging greetings, he started briefing us, 'The mountains don't care about people who show off. We need to be grounded and not hide any health problems that could occur during the trek to the Base Camp or beyond that altitude. It is better to take care of health issues at the initial stage. If the altitude sickness (with symptoms like dizziness, palpitations, severe headaches) continued, then returning to a lower altitude would be safer, as continuing to climb to a higher altitude could aggravate the problem and could even result in death. This had happened several times in the past.'

Everybody was listening to him carefully as he continued, 'Be careful when a yak crosses your path. Yaks may look calm and peaceful, but, sometimes, they become aggressive and unpredictable. Always stand on the upper slope of the path, away from the drop off and especially when a yak passes. Don't drink water from taps. You can drink mineral water but because the weather is so cold, you will mostly be given boiled water as the company will take care of your accommodation and food. You can use the water directly from the faucet at Namche as the water is clean. But it is also not advisable. You are not in the habit of drinking such water and it may cause problems for you at a high altitude.'

He continued, 'For your information, each one of you will be given one guide but you have to pay him bonus which is a minimum of 1000 USD; but you are most welcome to pay him more as money is one of the main sources of motivation for the guides. It is *why* they undertake this risky job in the mountains. You may be very experienced in your own area but here, in the mountains, please listen to the suggestions of your guide or Sherpa who will be with you. Your guide has more experience in the area and with the risks associated, so please follow him. In case of any problems, you can always approach a company representative, who will be with you while you are trekking as well as at the Base Camp. Don't go around the mountains alone. Always inform your guide and take one person along with you so that if something happens to you, then your friend can inform others and help may arrive in time. But if you go alone, then it would be very difficult and you may lose your life. There are hidden crevasses and you may fall into them, especially at the Base Camp area and above. If you are alone, then no one will be able to trace you and you will lose your life.'

Sherpa went on, 'Please don't display any heroism and always take extreme precautions while climbing or even walking above the Base Camp. Even a small mistake can ruin your chance of climbing this year. Always wear enough warm clothes and take enough warm water and food to recharge your body even if you are vomiting at first, after reaching a certain altitude. Altitude sickness is normal and everybody experiences it to some extent. But you have to act in a mature manner. Otherwise, if you give up eating food there is no option for us other than to call you back to a lower altitude and it may result in a cancellation of your trip. Especially, when you are leaving for the final ascent to the summit, check that you have taken all the necessary items with you. In any case, we all will always be with you to give you any kind of support. And now, we will enjoy this evening. I once again wish you the best of luck.'

Everybody seemed happy at his speech and felt proud that they were going to ascend the Everest under the guidance of a right and experienced person. I also felt that he had given us the best and very useful advice because I had heard about an incident where a foreigner tourist had lost her life because of her ignorance on taking precaution with yaks. She was happily returning after completing her trek to Everest Base Camp. As she was just outside Base Camp, she encountered a group of yaks coming with load meant for the camp. As the exhausted yak halted for a short break, she enthusiastically went near it, probably to play with its horn and had her picture taken with the yak. The tired animal instead pierced its horn into woman's waist and tore her stomach out. She died on the spot within a few minutes.

Anyway, after the speech, a series of introduction and informal chats continued followed by dinner. Thus, the dinner went well with live singing and dancing that reflected the local culture.

The next day was spent receiving equipments and clothing and checking everything properly by trying on every item. Once everything had been received, we were instructed to make separate packages, one which would go directly to the Base Camp and another would be carried by a porter while we were trekking. So we packed accordingly.

The day after, I visited the Indian Embassy and met a senior from the Indian Foreign Service, Sri Abhay Kumar. After meeting him, I visited the Boudhanath Stupa and offered prayer to God for my safety in the mountains. Located about twenty minutes from central Kathmandu, Boudhanath Stupa is one of the UNESCO World Heritage sites and one of the largest Stupas in the world. It is believed that the Stupa was built just after the demise of Gautam Buddha, and is said to have the remains of a famous Buddhist leader. It is one of the most popular tourist sites of Kathmandu. Within a radius of 15 kilometres, you will find Pashupatinath, the Swayambhunath, Boudha Stupa, Kathmandu, Bhaktapur and Patan Durbar Square etc. After returning from Boudhanath, I did some shopping at the Thamel market in the afternoon.

Boudha Temple in Kathmandu.

After a three-day stay at Kathmandu, the company's plan was to start the onward journey on April 9 and to reach the Everest Base Camp on April 17. On April 9, we would proceed to Lukla by flight and then start trekking from Lukla (which is at an altitude of 2843 metres) to reach Phakding the same day. The next day, on April 10, we would trek to Namche Bazar (at an altitude of 3445 metres) and get an extra day of rest to acclimatise. The day after that would be a trek to Pyangbuche where we would meet a famous Lama to receive his blessings. On April 13, we would trek to Pheriche (at an altitude of 4260 metres) and get one extra day's rest to acclimatise. Then, the next day we would begin our trek to Loubuche and the day after, a trek to Gorakshep. Finally, on April 16, we would trek to the Everest Base Camp(at an altitude of 5364 metres). One extra day of rest had been scheduled at two places (Namche Bazar and Pheriche) as the general rule; for every thousand metres gain in altitude, your body should become acclimatised to the change in the atmosphere by taking an extra day's rest.

April 9 was the scheduled date of departure from Kathmandu and as per the plan, we left for the airport again. But this time we took a flight to Lukla, the highest civilian airport in the world at an altitude of 9300 feet. It was also the most dangerous airport in the world. The airport was named Tenzing Hillary Airport based on the names of the people who were first to climb Mount Everest successfully. There was a lot of chaos when we arrived at the Kathmandu airport because each climber had a lot of luggage. On average, each climber had two big bags and a small one. One big bag had to go directly to the Everest Base Camp, and the other one had to be carried by the porter along the trek and the small bag would remain with the climber while trekking. I had three big bags and one small bag. One of my big bags was full of eatables, a few books, and some extra warm clothings. Mingma Sherpa had arranged for enough manpower to deal with all these bags. We were advised to tag the bags that would go directly to the Base Camp separately from the others. This was in addition to a small rucksack, which we would carry on our backs while trekking.

The Kathmandu to Lukla trip took forty minutes by flight. After reaching, we came to know that some of the group members' luggage was coming in another flight, so the whole group would wait there till all the luggage come. Waiting there was quite comfortable, as our Sherpa *Sirdar*, Temba Sherpa, had greeted us on our arrival. We called him Temba Dai out of respect. Dai means *elder brother*. He took all of us to the adjacent guest house where we took off our rucksacks in the big dining hall, and asked for tea or coffee, and later, lunch. A few people went outside and enjoyed taking photographs of the natural beauty of the air strip.

15

The Journey Begins

On April 9, at 2 pm, we started our march towards Phakding. Our Sherpa *Sirdar* was leading from the front and another experienced Sherpa was leading from behind. In between two, the members with colourful rucksacks on their backs and cool goggles covering their eyes and walking stick in their hands, looked very energetic. Everybody was walking leisurely, few of them talking to their fellow members, and some of them gazing at the shops in the streets of Lukla, as we passed through a long street full of shops with trekking items, lodges, and restaurants. Located far away in the mountain, Lukla seemed a very lively place to us in contrast to our expectation.

Lukla is a town in Sagarmatha zone of North Eastern Nepal situated at an altitude of 2843 metres (9300 feet) above sea level. The exact meaning of Lukla is 'the place with many goats and sheep'. But today, few goats and sheep are found in this area.

This place is famous because most of people start trekking from here to the Everest Base Camp. The Tenzing Hillary Airport, or Lukla Airport, has a very short and steep airstrip, which results in fatal accidents, especially in bad weather. There are daily flights between Kathmandu and Lukla, but they are limited to daytime when the weather is good.

Lukla airport.

Day 1 at Lukla-Phakding

Once we came out of the street and started on a narrow path alongside the valley, which was leading to Phakding. The place, indeed, was beautiful. As we moved ahead, we found that the area was full of trekkers, especially foreigners. People come here to trek to the Everest Base Camp. It took about an hour and fifty minutes to reach Phakding from Lukla and we reached there during daylight at 3:50 pm.

Phakding is a small village north of Lukla and is situated at an altitude of 2610 metres (8500 feet) above sea level. The whole village consists mainly of guesthouses and thus, it seems that the village is basically dependent on tourism. The tourists are mainly mountaineers and trekkers. After reaching Phakding, we put our rucksacks in our respective rooms (allotted to each pair). After freshening up, drinking hot water, tea, and having refreshments, some of us went to have a walk in the village. I found that all the houses on both sides of the road were either guesthouses or restaurants. I was amazed to see how people carried so many things to this far-flung place.

We stopped for a night in the guest house where a Nepali marathon runner, Sanjay Pandit, was my roommate. But I was mostly alone in the room as he was with a Nepali actress, Nisha Adhikari, who was also going to climb the Everest through the same agency. We spent a comfortable night in the guesthouse.

Mules and Trekkers passing over a narrow suspension bridge.

Day 2 at Phakding - Namche Bazar

The next morning we started the onward journey after breakfast. We reached Namche Bazar after four hours of trekking with a half-an-hour break at Jore Salle.

On the way to Namche Bazar, I saw Sherpas carrying a lot of weight on their backs. They were carrying the trekkers' big bags, heavy wooden planks weighing almost 60 kgs,etc. I met a very young Sherpa during a brief halt on the way, who looked hardly ten years old, with a bodyweight of about 30 to 35 kgs. He was carrying a big packet, almost more than double his size. Curiously, I enquired about the weight of the packet and he said it was 55 kgs. I had learnt little Nepali in Sikkim cadre and could comfortably communicate with the native Nepalese people. I was shocked to hear this and couldn't believe that he could carry that much weight. I tried to lift the packet to assess its weight. Although I could lift it, it seemed heavier than what he said, but

I could feel the level of toughness required to carry that much weight on uphill slope.

Being a civil servant, my mind immediately recalled the provisions of the Child Labour Act of India as well as the International Labour Organization, both of which have set a general minimum age of 14 years for introducing a child to employment. I enquired why he was carrying so much weight and he said that he would get more money for more weight. His father had died when he was very young. In his family, only his mother was there who worked as labourer. So he needed money for the family. I was silently listening to what he said. I gave him a few chocolates I was carrying in my pocket and helped him lift the weight as he struggled to lift it alone, and continued with my journey. But I kept thinking, *how could he walk with so much of weight?*

I understood that it wasn't his physical but his mental strength. Toughness doesn't come from the muscular strength; toughness lies in the mind. It comes from your deep inner belief and your visualization.

Namche Bazar.

As I continued my trek thinking about the tough life of that boy, at one point I realised that Namche Bazar was approaching. One of the most famous and popular stops on the way to the Everest Base Camp, situated at an altitude of 3445 metres (or 11315 feet) above sea level is Namche Bazar, famous for its market (managed by the locals). It is also a place where one can acclimatise to the altitude. The town is located on the slope of the hill with the Kongde Ri peak (6187 metres) in the west and Thamserku (6623 metres) in the east. This is the last place on the way to the Base Camp where you can buy all the necessary mountaineering equipments, in case of any need. Summer here, is cool, and people enjoy the weather. But winter is dry and extremely cold, so a lot of people leave the region and go to Kathmandu during that time.

We reached Namche Bazar at 2 pm. Col Neeraj Rana and Tashi Sherpa had already arrived directly from Kathmandu in a helicopter. I met them in the dining hall of the guest house and we had lunch. I can never forget the delicious cheese pasta, which I enjoyed just after arriving. It made me forget all the delicious kinds of pasta I had enjoyed on the ship during my last job when an Italian cook used to prepare them for us. This might had been because I was terribly hungry and exhausted after trekking for hours.

After my lunch, as we sat in the dining hall waiting for other members of the team to arrive and continued chitchat, I met a sherpa from my agency. His name was Mingma Dorjee, a young and strong sherpa. He said that he had been born and brought up in a village near the Base Camp of Mt. Makalu. He had started his climbing career in 2011 and would be climbing five peaks that were over 8000 metres high by April 2013. He had also climbed Mt. Everest twice, once in 2011 and once in 2012. I was amazed at how quickly he had successfully climbed so many peaks.

After everybody had their lunch, we settled into our rooms. My roommate was almost a kid, Raghav Joneja. May be he would become the youngest climber from Asia to reach the highest peak of the world. *Who can tell?*

Once we had settled in our rooms, I got a call from Sanjay Pandit, who had been my roommate at Phakding. He wanted to go for a walk and we started at 4:15 pm. We planned to move upwards so as to have a walk and acclimatise. While walking up, we took lots of photographs of Namche Bazar and nearby valleys continuing till the Everest viewpoint. By the time we reached, it was already evening and the sun was going down, so we took a few pictures and hurried down. But darkness caught us on the way and we reached at 6:45pm.

Day 3 at Namche Bazar

The next day, April 11, was for rest according to the acclimatisation schedule. It was recommended that for every 1000 metres, climbers take one extra day of rest. But a day of rest in the mountains doesn't mean eating and watching TV in your room. After breakfast, we were told to get ready and we would move uphill to get acclimatised. We started at 10 am and went up towards the same route I had taken the previous evening. After spending some time at 12,400 feet above sea level, we came back to the guesthouse by noon. We spent the afternoon buying some small items from the local market and visited a local monastery.

Day 4 at Namche Bazar-Thangbuche- Pyang-buche

The next day, we started trekking at 7:30 am. Initially, we had to climb up the ridge above Namche Bazar for about an hour and then descend for another one hour to reach Phungithanga alongside Dudhkoshi River, after two hours of continuous trekking. There, we waited for other members of the group and had some tea and chocolates. After a long break for one hour, we restarted at 10:30 am for a steep climb towards Thyangboche Monastery. This stretch was very tiring.

It was unusually tiring for me because the day before, I had exchanged my rucksack for a bigger one from Tashi sherpa and was carrying about 22 kgs. I kept panting and this was the first time after entering Nepal that I received a shock regarding my level of preparation. Although I knew that I was carrying more weight than the other climbers of my team, there were sherpas who were carrying as much as three times than what I was and were still going at their own pace, without panting, from Phungithanga to Thyangboche. The first stretch of the journey was through the woods and we walked in the shade. But once we had come out into the open, we climbed continuously up the slope under mid-day sun. My t-shirt got completely sweat soaked but I kept on going. After about an hour and half's continuous climb, I was desperately looking out for our destination. Finally, at one point, the slope became slightly less steeper and we reached monastery at Thyangboche after two continuous hours of climbing. I saw some of my teammates sitting outside a restaurant relaxing with cups of herbal tea and their rucksacks lying along the wall. Although our destination was further ahead, at Pyangboche, stopping for a lunch break made me feel very relieved.

Thyangboche or Tengboche is basically a village, which lies almost mid-way on the way to the Everest Base Camp. It is located on a hill at an altitude of 3867 metres (12,687 feet) and is surrounded by the Himalayan range. The majestic Mount Everest, Lhotse, Nuptse, Thamserku and Amadablam can be clearly seen from here.

The Sherpa community, who are said to have migrated from Tibet about five hundred years ago and who depended on pastoral, agricultural, and trading activities, inhabit the village. Now, they mainly depend on mountaineering and tourism activities which are seasonal and so, most of them do not stay in the village for almost eight months a year. Only a few families and lamas live here permanently. During the tourist season, a large number of trekkers and mountaineers pass through this place and stay here to acclimatise, which puts a lot of pressure on the village to cater to their needs, mainly in terms of accommodation and food. Tenzing Sherpa, the first person to scale the Mt. Everest in 1953 along with Sir Edmund Hillary, was born and brought up in this village.

The place is famous for its Buddhist monastery, the Tengboche Monastery, where we sat down for a break. It is the largest Gompa in the Khumbu region. The monastery had been built by an important spiritual leader of Sherpa community and is said to have a strong link with Rongbuk Monastry in Tibet. It was destroyed twice since it was first built in 1916; first time in 1934 due to an earthquake, and second time in 1989 because of a fire. However, it was rebuilt in 1993.

Around October to November every year, a festival, called Mani Rimdu, is celebrated in this Monastry, a tradition passed from the monastery at Rongbuk in Tibet. It is the most famous festival of the Sherpa community, where some blessed red pills are distributed to all those who attend it. A large number of tourists attend this festival, most of whom come for the Everest trek in autumn. The festival lasts for nineteen days, where, in addition to the traditional ceremonies and dances, some rituals are performed that are believed to ward off evil.

yeti's palm & skull at Pangboche monastry.

John Hunt, the leader of the 1953 Everest expedition, who visited the monastery on the way to the Everest Base Camp, wrote a book, *The Ascent of Everest*. Here's an excerpt from the book:

'Thyangboche must be one of the most beautiful places in the world. The height is well over 12,000 feet. The monastery buildings stand upon a knoll at the end of a big spur, which is flung out across the direct axis of the Imja River. Surrounded by satellite dwellings, all quaintly constructed and oddly mediaeval in appearance, it provides a grandstand beyond comparison for the finest mountain scenery that I have ever seen, whether in the Himalayas or elsewhere.'

We had a long break for lunch. A few of us went to the monastery to receive blessings from the senior Lama. The leader from the agency had decided to get blessings for the whole group at Pangboche. However, our Sherpa *Sirdar* told us that Lama at the Pyangboche monastery was the most learned Lama in the region.

First, we went to the big hall where there was a statue of Guru Rimpoche. After offering a *Khada* to the statue, I wished a young Lama and requested him to allow us to meet the head Lama. He asked us to wait and probably went to get the permission of the head Lama. After some time, he returned and told us to follow him. There were three of us. The young Lama took us to a place adjacent to the main Gompa, which seemed more like a home with a courtyard than a typical monastery. There, he told us to wait and went inside again. We guessed that the head Lama lived somewhere nearby. Then the young Lama came back and told us to follow him silently.

We passed through two rooms and then finally, he told us to wait there and come inside one by one. I entered first and saw that a Lama was sitting in a corner of the room on his customary *asana*, a raised chair-like structure, protected by a raised platform on two sides at the front, and the other two sides with raised walls behind him. I offered him *Khada* with a deep respect in my heart as I was meeting the man considered to be the most spiritual Lama in the area. He blessed me by touching my head. Then I wanted to clarify a few queries but

I had to ask his disciple, the young Lama, he had to be my translator. When I enquired about the weather that year, he said that it was going to be windy and when I asked whether I would reach the top, he said yes. Later, to my surprise, the wind was a major problem in attempting to summit the Everest and it came our way for many days. It was very windy from May 10 to 18, when the success ratio of reaching the peak was very low.

Later, I could understand the miraculous power of Lama to accurately predict the future in a scientific manner. Paramahansa Yogananda in his book, *Autobiography of a Yogi* had mentioned many incidents when yogis could read the thought going on in other person's mind and also could predict future correctly. He mentioned one incident where his spiritual teacher Sri Yukteswar had correctly read the thought erupting in a thief's mind, who was planning to steal a cauliflower from his ashram. He predicted this in advance and when his disciples went back to ashram, they found it happening exactly as described by guru. He wrote, 'The human mind, freed from the disturbances or "static" of restlessness, is empowered to perform all the functions of complicated radio mechanisms, sending as well as receiving thoughts and tuning out undesirable ones. As the power of a radio broadcasting station is regulated by the amount of electrical current it can utilize, so the effectiveness of a human radio depends on the degree of will power possessed by each person. All thoughts vibrate eternally in the cosmos. With deep concentration, a master is able to detect the thoughts of any man, living or dead (see p. 151-152).'

After receiving the Lama's blessings, we departed for Pyangboche at 2:15 pm. After lunch, I was feeling lazy but luckily, the climb was not as tough as it had been from river bed to Thyangboche. We reached Pyangboche at 3:45 pm after one and a half hour's continuous but easy trek.

Pyangboche or Pangboche or Panboche is a village in the region located north east of Thyangboche. Like Thyangboche, it is also inhabited by Sherpa community. Situated at an altitude of 3985 metres (13074 feet), it is famous for a Buddhist monastery headed by very learned Lama in the region, Lama Gheshe. This monastery also has yeti's hand and skull kept inside a small sealed chamber. According to information from various sources, the original hand and skull were stolen in the past and were replaced by replicas.

Yeti, also called the Abominable Snowman or the *Himamanav*, is a big ape-like mountain man, who is said to live in the Himalayan region of Nepal and Tibet. It is bigger and considered much stronger than the normal human being.

Religious tales link Yeti to an ape like creature, which was worshipped as god by the Himalayan people, especially Lepcha community. Some early accounts of trekkers from the nineteenth century and some mountain expedition members of twenties and thirties claimed that they had seen some footprints in the Himalayan region, which were similar to but larger than that of a bare-footed man and looked like the footprints of a snowman. Few others (a Greek photographer and geologist Mr Tombazi during 1925 British Geological Expedition) even claimed that they saw a dark human-like creature walking upright in the snow without any clothes. Some write-ups also described Yeti as wildlife of the Himalayan region like a Himalayan bear or a monkey of low altitude, which has been misidentified and considered as Yeti. For example, famous mountaineer Reinhold Messner in his book, *My Quest for the Yeti*, described Yeti as an endangered Himalayan brown bear, which can walk upright as well as on its all four limbs. But till now, scientific community considers it as an unrecognized animal.

There is a great view of the Everest from Pangboche. We spent the night in a tourist lodge. Both day as well as night were very cold but I was waiting for the morning when we would go to meet 'Lama Gheshe', perform *pooja*, and receive his blessings. We planned to depart from the tourist lodge after breakfast in the morning with our luggage and resume our trek towards Pheriche.

Rising price as we go further while trekking.

The following day, we started at 8 am and after a twenty-minute walk, we reached Lama Gheshe's place. We were asked to leave our rucksacks outside and be ready with a *khada* in our hands. We did as we were asked and then waited outside the main entrance gate to the room where the Lama was supposed to be sitting. After about ten minutes, we entered and went into a hall where about thirty people could be seated comfortably. In one corner of the hall was an asana for the Lama. We all took our seats and waited for the Lama. The wall was decorated with embroidered wall hangings and several pictures of climbers. These climbers must have visited and gifted these photographs after successfully summiting the Everest, believing that it had been due to the Lama's blessings.

After some time, the Lama came in. He looked old but it was difficult to guess his age because there was a fair chance of being wrong. He was dressed in a traditional red Tibetan robe but had a cheerful yet peaceful expression on his face. He took his seat and rearranged the *pooja* items: dry fruits, biscuits, fruits, a bottle of liquor, and incense sticks. He started by lighting several incense sticks and chanting Tibetan mantras. The fragrance of the incense filled the room and we began to feel a very positive aura.

After the chanting was over, everybody went to the Lama one by one and received his blessings. As I had heard, protective holy amulets blessed by the Lama would really help us in the mountains, so on our last evening I had talked to the representative from the company, Tashi Sherpa, about this. He had arranged for the amulets for a few of us including himself, Col. Rana, me, Nisha Adhikari, etc. We had the amulets blessed by the Lama and put aside some money as an offering. As he blessed us, he said something in Tibetan, which I didn't understand. Later, when I enquired about it with another Sherpa, he said that the Lama had been suggesting some general precautions to follow in the mountains.

I kept the amulet blessed by the Lama with me throughout my stay in the mountains and took it off only after returning to Gangtok after a successful expedition. It was the third such thing that I kept with me throughout. The first one was the sacred rice (*prasaad*) in a small polythene packet that the principal of SGMI had given me. The second was some *prasaad* that the Lama at the Thyangboche monastery had given me. It was also in a tiny polythene packet. These were the most valuable things, which I had to keep always with me throughout my stay in the mountains. We departed for Pheriche at 10 am and reached at 12 pm, after two-hour trek.

Day 5 at Pyangboche- Pheriche

Pheriche, similar to the other stops, is a village situated at a 4260-metres (13980 feet) height. It is full of guesthouses, which offer accommodation, food, small libraries, telephones, and internet facilities. I found that the quality of service was better, might be because of the presence of a landing area for a helicopter. Perhaps there was comparatively more of a demand for expensive items as only the affluent folk could afford a helicopter to reach here directly, avoiding some stops behind us. Here, I found out that earlier, the villagers used to earn their livelihood by farming and keeping yaks but these days, with the increase in opportunity in tourism, most of the youths were engaged as trekking guides or bearers, especially during the summer season.

I found Pheriche very interesting because as I entered the guesthouse, I saw various kinds of T-shirts decorating walls and ceiling of the hall. Overthem were names of members and expedition teams alongwith the year they had come here. They were a token of remembrance gifted to the guesthouse. How fascinating it is that people remember you after so long through this small gift of your clothes. The owner also enjoyed displaying and taking care of these clothes. Waiting in the dining-cum-reception hall for other members of the group to arrive, I saw a chessboard on the rack behind my table. I was happy to see it and tried a game with a member of the group, although I was playing after long time. I won the game. Then I played two more and won those, too. This was very motivating for me as after reaching Base Camp I luckily found that Temba Dai, Sherpa *Sirdar* of our group, had another chessboard. After this, playing chess was a favourite activity to pass the time and I won around a hundred and fifty games, which I played during my one-month stay at the Base Camp. In fact, later, people at the Base Camp stopped playing with me because they were afraid they would surely lose the game.

After winning the game of chess, I noticed that one boy from Lawrence School was standing outside the bathroom with a towel and some clothes in his hand. I immediately guessed that a hot shower might be available and I was thrilled to learn that it was. I booked my turn because there was only one shower in a place like this. With so many people around I had to reserve my turn. When I went inside, I found that there was a system to heat the water with the help of an LPG cylinder. I enjoyed the shower, as it was the first bath I had taken after leaving

Kathmandu on April 9 although I had to pay four hundred rupees for it. We had to rest the next day and acclimatise, so I slept well at night.

Day 6 at Pheriche

The following morning was warm and pleasant with a bright sun over the horizon. After breakfast I met Capt. Ankur from Gurgaon who was from T. S. Rajendra, batch of 1978-79. He was waiting for the helicopter to fly back to Kathmandu. The helicopter landing area was just behind our guesthouse in the open field. Capt. Ankur said that he had quit his job after twenty years of sailing. Then he was in the ship brokerage business and was an adventure lover. He came on this trip to accompany Col. Satya Brata and had climbed Loubuche East peak, which is 6119 metres above the sea level.

While I was talking to Capt. Ankur, other members of my team left for acclimatisation. I hurried up to catch with them. It was 9:30 am but it took almost one hour to catch and I could only do that as they were just about to reach 4500 metres above the sea level. They spent some time at this altitude and started returning but I was not satisfied. So, I began going further with a Sherpa and another member of the group, Saachi Soni. But Saachi gave up on the way, so we told her to wait at a safe point without going anywhere and we continued to 5070 metres (16634 feet), the highest point on that ridge, which was the Nangkartshang Peak or Nangkar Tshang Peak, also called by locals as Nangar-joong peak. It was basically an uphill walk and relatively an easy ascent, except some minor scrambling near the peak.

When we reached at the top, there were already two foreigners there, probably a couple. There was a magnificent view from the top with a steep slope on the east side. The guide showed me a clear view of peaks in the surrounding like Amadablam, Nuptse, Lhotse, Makalu, Cho Oyu, etc. One by one, both of us went on top of the highest stone there, behind which there was a very steep slope. We had fun taking photographs in these dangerous locations without looking down much, on the other side. Then we started to descend. But when we reached the point where Saachi was supposed to be waiting for us, she was missing. We looked around and thought that she might have left. Sure enough, after descending for thirty minutes, we found her on the way descending slowly. We were glad to find she was safe and then continued our return until we reached the guesthouse at 1:30 pm. After lunch, the chess started again. I won ten games without losing to anyone.

Ready for trekking at Pheriche.

Day 7 at Pheriche–Lobuche

After having breakfast the following day, we started for Lobuche at 7:50 am and reached at 10:25 am. We saw some snow along the way but as there was no tree line anymore, a significant lack of oxygen made us pant along the way.

Evening view from loubuche.

Lobuche was our second last stop before we could reach the Everest Base Camp. Located at an altitude of 4940 metres (16210 feet), it is a small settlement situated at about 8.5 kilometres south-west of the Everest Base Camp. It is famous for the peaks in the surrounding areas like Loubuche West, Loubuche East, Lobuche Kang, etc. Many new climbers try their luck there. People on the way to Everest also try them for acclimatisation but we didn't get to scale any of the peaks, as we had not planned for it. After reaching, we sat in the dining hall, sipping hot water and tea, and later, had lunch. At 1 pm, I went up to a height of 16,450 feet on the hill along with a Sherpa to acclimatise, stayed there for some time and came down at 2:30 pm.

Day 8 at Lobuche-Gorakshep

The next day was April 16. We started from Lobuche at 8 am and reached Gorakshep at 10 am after a good two-hour trek.

This is the last stop on the way to the Everest Base Camp at an altitude of 5,164 metres (16,942 feet) but it has an interesting history. It is said that Gorakshep village is sitting on the edge of a frozen lakebed, which is now covered in sand. In 1952, the Swiss team on their Everest expedition had established their Base Camp here but with global warming and the shrinking of the glaciers, the Everest Base Camp has been shifted further north near the foot of the Khumbu Icefall.

Tourist lodge at Gorakshep with Pumori Peak in the background.

Additionally, it is considered the best place for climbers to reach Kala Patthar at an altitude of 5550 metres (or 18209 feet) for acclimatisation before leaving for the Everest Base Camp, which is situated at an altitude of 5,364 metres (17,598 feet). The idea is that once the body is habituated to a higher altitude (meaning the thinner atmosphere) then climbers can sleep well and feel comfortable when they arrive at the camp. Trekkers who are not allowed to spend the night at the Everest Base Camp generally don't go to Kala Patthar, unless someone is interested in doing so because the Everest summit is not visible from the Base Camp. But there is a clear view of it from Kala Patthar. Also Lhotse, Nuptse and many other peaks in the surrounding are clearly visible from Kala Patthar.

After arriving at Gorakshep, we first went into the dining hall as usual and rejuvenated ourselves by some hot water and tea. After some rest and chitchat, three of us, Sanjay Pandit, Nisha Adhikari, and I moved towards Kala Patthar to acclimatise. The route to Kala Patthar is a gradual but continuous climb. We kept on moving with a few small breaks to acclimatise our bodies as well as to take some snaps of beautiful surroundings. The last ten minutes needed scrambling over boulders before we reached onto the top. It took an hour and forty-five minutes of climb to reach Kala Patthar. The top is marked with prayer flags. I was happy to reach about 18,200 feet, the highest point in my life till then and I offered prayers to the mountain god facing the prayer flags. By the time we had reached, it was very windy and we were cold. So, we didn't spend any more time there and after taking few photos, we started descending fast but it still took us forty-five minutes to reach the guesthouse.

In the afternoon, everybody checked their pulse and oxygen content with the help of a pulse oximeter. My pulse was 103 BPM and my oxygen content was 58 percent. The oxygen content was low; it should normally be above 80. This was concerning as someone explained to me that my RBC count was low. I felt a little low for some time but later consoled myself by thinking about the different reasons for the low oxygen content, and tried to remain calm about this, thinking that I had never gone beyond 18,000 feet in my life except that day at Kala Patthar. In addition, I had only reached 18,000 feet once during the advanced mountaineering course, when trainees had been taken for height gain. There too, we had descended after a short stay of about thirty to forty five minutes, during which trainees and instructors offered *pooja* to the mountain God by burning juniper leaves (which act like an incense stick) and offering some *prasaad*. It, indeed, had been a very short exposure to that altitude. Other than that, I had spent most of my life in the plains and then at sea. My posting in the hilly area of Sikkim had not been for very long. So, my RBC count was normal for this altitude acclimatisation. I felt a little reassured thinking these symptoms might be temporary. In any case, Col. Rana gave me a capsule saying that it would artificially increase my RBC count.

At Gorakshep, the tourist lodge was very crowded and the room, I got, had no ventilation. It was a hard night for me. I found breathing difficult and could not sleep properly. I remember the gurgling sound my breathing made as I woke frequently from sleep. In the morning, I felt nauseated, which was aggravated by the terrible smell of the closed toilet. This toilet was small and ventilation was naturally restricted. But somehow I controlled my desire to vomit but still felt weak. I did not know how things could change so quickly in the mountains. I had been so full of energy while climbing Kala-Patthar the previous day and had found myself to be one of the strongest members because apart from the three of us, none of other members had tried Kala-Patthar. Now within one night, I was feeling weaker than many other members. Some of my team members had gone to Kala-Patthar early that morning and were feeling fresh after returning from the higher altitude.

Day 9 at Gorakshep —Everest Base Camp

The next day was the auspicious day of April 17. We entered the Everest Base Camp area and stayed there for more than a month. We would return only after returning from the Everest summit. Although, my health was low since early morning and I was not willing to have breakfast due to nausea, I had to have something to survive in the mountains. I was also not feeling like trekking or gaining altitude any further but finally, I decided to get to the Base Camp at a slower speed and with minimum weight in the rucksack on my back thinking that it was better late than never. So, I lightened my luggage and put some into the bag which was carried by porter.

After a light breakfast, we started for the Base Camp at 9 am. Initially, I was slow but I kept up my pace and later, once I found my rhythm again, I overtook many of other members and reached the Base Camp at 11:45 am after two hours and forty-five minutes. In fact, I entered the Base Camp after about two hours but our agency had established the camp at the other end of the glacier, at the foot of the Khumbu Icefall, which took almost forty-five minutes to reach. Once we entered the area, a Sherpa was ready with warm juice at the entrance to serve us. I felt better after having two full glasses of hot juice but it didn't increase my speed. In fact, I became lazier and walked slower, thinking that I was now inside the Base Camp zone and would move at a more gradual pace.

16

Life at the Everest Base Camp

The Everest Base Camp is situated at an altitude of 5364 metres (17600 feet) above sea level, on top of rubble from glacial moraine of Khumbu icefall. There are hundreds of feet of ice below groups of tents erected for the climbers to stay for about one and half months during which they go up and come back here to recover. Mountains on three sides surround this area and there is a river, with chunks of ice floating on it, on the fourth side. People have to walk on the flanks over the river to enter or leave this area.

As mentioned earlier, our agency had set up a camp at other end of the area, near the foot of Khumbu icefall, so it was a longer journey for us than for members from other agencies. The Khumbu icefall was on our right as we entered the Base Camp. As I understood, the difference between glaciers and icefalls is similar to the difference between rivers and waterfalls. A glacier is like a river of ice that moves very slowly and an icefall is like a waterfall, which forms when a snow mass passes down a steep slope and so, its speed increases. The Khumbu icefall moves at the rate of three to four feet daily and the glacier is slower than that. Our route to Mount Everest passed through Khumbu icefall, which is considered one of the most dangerous parts of the whole route. In fact, it is the first obstruction above the Base Camp and we had to cross it before reaching camp 1. Our Sherpa *Sirdar* told

us, "If you cross Khumbu, you can consider yourself completely
fit for the summit. " Although there were more challenges ahead,
his statement was worth believing.

Bird's eye View of Everest Base Camp while coming from outside.

Our camps were set up just outside the foot of the icefall from
where the glacier takes a sharp turn of almost ninety degree and
its slope becomes gradual, and thus the rate of movement of the
mass of ice also becomes slower. In fact, the whole Base Camp
is located over the glacier on top of hundreds of feet of ice but
the main channel of ice is on the right side and its movement is
relatively faster which can be observed from the changing shapes
of the ice blocks. The change in shapes of ice blocks becomes
clearly noticeable almost every two or three days. The part of the
glacier, where the Base Camp was established, was adjacent to
the main channel and was covered under a thin layer of gravel
and soil, which were brought down from the surrounding peaks
by the frequent rock fall and landslides, so it was difficult to see
that it was moving. While walking inside the Base Camp area,
one could see that the blocks of ice were straight and some were
broken down. There were also some tents rigged on top of the
blocks of ice. Entering the area makes one feel like he is inside
the glacier.

Tents are erected over glacier at Everest Base Camp.

On reaching Base Camp, normally the first problem visitors encounter, is the severe headache, vomiting, sleeplessness, and the resultant weakness. This may persist for two to three days depending on the rate of acclimatisation, which may vary from person to person. On an average, people start feeling better from the second day onwards and the signs of altitude sickness disappear after a few days. But by that time, a new health problem appears and remains as long as you stay at the Base Camp. It is the terrible Khumbu Cough.

Various reasons have been cited for this cough. According to Sherpa and a few climbers at the Base Camp, there is mica in the rock, which adulterates the atmosphere. These particles enter the body as you inhale and they accumulate in the throat causing irritation, which leads to coughing. According to studies available on the internet, the cold and dry air at this altitude has been assumed to be responsible for this cough for a long time.

A research study was done on Khumbu cough in nineties and the conclusion was that the low atmospheric pressure prevailing at that altitude is the cause of the cough. A few people were kept under observation in a hypobaric chamber and the chamber was subjected to low atmospheric pressure, equivalent to what would be present at a 7000-metres altitude.

Further, during a research expedition, called the Caudwell Xtreme Everest Expedition conducted by a few universities from United Kingdom and USA in 2007, the conclusion reached was that Khumbu cough might be caused by the tiny pulses of acid refluxing up from the stomach and irritating the larynx and trachea. The exact reason for the cough is still unknown. It is said that there is no medicine, which can effectively cure it but depending on the extent of acclimatisation, the cough varies from negligible to serious, varying from person to person.

The atmosphere in and around the Base Camp is dry, and as you breathe, your body loses moisture and dehydrates. Climbers are advised to drink a minimum of three litres of water every day to maintain good health and avoid dehydration. It has to be warm, boiled water. So people continuously sip hot water during the whole day and would routinely go to piss almost every hour.

Another danger at the Base Camp is the probability of avalanches and these can be big enough to wash out the whole Base Camp killing all the people present there. Although big avalanches are not very frequent, you see many small rock falling from the surrounding mountains every day and can also hear them falling at night. Other than this, you are always to be accompanied by somebody if you leave the living area and go out because you never know if there is a hidden crevasse or water under the thin layer of ice, which you can fall into and die.

The weather is very variable. You may be enjoying a sunny day around noon and within a few minutes, you find that the entire area has become foggy with visibility reduced to almost zero. This is quite frequent. Similarly, it often goes from being sunny to snowing within a few minutes. When there is no snowfall, the ground below your feet is dark because of the thin rock particle layer above the glacier. These rock particles are brought here from surrounding hills by rock-falls. If it snows at night you wake up to find a completely different sight in the morning, everything is white surrounding you and your tent. Even the top of tent is covered with snow and when there is heavy snowfall, you need to wake up frequently at night, to shake the top of the tent from the inside to bring down the snow accumulated there. There is a fair chance that your tent would collapse under the weight of the fresh snow.

Bird's eye view of Everest Base Camp from khumbu icefall.

After reaching our camp, I was allotted a separate tent and I was happy. My tent was very close to the dining tent. I went into the tent to rearrange my luggage as my two other big bags had arrived directly from Kathmandu, in addition to the two bags which were being carried during the trek. But I was not feeling well and thus, lied down to rest. I vomited into a pee bottle, which I had kept ready, and it saved my precious tent floor, which would not have dried for several days if it had been ruined by vomit.

After some time, we were called for lunch and everybody assembled in the dining tent. Here, I saw most of the members were in a worse shape than I was. I had a little rice and *dal* so I could digest my food easily and came back to my tent. Although we were told strictly not to sleep in the tent during daylight hours, I took a short nap. I had great difficulty in breathing and had a severe headache. Finally, I vomited again in the evening, just before dinner.

When I entered the dining tent for dinner, I was in a bad shape but after a light dinner and a long conversation with other members of the team and the Sherpa, I felt better. We measured our oxygen content in the dining tent itself. I was happy that mine had started improving and was now 64 percent. In the night, I kept the zip of the tent slightly open, although it was quite cold outside with the temperature dropping to –10 °C. It ensured fresh air and relief from suffocation due to lack of oxygen.

In spite of my physical problems at the Base Camp, I was happy to be free from a daily routine of my normal life. In Gangtok I used to start my day at 4 or 4:30 am and would get trained for almost three hours of rigorous self-imposed physical activity to prepare for this long awaited expedition. Then I had to go to work from 10 am to 5 pm after which I returned home at about 6 pm in the evening. During holidays, my routine used to be more rigorous, as I had to trek for almost the whole day or at least half of the day. Here, at the Everest Base Camp, I did not have a morning exercise schedule or office. Every day was a holiday and unlike the holidays in Sikkim when I used to go on a self-imposed long trek, days were completely relaxed here. Although there were set activities planned for acclimatisation, it was going to be slow and steady. There would be no jogging and running the way I had been doing over the last one year when my life had seemed almost computerised with a fixed routine every day.

Medical arrangement at Everest Base Camp.

Here, at the Base Camp, our day started when we woke up in the morning, which was normally after first rays of the sun hit the tent. But there are always some exceptions as I was used to wake up early throughout my stay at the Base Camp. I found that amongst all the guests in our team, I was either the first to wake up, or some days, Col. Parry (father of Hakikat Singh, one of the boys from the Lawrence School) woke up earlier than I. But before both of us could wake, the mess staff and the Sherpa cook would already be in full swing in the kitchen preparing the meals for the day and heating ice (to melt it into water and heating it further to make it fit for us to drink) or tea or coffee. There was another advantage of waking up so early: I would avoid the foul smell of human excreta that would accumulate in the drum that was used to collect waste in the toilet tent.

Rear view of Toilet Tent.

There was a unique system of toilet arrangements at the Base Camp. It consisted of a plastic drum inside a temporary toilet tent made of canvas wall, with two stones that acted as a platform where we could place our feet to balance. Toilet paper hung from the side on the canvas wall. There was no system for using water in such freezing cold. There was no system to lock the toilet from inside no matter what gender you were. There was only a zip which you had to pull down once you were inside. Everybody would come and defecate in the same drum. So you had to keep on defecating everyday into the same drum, irrespective of how full it was! and how bad the smell was! The drum was open until full. When it got full the drum was sealed and transported back to the nearest town for safe treatment and disposal of the waste. In this way, the serenity of the mountains and the environment was maintained. The advantage of waking up early was that all bad smells would dissipate during the night and you would think that inside the toilet tent, it smelled normal, as well. I was grateful to the porter or the yak that carried these full drums a great distance on their backs.

After freshening up, I would do some *pranayama* like Bhastrika, Kapalbhati, Bahya, and Anulom Vilom. These four *pranayama* techniques were my friends for the ten years and I had been practising it intermittently since my days in shipping. I had also used it for many months during my civil services preparations and sometimes, during trekking and mountaineering in the past. Although I could hardly practice it on a regular basis, I had used it successfully as a stress buster in the past and sometimes, also to improve my health and to enhance concentration power. I was well aware of its immense benefits. *Pranayama*, if practised correctly, works like a miracle to pour out stress from your body and mind.

Here, I couldn't continue *pranayama* on a daily basis. Mostly, I would prefer to go for a morning walk out of the camp to the other end to rejuvenate myself with fresh morning air, either along with a Sherpa or sometimes, some other member. After getting a fair idea about the area, I went alone most of days.

Breakfast was served at around 8 am in the dining tent, rich in a variety of food items. There would be *aloo paratha* and curd, plain *paratha* and *hari sabji* (green vegetables), *khichdi* (a mixture of rice, pulses and vegetables), oats porridge, upma, pancake, chicken sausage, salami, bread and jam and butter, sandwich, omelette, boiled eggs, boiled milk, cornflakes, muesli, tea, coffee, etc. were common menus during breakfast time. Aloo *paratha*, *khichdi* and chicken sausage were my favourite items but I would also opt for oats porridge and boiled eggs if I didn't feel quite well. After a heavy breakfast, we went about our daily activities.

Relaxed time at Everest Base Camp.

Life here was relaxed except for when we have to move beyond the Base Camp to acclimatise. Some days we'd visit Gorakshep (the last stop before the Base Camp) or climb to Pumori Advance Base Camp to gain some altitude to get our bodies moving. Sometimes, there would be trainings held on the correct use of oxygen bottles, mask, etc. Other days we'd simply relax. Sometimes, we would simply sit in the dining tent and watch movies, and just chill. Some of the Lawrence School boys were the most enthusiastic lot in teasing each other, pulling each other's legs, but their hot target was Nepali movie actress,

Nisha Adhikari. Their other target was Sanjay Pandit, the Nepalese marathon runner and even the team leader, Col. Rana. Sometimes I was the target. I would also enjoy it sometimes. But some of them would exceed their limits and I felt awkward, sometimes also got annoyed, but eventually ignored. All these group activities were likely to happen as we were advised to stay out of our personal tents during the daytime because there was a fair chance that we might go to sleep if we were inside our own tents. Sleeping during the day was not advisable. Also, during a sunny day, the tent would be heated and it was unpleasantly warm inside.

We would mostly hang out in the dining tent, which was spacious enough to accommodate all of us. The floor inside the tent was covered with a carpet. It had a long table in the middle with chairs around it. The table was full of eatables like biscuits, bhujia, Bournvita, glucose, honey, *chyawanprash*, and thermoses with warm water, tea and coffee. There was also an LCD TV with a DVD player and lots of charging points, which were located at the other end of the tent. There were long pockets in the canvas wall of the tent, where we used to keep our chess board or books; so it was easy to find them whenever we wanted to play or read, and there was no chance of their being misplaced. However, this tent was temporary, and had only been put up for the time and would be dismantled at the end of climbing season.

Other than the activities outside our camp area, my activities inside the camp were limited to mainly reading books or playing chess, both of which would give me mental strength. I didn't like killing precious time by chatting and talking about social issues, or watching the same movies over again, except on a few occasions. Mostly I wanted to keep to myself. I enjoyed reading. Other than mountaineering books, I couldnot forget the effect of reading *Old Path White Clouds*, a biography of Gautama Buddha. I often used to compare my life with Buddha's whenever I faced struggles. That's how I learned how to overcome problems by keeping calm. This book pacified me, to some extent, and my surroundings.

Lighter moments inside Dining Tent.

Chess also helped me a great deal. It would lift up my spirits in any situation, make me feel confident again, and I would believe that my mind was in its place. While focusing on the game, I would forget any kind of physical ailment. I never lost a game out of the hundred and fifty games I played at the Base Camp. My competitors would say, 'Haar to jayenge par phir bhi khelenge aur kosis karenge (I know I'll lose, but I'll try my best and play).'

Lunch was used to be served around 1 or 2 in the afternoon. Unless some member had gone outside the Base Camp or was invited for lunch by another team, our team would had lunch in the dining tent. For me, breakfast was more special than lunch, unless they had added something new to the menu. Anyway, I used to have light lunch after heavy breakfast in the morning. Evenings would be cheerful with a lavish dinner. Starting with soup and other starters, the main course included *pulao*, stuffed *paratha*, *hari sabji* (green vegetables), chicken, fish, mutton, *paneer* and mushroom items, salad, roasted *papad*, curd, etc. Sometimes,

Chinese, South Indian, and continental cuisines were also served for a change of taste. As the dessert, we were served ice cream, canned fruits, *gulab jamun*, *kheer*, cake etc.

Dining Tent is kept heated by using cooking gas.

It was a surprise to have fresh, green vegetables at such a place, but big agencies ensured a regular supply of green vegetables through the helicopter service. After dinner, some would be treated for the Khumbu cough. They would have a glass of hot milk with turmeric powder and ghee mixed. They had to inhale hot water vapour with some Vicks, eat raw garlic, roasted ginger, etc. Although these treatments were not fully effective enough to cure the ailment completely, it would still provide a temporary relief from the cough. At the end, members used to fill their thermos with hot water before finally leaving for their individual tents, to drink it throughout the night. The mess boy, Gyaltsen, was very caring for the team members and provided smooth services to us at any given time and would meet most of the demands of the team members.

Here, I would like to say that my agency, Seven Summit Treks, was famous at the Base Camp for its three unique features: a bar, a bakery, and an open-air theatre. There was a separate tent for the bar and different drinks were available, although I never went inside to find out which brands were on offer. Members were given limited coupons, all free, to avail a certain number of drinks per week. People could opt for canned juice in the place of beer. I had juice only a few times. As the temperature would be excruciating, even the juice had to be heated, which tasted weird. I preferred to drink hot water instead of juice.

There was a separate tent that served as a bakery. Everything available there, was free for the members who had come for the expedition through Seven Summit Treks. Different types of biscuits, donuts, and special coffee were always available with cake and pizza to be ordered, as well.

The third unique feature was the open-air theatre. A foreigner climber had come to make a movie on mountaineering and he had brought a projector, so the people from the agency used it and erected a big canvas screen out in the open. In the evening, they would project English music videos on the screen and people would dance in the spine-chilling cold on the icy-slopes at the open area in front of the projector. This was called the open-air theatre. No other agency enjoyed these privileges.

So the life of the Base Camp was quite different in some perspectives than what I had imagined before coming here. My visualization was according to my experience at the HMI Base Camp at Chowrikiang, my first substantial interaction with the mountains in September-October 2012, where there was no mode of entertainment at the Base Camp.

Thus, life at Base Camp was a mix of pleasure and pain, comfort and toughness, but my main focus was keeping myself fit by all means. One of the ways to acclimatise quickly and keep fit was to keep moving rather than sit idle at one place. So, other than my favourite activities of reading and playing chess, I tried to keep myself active by moving my body so that I wouldn't face sudden difficulties while climbing the final summit.

Leisure time with parents of sanawar kids.

The day I arrived at the Base Camp, I did not do anything for rest of the day and rested due to bad health. The next day, April 18, I went to the glacier to have a round of the area although I wasn't in a good shape. While returning, I met Commander Satya Dam, who had come to guide a Portuguese lady in climbing the Everest. He offered me general information about mountaineering, and I felt great.

Pooja being offered to please goddess chomolungma.

The day after, I was introduced to Passang Sherpa who was an Everest Summiteer for over eleven times and would be my guide for the expedition. The day proved to be pretty good because after getting an experienced climber as a guide, I also took a bath for the second time since I had left Kathmandu ten days earlier. In addition, I participated in the *pooja* being offered to please Goddess Chomolungma, the mother goddess of Everest. After my bath, I put on a completely new set of clothes to participate in the *pooja* and brought all of my climbing equipments to get them goddess' blessings as well. The *pooja* continued from 11:30 am to 2 pm, during which the Buddhist lama chanted mantras in Tibetan and offered different types of eatables, chocolates, juice, biscuits, and alcohol to God. When the *pooja* was almost over, long threads with hundreds of prayer flags tied on, were erected and spread in all directions starting from the pole at the centre of Lhapso. *Khadas* were exchanged, people put coloured powder, *abir*, on each other's faces, and drinks were served. Even the lama enjoyed the drinks.

Lhapso.

Finally, a Sherpa dance was performed. The Sherpa and a few interested climbers stood in a line and wrapped their arms on the shoulders of the person standing either of their sides and sang in their own Sherpa language while dancing. It was a relaxed tune and the dancer's movements were slow. After the *pooja*, we enjoyed special lunch.

The next day, April 20, was supposed to be the first day of training but heavy and continuous snowfall had it postponed.

The day after was our first day of training. After breakfast at 9 am, we changed into snow boots, put on harnesses, and went to the training ground where we practised climbing an ice wall, by jumaring, ladder crossing, and descended the ice wall by rappelling. The training continued till 12:30 pm, and then, we returned for lunch. In the evening, we enjoyed a chicken sizzler and after one last game of chess, I came back to my tent at 9 pm to go to sleep so that I could start another day afresh.

Climbing Ice wall.

As I opened the tent's zip the next day, everything around us was white because of heavy snowfall in the night; the day's training was cancelled.

After breakfast, I was just planning the day's activities when Kazi Sherpa came to meet me. He was also from Sikkim along with

Anand Gurung. The former had come to climb Mount Everest as a member of the first North East Everest expedition and his camp was set up at some distance. He had returned from camp II the previous day, where he had gone as part of his team's acclimatisation schedule. His team had arrived at the Base Camp about ten days before ours. We knew each other from before. In fact, he had been my trainer during the pre-Everest training at Chemchey. He was a soft-spoken gentleman with a helpful attitude. After talking with him in the dining tent and sharing breakfast, we went to his camp together. I met other team members and we had lunch together. During lunch, I was told that an eighty-year-old man from Japan had also come to climb the Everest and was staying just nearby. I was very excited to meet him and planned to visit his camp along with Sri Kazi Sherpa immediately after lunch.

Ice climbing practice at Everest Base Camp.

After lunch, two of us went to meet the man, Mr Muira, who had come to climb the Everest with his team of a very good Sherpa, and his own news reporters.

We met in his tent. As I shook hands with him, I could feel that he did not seem as eighty at all. He looked like he was in his fifties. I saluted his determination and hard work to maintain such level of physical fitness and further, his courage to take on the challenge. The Roman Emperor Marcus Aurelius in his book *Meditations* wrote,

'Look well into thyself; there is a source of strength which will
always spring up if thou wilt always look.'

Although this man was eighty, his mind and body were as fit as
a fiddle. And he was determined to climb the Everest not by his
physical body but with his will power.

Kazi Sherpa introduced me to him as the first IAS officer of
India who had come to climb the Everest. I clarified that IAS
is like the counterpart of the premier civil service in Japan. He
conducted a television interview with me for a Japanese news
channel. Later, he did climb the Everest and set the world record
for the oldest man to reach the peak. He broke the record of Min
Bahadur Sirchan of Nepal who had held it for climbing Everest
at seventy-eight years old.

With 80 yrs old japanse climber Yuichiro Miura.

April 24 was a very important day for us as we were going to the
area above the Base Camp for acclimatisation for the first time.
We went half way to camp I, and then came back. But obviously,
people needed to rest after climbing such great heights around
the Khumbu icefall. Hence, the next day, we all relaxed. But
as usual, I woke up early and went for a morning walk alone.

But walking at the Everest Base Camp is not like taking a normal walk in Gangtok. As the whole camp is established on top of a glacier, in many places the route, which connects the whole camp to its entrance, passes over loose ice sheets with water rushing below. Going for a walk alone in this hazardous area without informing anybody is like taking unnecessary risk. So, as a precautionary measure, I told a Sherpa who was around, that I would return after an hour.

The following day, too, I went for a walk at 6 am and on the way, walked into the Sashastra Seema Bal camp, and met their leader along with a few other members. After returning, I had my breakfast and walked into the Indian army's camp. Major Jamwal was the leader there. I had been having telephone conversations with him since February when I had come to know (through the army set up in Sikkim) that he would be leading the Indian Army team to Everest. He was one of the most amiable men I had ever met. When I walked into their camp, their tents were being set up; they had reached the previous day (April, 23, 2013) and had probably been the last team to arrive. But they had a well-planned acclimatisation schedule with a four-day stay at Namche Bazar so their members were fit. Major Jamwal welcomed me very warmly and we had a long chat.

With Major Jamval (leader of Indian army expedition team)
-friendship in mountain.

After returning from the army camp, I planned to take a round of Gorakshep to warm up my legs, which seemed a little lazier to me at the Base Camp. So the next day, after breakfast, I went to Gorakshep along with some other members from my team. Normally, people from the Base Camp go to Gorakshep to make phone calls or to access the internet or simply to trek and keep themselves fit for climbing. It is a two-hour walk at a slow pace from the Base Camp and is located at a slightly lower altitude, so you get a lot of fresh air while walking down along the ridge. People feel better after a visit there. I returned in the afternoon and met Major Jamwal, then visited Commander Satya Dam along with him. He had been in the Indian Navy a long time ago, had quit and had taken up mountaineering and climbing as his career. He was an expert in the alpine style of climbing and used to spend most of his time outside India, either climbing or delivering lectures in different parts of the world. Later, we went to meet Col. Sharma and Wing Commander Kutty (the leader and deputy leader of the National Cadet Corp or NCC Everest team) at their camp. The leader of the North East Everest team also came with us and we all had a good chat. Major Jamwal invited everybody for lunch that was to be organized on the following day at the army camp.

As expected, the next day was wonderful and felt like a party day. There were over hundreds of feet of ice below our feet in sunny noon time and the shimmering ice from glaciers hung on slopes of mountains all around, when all the invitees gathered in the army camp located near the foot of Khumbu icefall. It was a good gathering and the leaders of the NCC team, North East team, and a few important members from our agency like Commander Satya Dam, Nepali film actor Arjun Karki, actress Nisha Adhikari, and Col Neeraj Rana etc. were a few noticeable figures amongst guests. We had a good chat and a delicious lunch.

After returning, I read a book on mountaineering, *No Shortcuts To The Top* by Ed Viesturs. He had climbed all the fourteen highest peaks of the world without aid of supplemental oxygen. I was very impressed by his motto, 'Reaching the summit is optional, getting down is mandatory.' This small statement held a lot of meaning and was a very good warning for those who only aimed to reach the top and lost their lives due to over exhaustion while descending.

With Commander Satya dam and Our Sherpa Sirdar Temba Sherpa at Everest Base Camp.

In the evening, the open-air theatre was lots of fun. Many people danced, including me, although later, the theatre was closed because of sudden snowfall. I was thinking about the day when back to my tent and entering my sleeping bag. It had been a crazy lot of fun and hadn't seemed like it was a trekking camp. It was like we had all come for an eco tour in the lap of nature, with good music sessions as DJ played music in evenings. Obviously, it was an expensive holiday, but was all worth it. With a smile on my face, I said to myself that I came here expecting that life would be tougher, more or less like at Base Camp of the Himalayan mountaineering institute at Chowrikiang in West Sikkim. But life appeared more luxurious here. I had to break this chain of luxury because there would be none beyond the Base Camp and I had to be ready for the final show. Immediately, I decided to make a long trek to Pumori Advanced Base Camp the next day, provided that I found a companion. And with this new decision, I surrendered myself to the night.

After freshening up early the next morning, I met Col. Parry in the dining tent and discussed Pumori visit. He agreed to come and both of us departed immediately after breakfast. After two hours of a slow uphill walk, we both reached an altitude of about 19,200 feet around Pumori Advanced Base Camp. After spending approximately one hour there in acclimatising and taking pictures of Everest's peak (which was clearly visible from that altitude), we started descending and walked for roughly an hour and a half to reach the Everest Base Camp again. Everest's peak is not visible from the Everest Base Camp, so it was a good trip and I got a very clear view of my destination for which I had come all the way from Sikkim.

On reaching, I was informed that the team was planning to go up to camp I on the day after next and then further uphill for acclimatisation. I thought I would rest the next day to store my energy for going up to camp II, which was at an altitude of over 21,000 feet, and which I would be going to, for the first time in my life. Thus, the next day was a day for resting and I spent it reading, relaxing, playing chess, checking my equipments, and preparing my rucksack for the following day's climb.

The following day, in the dawn of April 29, I left for camp I, along with other members of the team and their guides. The plan was to spend the night at camp I and then move to camp II, the following day. But after reaching camp I, I moved further as suggested by my guide and reached camp II at 21,300 feet although remaining members of my team, including Col. Rana stayed back at camp I itself. The next day, remaining members of team also joined camp II. After taking one extra day of rest at camp II, the team moved further towards camp III on May 2, but returned back to camp II after reaching a jumar point at the base of Lhotse face as planned by the leader, Col. Rana. Finally, the team came directly back to the Base Camp on following day, May 3, 2013.

The next day, I thought I would take a luxurious bath with warm water because it had been about two weeks since I had last taken one; it had been on the day of the *pooja*. Taking a bath at that altitude was a luxury in itself because I had seen the price of hot water in the guest houses while trekking to the Everest Base Camp. It was five hundred Nepalese rupees for a jug of hot water. Staying in that area, I could count the number of baths I had taken after leaving Kathmandu; it was the third bath since then. Still, the frequency of baths was good enough and in addition, it was a warm water bath. Otherwise, I had studied that in the past the standard norm at the Everest Base Camp had been to have a bath once a month.

The next day, May 5, was not a great one; we heard that a Sherpa named Da Rita Sherpa from an agency, International Mountain Guides, had died in his sleep after eating at camp III, probably due to cardiac arrest, and also that a Chinese climber at the same camp was in a bad condition. One keeps on getting such news in the mountains. So, one must listen, pay sympathies, be careful, and forget. We had to move on if we wanted to reach the top, so I decided to take a round of Gorakshep the next day to keep myself active. I went along with members of the North East Everest team while members of my team didn't want to go.

On the way to Gorakshep, I met a differently-abled Indian girl, Arunima Sinha, from Uttar Pradesh, who had also come to climb the Everest but was going through a different agency. Later, she became the first female amputee in the world to climb the Everest. I was impressed by her degree of determination to take on this feat. Mountain climbing, I realised, is more your will and perseverance, than physical activity. Arnold Schwarzenegger, seen as the symbol of physical strength and muscle power for many years, also accepted the power of mind and visualization and said, 'The mind is the limit. As long as the mind can envision the fact that you can do something, you can do it, as long as you really believe hundred percent.'

View of Everest in cloudy weather.

In this manner, life at the Base Camp continued with both relaxation and activities to keep our bodies moving till I received the forecast that the weather was favourable for us to make the final climb on the morning of May 16, 2013.

17

Family Dilemma

'At 6:20 P. M., Cotter contacted Hall to tell him that Jan Arnold was on the satellite phone from Christ church and was waiting to be patched through. "Give me a minute," Rob said. "Me mouth's dry. I want to eat a bit of snow before I talk to her. " A little later he came back on and rasped in a slow, horribly distorted voice, "Hi, my sweetheart. I hope you're tucked up in a nice warm bed. How are you doing?"

"I can't tell you how much I'm thinking about you!" Arnold replied. "You sound so much better than I expected. ... Are you warm, my darling?"

"In the context of the altitude, the setting, I'm reasonably comfortable," Hall answered, doing his best not to alarm her.

"How are your feet?"

"I haven't taken my boots off to check, but I think I may have a bit of frostbite.... "

"I'm looking forward to making you completely better when you come home," said Arnold. "I just know you're going to be rescued. Don't feel that you're alone. I'm sending all my positive energy your way!"

Before signing off, Hall told his wife, "I love you. Sleep well, my sweetheart. Please don't worry too much. "

These would be the last words anyone would hear him speak. Attempts to make radio contact with Hall later that night and the next day went unanswered. Twelve days later, when Breashears and Viesturs climbed over the South Summit on their way to the top, they found Hall lying on his right side in a shallow ice hollow, his upper body buried beneath a drift of snow.'

—Jon Krakauer, Into Thin Air

At the Base Camp, we are completely isolated from the outside world. As far as connectivity was concerned, we would sometimes get a signal on a local mobile network, called N-cell at specific locations, and telephonic conversation would be possible somehow. Sometimes, we were also able to catch the internet signal especially early in the morning. But for uninterrupted communication, we would prefer to walk down to Gorakshep, the last stop during trek just before the Base Camp. It was a two-hours walk downhill along a gentle slope and an uphill walk while returning. On a fine day, I walked down to Gorakshep after about a week's stay at the Base Camp, and called my family.

The first person I talked to, was my *Mamaji*, who told me that my family was worried for me as there had been no communication between us for the past week. When I enquired, I learned that I had left behind the mountaineering movie *Touching The Void*, which had created a nuisance when my family saw it. When I had been preparing, I would carry movies and books on mountaineering, during my tours or travels out of Sikkim, and would read more and more. I had carried a few such copies during my last visit to my hometown. I told *Mamaji* that the movie was based on one accident that had taken place in the South American mountains and not at Everest and so there was no reason to worry. I added that I was very comfortable at the Base Camp and would update them regularly, at least by SMS, which was possible with the intermittent mobile signals available at the Base Camp.

I knew that things at the Base Camp had not been as comfortable and simple as I had told my family, to be. I had faced a dilemma when my oxygen content was very low and then my initial stay had been filled with sleeplessness, vomiting, and severe headaches. Then, the continued Khumbu cough had been troubling me a lot. But if I told them all of it, they would worry a lot, which would in turn, bother me back.

When I spoke to my cousin, I learned that my younger brother Birendra, who had been working on a ship with a European company, had called home enquiring my father about me as I had sent the former an email a few days back, before leaving for Kathmandu. The email had contained details of all my assets and liabilities, insurance, bank accounts, the places where all original papers for my insurance and immovable assets were kept, etc. It had included information about the money borrowed for the Everest expedition. There had been a specific mention about the special insurance taken to cover risks during mountaineering expeditions. As we were pretty close, I thought I would let him know everything in advance, so that the family did not fall into the doldrums in case something happened to me in the mountains.

In the four pages of information, I had provided all the details including how to pay off the borrowed money. I thought that some people could make false claims that I had borrowed from them if there was no concrete information regarding all my assets and liabilities with my family. This was a part of my strategy to prepare for the worst but I hoped for the best. Although I had the confidence that I would be returning safely, it was my duty to pass on the information.

Talking with some other near and dear ones in my village, I came to know that my father had been very annoyed, shouting around, questioning my worthless intentions of going to the mountains. I knew that if I had told them about my plans and the risk associated, I would had never been successful. As I had already been struggling and was occupied with sponsorship matters in Sikkim, I didn't want to entangle in another dilemma and to have an undue argument with my family on this matter.

Another very important precaution was postponement of my marriage. I was not sure whether my life partner would support me on taking such a big risk if I got married before completing the journey to the Everest. My doubt was very justified because fear of the unknown is quite normal with any human being. I had earlier read a famous book on mountaineering named *Into Thin Air*, which is about the 1996 Everest disaster and described the heart wrenching scenario of death of a thirty-five-years-old mountaineering guide from New Zealand, Rob Hall. He died on the slope of the Everest while his newly-wed wife, Jan Arnold was pregnant with her first baby. A brief account of his death is given earlier at the start of this chapter. Therefore, I thought not to endanger two lives by marrying at that time.

I decided to keep them updated from the Base Camp by SMS. I planned to regularly update *Mamaji* and told other people to get news from him.

As long as I was at the Base Camp, I sent almost one SMS every day. While going up to acclimatise, I used to leave a message that I would be going up and wouldn't be sending messages to them for the next couple of days. Even when I was going up for the final climb, I told them that I had created two systems for sending them information and they would be informed by both or at least one when I reached the top. So, I had left the key contacts with the company representative at the Base Camp as well as with the Indian army team doctor, and had told them to inform people such as my DM in Gangtok, my *Mamaji* in my home state and my boss from the last job in Mumbai.

18

Much-needed Acclimatisation

'I would rather attempt to do something great and fail than to attempt to do nothing and succeed.'

—*Robert H. Schuller,*
Tough Times Never Last, But Tough People Do!

Mountain climbing is a slow process because we don't climb directly, but in stages. Even if somebody wants to go directly, he or she can't because the human body is not habituated to move in the thin atmosphere so suddenly. That's why climbers go up slowly in planned stages and take adequate rest in between to adapt to the low pressure, low temperature, low oxygen, etc. This slow adaptation of the body to the changing atmospheric conditions is called acclimatisation.

The IMAX film *Everest* (1998 movie), which is based on the exploits of three climbers who survived perils of the 1996 disaster on Everest, reveals that the difference in the barometric pressure and oxygen content between the sea level and top of mountain is so vast that if a human being were taken directly from the ocean-side and deposited at the peak, he or she would immediately fall unconscious and die within a few minutes.

This happens because body of a person who lives at the sea level cannot take the sudden drastic change in the atmospheric conditions. That's why climbers go up slowly. The general recommendation in the mountains is, not to climb too high too fast. It is specifically advised that we take one extra day of rest for every thousand metres of ascent.

Although the idea of slowly trekking from Lukla to the Everest Base Camp is also to acclimatise the body to the change in the atmospheric conditions, the acclimatisation schedule beyond the Everest Base Camp is to make the body fit for higher altitudes as well as to test it to see whether it is fit for the final climb.

Generally, after reaching the Base Camp, the climber has to rest for an average of two days and then, a *pooja* is performed in honour of Mother Chomolungma. This is followed by a climbing practice on a nearby ice-slope in the glacier. After this, the acclimatisation schedule is decided by the team's leader in coordination with Sherpa *Sirdar* and a representative of the agency duly considering weather conditions and whether to route through Khumbu icefall and further in an option.

Normally, most of the teams undertake the acclimatisation in two stages. During the first shift, they go to camp I and stay there for a few hours and come back to the Base Camp and rest for a few days before moving to the second stage of acclimatisation. During acclimatisation, particularly during the second stage, the weather is carefully monitored, especially to see if there are chances of snowfall because the climber has to spend a night in camp III at the altitude of 24,000 feet (7315 metre). It is on the slope of Lhotse face and any heavy snowfall that might lead to an avalanche, which could sweep away the whole camp claiming all our lives.

For the second stage of acclimatisation, the team first reaches camp I at altitude of about 19,900 feet (6065 metres) and takes a break where they have warm water, tea, etc. Then they move towards camp II at an altitude of about 21,300 feet (or 6500 metres) where they spend the night. If everything remains normal, then next morning, the team may move towards camp III, or may take one extra day of rest at camp II before moving further. After spending a night at camp III, the team comes back to camp II on next day and depending on the team, they may spend the night at camp II and come back to the Base Camp on next day or the same day. If a climber spends the night at camp III without supplemental oxygen, and his or her health remains normal, then he or she is considered fit for the final climb to the top.

Sometimes, a climber develops abnormal symptoms during acclimatisation, so they have to be careful and look for solutions. Depending on the case, the climber goes to Kathmandu for medical treatment, and in many cases, abandons climbing further. For example, when the North East Everest expedition team was acclimatizing, a young boy, James, from Manipur, had a severe headache at camp III. When he could not tolerate the headache any longer, he started crying aloud. Somehow he returned to the Base Camp with the support of his team members but he was in a bad shape by the time he came down.

Initially the doctor at the Base Camp checked him, trying to diagnose the cause, and later, he referred him to the Kathmandu Hospital for a further check-up. So, he was evacuated from the Base Camp in a helicopter and after the check-up at Kathmandu Hospital, doctors found that there was internal bleeding in his brain that had led to blood clotting. He had to abandon the expedition. Luckily, the problem had surfaced during acclimatisation, and he was saved due to timely evacuation and medical treatment. If the same problem had occurred above camp IV, his chances of survival would had been questionable.

Our acclimatisation, above the Base Camp, started on April 23 when we went only half way till camp I and came back. Since it was the first climb above the Base Camp, I was taught that timing is very important in the mountains. To make sure that I wouldn't get late, I couldn't sleep well the night before, thinking my phone alarm wouldn't work as mobile phones stop working at very low temperatures. So I slept intermittently.

I finally woke up at 2:45 am and got ready at 4 am. I rigged up all the equipments like the climbing boots, harnesses, karabiners, descender, warm clothes, head lamps, and put my rucksack on my back and came to the dining tent where the other members and their guides had to assemble before the final departure. The dining tent was the assembling point for members as it was big enough to give us enough space to move around and so, some climbers preferred to don the climbing gear here in contrast to personal small tents, in which we could not stand. Once everybody was ready and had something like tea, coffee, honey lemon water, etc., we departed. We turned on the main head lamps to test them because we would use them for the final climb. Otherwise, I had another head lamp (that was less powerful) to use at Base Camp. First, everybody went to Lhapso and after praying to Mother Chomolungma, made one circumambulation of Lhapso clockwise and moved on to the Crampon Point. We donned our crampons here and moved ahead.

Climbing ice wall with the help of aluminium ladder in Khumbu icefall.

Since it was our first visit to Khumbu, which has its own special history and has particular significance during the whole Everest journey, I was well prepared because I had read a lot about it and its history. It is situated between the Base Camp and camp I, i. e. between an altitude of 17,600 feet and 19,900 feet and is like a fast moving river of ice. Its main feature is big and deep crevasses and big blocks of ice, which are as high as ten-storey buildings. The movement of ice is about three or four feet in a day, so the fixed ropes set up for our route can break within a day. Due to the daily movement of ice, the aluminium ladders which are put across the crevasses and tied on both sides of them, would either be hanging on one side, or would become compressed between the sides of two crevasses. This happens due to tension and squeezing caused by the movement of the ice, and the resultant widening and shrinking of crevasses at different places. Crossing Khumbu icefall is so dangerous that the famous mountaineer Ballinger said, 'If it wasn't the tallest mountain in the world, you would never put yourself on a glacier this active.'

Many deaths have been caused when the climbers or guides fell into crevasses or were buried under the breaking seracs. Jon Krakauer, a team member of the 1996 Everest expedition and author of the book *Into Thin Air* described every journey through the Khumbu icefall as, 'A little like playing a round of Russian roulette.' Sometimes, bodies buried under ice in the Khumbu are seen when they resurface after a few years when the shifting ice takes the body down near the Base Camp. Knowing this much about Khumbu, I was not surprised when I, later, read that the legendary mountaineer George Mallory had also turned away from Khumbu Icefall in 1921, saying it was impossible to pass.

Climber encountering crevasse in Khumbu icefall.

Nowadays, every climber aspiring to climb the Everest from the south side has to pass through this treacherous Khumbu icefall. There is no other option and my case was no exception. After climbing, descending, and crossing so many crevasses using the aluminium ladders, we finally reached the dam area inside the icefall, after one and a half hour, and after a short break, started descending. It took us another hour to come back to the Base Camp. The first interaction with Khumbu was good and memorable and we waited for our next visit when we would go further up till camp II, or may be further till camp III, as would be decided by the Sherpa *Sirdar* and the leader Col. Rana.

The next phase of acclimatisation started on April 29, when the team went up and remained above the Base Camp for four days. We came back to the Base Camp on the fifth day. Our actual plan was to go to camp I on the first day, rest there during the night and move to camp II on the next day. After spending one extra day at camp II, we could go further, depending on the situation.

The first day, April 29, started with us waking up at 12.30 am. After we were ready and had donned all the climbing equipments, we moved out of the dining tent. As usual, the first stop was Lhapso, where we prayed to Mother Chomolungma, and made a clockwise circumambulation of Lhapso and moved ahead to the Crampon Point, where we put on our crampons and moved ahead. We started from Crampon Point at 2 am.

Passing below ice seracs.

Initially every member and guide were moving slowly and closely in a line following the light from the head lamp of the members moving ahead at the gap of about a metre but slowly, the gap started increasing as everybody started settling at their own pace. My guide and I kept on moving up and down in the Khumbu and crossing many dangerous crevasses by balancing crampons on the steps of aluminium ladders, passing below big, high, and slant ice blocks, crossing many sherpa coming down from higher camps, and overtaking many slow climbers. When we used to get tired, we would take a break for a few minutes at a safe point while our anchor remained hooked to the fixed rope. When we looked behind, sometimes some members were sighted and sometimes none of them could be spotted depending on the gradient of the place. But it was obvious that the team members were scattered and no more moving together.

Climber crossing crevasse on aluminum ladder in Khumbu icefall.

After about four hours, Khumbu seemed unending, and I was eagerly awaiting the sight of the camp I. My guide, Passang Sherpa, and I were much ahead of the other group members. Only Commander Satya Dam (who was a member of the international team) and some Sherpa from our agency crossed us on the way. But I was feeling tired. It was my first time at this altitude, so low oxygen content in the atmosphere was another problem. Normally, Sherpa are very strong and they walk faster than climbers at that altitude. I could make out the physical strength of Sherpa by their pace while descending down from the higher camps whenever we used to cross each other on the way, and they used to greet my guide, who was familiar to many of them. I observed smile on the faces of Sherpa as they greeted my guide. They really seemed happy and peaceful; although one would make out they were tired. What was important for me that they really seemed to be enjoying the process in spite of the physical exhaustion. That was probably a habit they had developed over a period of time when they had happily accepted their destiny and found enjoyment in it.

It also came into my mind to try finding enjoyment in the process, which would also withdraw my focus from exhaustion. I diverted my focus from my tiring body to silent ice seracs in the surroundings, and deep crevasses as I crossed them. I wanted to connect with them, spiritually. And I knew they were watching us too, like silent spectators. I felt that as I was passing by, they were welcoming me. As I moved ahead and came to a gentler slope leaving them behind, I looked back to watch the seracs looking back at me.*

Climber passing through Khumbu Icefall

Khumbu is combination of crevasses and ice seracs.

I felt like I reached camp in no time. I noticed a few tents standing ahead and some people standing outside busy with their rucksacks. I looked at my watch and found that it was almost an hour since I was busy observing the mountain features and I felt as if time had passed very soon.

Sign of life in non-living substances has been a matter of excitement for the scientists for more than a century. Indian scientist Jagdish Chandra Bose was one of the pioneers in the area, who did a series of experiments around the year 1900, based on stimulus response system on animal, plant and metal. He found that all three responded to stimulus applied on them. He experimented by passing electrical current, exposing to chemical reagents like anaesthesia and poison, variation in temperature, effect of light, and found that the inorganic substance like metal (for example tin) responded in a similar way like living tissue of animal and plant. He, in his book Response in the Living and Non-Living, wrote, 'We have seen that the criterion by which vital response is differentiated is its abolition by the action of certain reagents—the so-called poisons. We find, however, that poisons also abolish the responses in plants and metals. Just as animal tissues pass from a state of responsiveness while living to a state of irresponsiveness when killed by poisons, so also we find metals transformed from a responsive to an irresponsive condition by the action of similar poisonous reagents.'

Similarly, he experimented the effect of light on artificial retina made up of inorganic substances and mentioned the effect in his aforesaid book, 'Even the responses of such a highly specialised organ as the retina are strictly paralleled by inorganic responses. We have seen how the stimulus of light evokes in the artificial retina responses, which coincide in all their detail with those produced in the real retina. ....These similarities went even further, the very abnormalities of retinal response finding their reflection in the inorganic (see chapter xx - General Survey and conclusion).'

Thus, on the basis of above experiments, we can't ignore the possibility of sign of life in inorganic substances like ice seracs and crevasses, although it looks strange presently.

A French physiologist Charles Robert Richet, who was 1913 Nobel laureate in physiology or medicine for his work on anaphylaxis, said, 'Metaphysics is not yet officially a science, recognised as such. But it is going to be.... At Edinburgh, I was able to affirm before 100 physiologists that our five senses are not our only means of knowledge and that a fragment of reality sometimes reaches the intelligence in other ways.... Because a fact is rare is no reason that it does not exist. Because a study is difficult, is that a reason for not understanding it?'

I was amazed by the fact how easy work becomes, when you change the focus of your mind. The process of climbing through Khumbu icefall, which seemed so tiring, boring, and dangerous previously, seemed enjoying and interesting and I also found new friends like seracs and crevasses, which I knew, would always welcome me with open hearts.

In Khumbu Icefall.

As my mind returned back to the physical world, I realized that I was at an altitude of 19,900 feet and in the western CWM area located just above Khumbu icefall, what I had read previously. At the same time, I became fully conscious of my physical body, I was very exhausted. I wanted to collapse in my tent and rest for the day, but after drinking some hot orange juice, I regained my energy quickly and was more confident of reaching ahead of others. After spending some time in the mess tent, Passang Sherpa suggested me to move ahead to camp II, saying there were better arrangements for food, tents to stay in, toilet facilities, and also less wind there.

Camp I was only for the transit between the Base Camp and camp II. It was also subjected to a windy weather most of the times and so, climbers had to tolerate it. I also recalled, I had read that while resting in the tent at camp I, climbers listen to deep murmuring and cracking sounds of crevasses opening and closing deep down in the glacier beneath. It was also not sure whether a crevasse would open beneath your tent in dark of the night and you fall deep into it. I thought the suggestion was logical. Commander Satya Dam was also moving towards camp II, so I also made up my mind to try and move further up but I told my guide that I would go after other members of my team arrived and that I would just inform Col. Rana. When the others arrived, I informed Col. Rana and moved towards camp II. It needed another three-hours trek through the gently rising glacial valley of the western CWM, also called the *valley of silence*.

It is a large, flat glacial valley between Nuptse on one side and the Everest and Lhotse on the other side. The glacier of western CWM is made up from the ice and snow that comes off from the Everest, Lhotse, and Nuptse face, and gets accumulated in the valley. The undulating valley has a gentle pitch from camp I to camp II. It is featured by many large lateral crevasses in the centre, which necessitates the climbers to move from the far right side of the valley near the base of Nuptse and keep themselves hooked on to the fixed rope most of the time while moving due to presence of hidden crevasses in the area. The upper portion of the Everest was for the first time visible from here since we reached the Base Camp as it was not visible from there. The name *valley of silence* is given because the topography of the area generally cuts off the wind from the climbing route but a windless sunny day becomes very hot and unbearable for climbers to cross it.

The first hour was normal as the gradient was less and the slope was gentle along the route. But after about an hour, there was a slow but continuous gradient upwards. It was also sunny day and so, walking upslope with the heat of the sun getting re-radiated from the ice surface made the journey quite unpleasant with our warm clothes on the body. I tried to connect to the surroundings of the western CWM but didn't find anything except the large undulating plain with a few very small crevasses, which made me a little uncomfortable with all the heat radiating from it. Looking ahead, I could only see camp II, which was clearly visible. It seemed near and looked like, it was hardly half an hour away but my guide said that it would take two hours to reach there. As I continued walking towards it, my exhaustion increased and the path seemed to be never ending.

As the time passed, I started thinking that my guide's estimation was correct and I was yet to gain experience to estimate correctly in the mountain and glacier. The last half an hour of the trek was comparatively tougher than before. I stopped to breathe and was trying to store my energy closing my eyes. But the moment I did so, I almost fell asleep on my feet for a while and after a few moments, my eyes opened and I resumed again. I felt dizzy and almost lost balance many times while I closed my eyes. But, I had no option but to continue as it would be tougher to return in such a hot, sunny day and traverse the glacier. Finally, when camp II seemed to be 200 metres away, surprisingly, I felt more energetic and my pace increased. I finally reached it at 12 o'clock. I realised that the second part of the journey was very tough and exhausting.

Camp II at an altitude of 21,300 feet (6500 metres) is located on a rocky patch below the Lhotse face. The camp is generally erected near the Lhotse wall and a little away from the west face of the Everest to avoid sudden avalanche. It is higher than all the mountains of Europe, North America, Africa, Australia and Antarctica. Only a few peaks of South America are higher than camp II.

The Sherpa there welcomed me and I was given a tent near the mess tent where Sherpa cooks were preparing food. But after a while my guide shifted my luggage to a different tent away from the mess tent. He said that I needed more fresh air. Some time after reaching camp II, I started having a splitting headache and so I thought that I had made the wrong decision by coming directly to camp II. I should have thought about it because, first of all, I had never been at a height over 19,200 feet before and so I should have come slowly taking a night halt at camp I. Secondly, my guide, who made the suggestion, was an Everest Summiteer eleven times over and even Commander Dam, who had covered it in one stretch had been pursuing mountaineering for over two decades. I shouldn't have compared myself with them as I had come to a big mountain for the first time in my life.

But I decided not waste my energy whining over what's done and regain my positive outlook. I tried my best to overcome the pain thinking that I had covered both the camps in one day and have an upper edge with respect to other members of the team who were resting at camp I. The pain was there due to the decreased oxygen content in the atmosphere at camp II in comparison to Base Camp and would disappear in some time when my body would adjust to the prevailing atmospheric condition. I shared this with my guide, who told me that the members at camp I also suffered from the same symptoms and it was windy over there. Thus, I thought that moving to camp II directly had been a good decision.

The next day, other members of the team came from camp I and they told me about their problems faced at camp I including headache, sleeplessness, wind, and extreme cold. As per the plan, we were going to move further ahead after staying at camp II for one more day. After having lunch and chatting with the other members of the team, I played chess with my friend from our team and won as usual. Playing chess at that altitude of 21,300 feet was a unique experience for me. It also made me certain that everything was alright with my mind. The next day too, we were at stand by atcamp II. The team had to spend an extra day to acclimatise before moving on.

Enjoying chess with Sanjay Pandit at 6500 meter altitude.

The day after, May 2, was another climbing day. As we had planned, after breakfast, we donned all our gear and moved towards camp III. But unlike the other team, who used to go to camp III and spend one night there, our team leader Col. Rana decided to go only till the Jumar Point, which is halfway to camp III, at the base (bergschrund) of Lhotse. From this point onward, the slope is very steep and the climbers have to attach themselves to the fixed rope with the help of an anchor and move up with the help of the jumar on the rope. This Lhotse face is very steep and risky especially because of ice chunks that keep falling there, rubbles and boulders, and also the chances of getting head injury, so our leader had decided to avoid this risk and to return from the Jumar Point because of some recent incidents of injury on this slope.

I started with my guide at 8.30 am. A few members of the team had gone ahead and a few were coming from behind us. During the first hour, I moved at a normal pace and everything seemed fine. But the pain started acting up. However, I continued moving up. Slowly, I felt like it was increasing and my pace was decreasing. I felt helpless when two others overtook me. But I tried to ignore the pain and progressed. The pain kept on surging and I was a little worried about my health.

I was walking alone with my guide some distance ahead. Then, at some point, I decided to return to camp II just to be on the safer side so that if there was some internal problem then I could first get it treated and avoid unnecessary risks of aggravating the problem by climbing further up and gaining more altitude. I was about to return but I saw our Sherpa *Sirdar* Pemba Dai some way ahead. I decided to reach him, so that he would contact my guide on VHF radio to return him back to accompany me on the way down. My guide seemed much ahead and I couldn't recognise him amongst a bunch of people moving ahead at some distance. So, I increased my speed to catch up with him and as I focussed on it, the pain was automatically subsumed in the process and I felt comparatively relaxed when I reached him finally.

As we met, I told him about the pain and he said that our destination jumar point was near, which would take some thirty minutes of further uphill walk. He left the decision to me whether to continue or return back. I decided to continue but simply walk leisurely and to enjoy the nature without putting much stress on reaching before others. The Everest and Lhotse face was on the left side and Nuptse on the right. The steep white coloured ice wall of Lhotse was clearly visible, which was shining in the sunlight. I could see the thin dark line of climbers over the white wall, who were trudging on this steep face. I could make out that they must be either climbers, going up for acclimatisation or Sherpa carrying loads uphill for camp III. I could feel their difficulty level and compared with myself as I was just trudging a gentle slope when compared to them. I felt that I must uplift my performance standard because I was about to give up on such a gentle slope some time back.

Winston Churchill, the British Prime Minister during Second World War, had said, 'It is not enough that we do our best; sometimes we must do what is required.'

I thought that it wan't helping me to be giving excuses and slowing down. The people trudging on the Lhotse face were going to camp III for acclimatisation and I was given an easier target, to reach just the jumar point. I shook off the negativity that was bugging me and increased my speed, completely oblivious to the pain in the process and finally after three hours, reached the jumar point below the Lhotse face, at an altitude of 22,000 feet (6705 metre). On reaching, I realized that the pain was still there but it seemed submersed. I was relieved that I was able to make it in spite of the severe pain. It was better that I didn't return midway otherwise it would have decreased my motivation level. I took a ten minute break and started downwards, reaching camp II after an hour and fifteen minutes. The pain also vanished on the way. But I was a little worried about the reason for the pain. At dinner I explained the problem to Col. Rana, who said that the chest pain had been due to gastric problems. He said he would give me medicine at the Base Camp.

While retiring in the sleeping bag in my tent that night, I analyzed that somehow, I did complete my target for the day. First, I was motivated from the climbers on the Lhotse wall, and next, I wanted to do what they did, if not, overtake them. The zeal that I had in me was something that made the whole thing possible.

Climber descending down in the Khumbu Icefall.

We would return to the Base Camp the next day, May 3. So after breakfast, we started from camp II and reached camp I in forty five minutes. After a short fifteen-minute break, we continued our journey to the Base Camp and by noon, reached it after about three and a half hour later. On the way down in the Khumbu icefall, I experienced a little pain again.

One interesting incident occurred while descending down the Khumbu Icefall. The team members on the icefall were split up and some were further down and some, still trying to match up to their pace. My guide and I were walking together and suddenly, we heard a noise. We saw that an avalanche had been triggered from the Lola face on the right and a big rock flew off from it and towards us. My guide told me to hurry down and take the cover of a big ice wall; I did so. The rock passed some distance away from us. When we reached the Base Camp, Col. Rana was saying that they saw the same boulder hurtling towards them and for a moment he had thought that it would hit somebody. Luckily, everyone was safe.

With a safe arrival of all the members at the Base Camp, our team completed the acclimatization schedule and we were pretty relaxed. Further, we would wait for a favourable weather forecast to start the final journey for the zenith.

People returning from Khumbu Icefall.

19

Sherpa: The True Heroes of The Mountains

'A man should do his job so well that the living, the dead and the unborn could do it no better.'

—*Martin Luther King Jr.*

While the climbers are busy with their own preparations by doing rounds of camps above the Base Camp and acclimatisation taking part in recreational activities as they wait for fair weather to attempt the final climb, acclimatise the Sherpa have their own activities, which they have to complete before the forecast for fair weather arrives. Their important responsibility is to fill up each camp with the necessary items for the final climb. Camp III and camp IV are especially set up in advance and the necessary oxygen bottles, butane gas canisters, tents, food items like juice, fruit, chocolates, etc. are carried up along the dangerous route of the Khumbu icefall and above. They carry loads from 20 to 40 kilograms above the Base Camp, where it is difficult for a normal climber to even carry 10 or 15 kilograms. Once, all camps are set up and loaded with the necessary stuff, the Sherpa are ready to accompany climbers to the top.

In fact, their activities start a few weeks before we arrive at the Base Camp because they set up the Base Camp and carry the necessary items for setting up tents, kitchen provisions, generators, climbing gear, etc. They also start identifying the route and start fixing up ropes along the route beyond the Base Camp before we arrive. They do this so that the climbers can go up for acclimatisation without losing much time at the Base Camp waiting for rope fixing. When we reach the Base Camp and start our acclimatisation schedule, the Sherpa continue fixing the route further uphill depending on the weather conditions. While the climbers trek to the Base Camp, some of the Sherpa also work as porters and carry extra baggage of climbers daily from one stop to another and finally bringing it to the Base Camp. During the climbers' stay at the Base Camp, they also carry necessary consumables on their back for many kilometres and bring them to the Base Camp. Some people also carry the sealed drums of human excreta on their backs so they can dispose of them outside the area to keep the hygiene and pollution of the area under control.

Sherpas carry and stack oxygen bottle at higher camps.

There are different kinds of Sherpa as one enters the mountaineering sector. The least experienced and new entries are employed as porters who carry loads to and from the Base Camp. As one learns mountaineering and starts climbing, they become climbing Sherpa, and work as climbing guides for climbers. They also load ferries going to and from different camps beyond the Base Camp. The third category includes the most skilled ones, who are route openers; they identify the safe climbing routes on the mountain slopes during each climbing season, and fix up ropes for the same.

My guide passang sherpa while returning after summit.

Normally those Sherpa, who have summited the Everest the maximum number of times, are the ones who carry maximum load and those who undertake route opening become well-known amongst the climbers. Their charges also vary according to their strength and experience. Born and brought up there, and then, living at that height gives them a natural advantage in terms of adaptability as well as stamina at high altitudes. So they are the most suited for carrying heavy loads at that high altitude.

Nyima, Dawa, Migmar, Lhakpa, Phurba, Pasang, and Pemba are the common names you hear on entering the Sagarmatha National Park region for trekking or mountaineering. This is because they are named after the day they were born. They believe that the child, who opens his eye on the particular day of the week, is protected by that day's deity. For example, the name Nyima indicates that he was born on a Sunday and thus, he gained the protection of the Sun god. Similarly, other common names, Dawa, Migmar, Lhakpa, Phurba, Pasang, and Temba indicate the children born on Monday, Tuesday, Wednesday, Thursday, Friday and Saturday respectively. Thus, they would be under the protection of the Moon, Mars, Mercury, Jupiter, Venus, and Saturn respectively.

Group of sherpa carrying heavy load through khumbu icefall.

They are inhabitants of the Khumbu Valley region, the Sagarmatha National Park surrounding the Everest in Nepal. History says that the Sherpa were nomadic people, who first settled in the Khumbu region of Eastern Nepal. *Sherpa* is a Tibetan word, which means *Eastern people*. *Shar* means east and *pa* means people. It is said that the Sherpa migrated from Eastern Tibet to Khumbu around four to six hundred years ago. Tengboche is considered the oldest Sherpa village in Nepal. Later, some of them shifted to Western Nepal too.

Trading is their main economic activity. They have often been working as middlemen between Tibetan traders and other people of Nepal. Tourism, especially trekking and mountaineering activities, provide them an alternative source of income, where they have taken a wide range of activities. The increase in tourism in the Khumbu region of Nepal has given a good boost to their economy. Tourism has made some of them well off and they send their children to the western countries for education and work.

Sherpa are very religious in nature and they follow Tibetan Buddhism. Some people have commented that they are very superstitious. They believe that all non-human objects have spirits and so, they see sprits everywhere. Some say that they have an intuitive relationship with the environment, and what we call superstition is their faith. For example, they believe that sexual liaison between unmarried couples above the Base Camp is forbidden by the mountain. It is disrespectful to the mountain god if somebody does it. They believe that the mountain gets angry in such case and bring disaster to the people by bringing unpleasant weather. This has also been shown in the movie *Everest* (2015), which is based on the 1996 Everest Disaster.

They are simple and happy people. After working hard, they enjoy their life in their own way. Life for them is hard, and they are extremely vulnerable to natural mishaps. They take pride in their job and have a lot of self-respect. They cannot tolerate misbehaviour and ill treatment. Sherpa do not tolerate being treated like servants. There were a few clashes between Sherpa and climbers whenever the latter tried to disrespect them. During the 2013 climbing season itself, there was a clash between a foreign climber and a Sherpa. I remember that once we landed at the Lukla airport and were getting ready for the Base Camp, I was told to call the Sherpa *Sirdar* 'Dai' in addition to his name or he would get angry.

But at the same time, they have also saved lives of many climbers high on the slope of mountains during emergency. This is not limited to saving their own clients who had paid them for the service as guides but also many unknown climbers by risking their own life. I have heard brave rescue stories by Sherpa. In 2013, the year I climbed, a climber of the first North East Everest Expedition, Mohan from Manipur, was rescued by a Sherpa from my agency, Seven Summit Trek. Mohan was on his way down after the summit and he had exhausted his bottled oxygen. He was unable to move even a single step and in the absence of oxygen, his condition was deteriorating. His own guide had earlier moved ahead thinking that his client can reach alone without any risk, as camp IV was half an hour away. Luckily, the Sherpa from my agency spotted him while he was also on his way down from the summit and shared his oxygen mask, which too, was limited. He alternately gave him a few breaths and took fewer breathe sand somehow assisted him to reach south col. That's how he saved Mohan's life.

Some of the famous climbing records on Everest are also dedicated to Sherpa. The first person to climb the Everest in 1953, Tenzing Norgay, who reached the summit along with Edmund Hillary, was a Sherpa from the Khumbu region of Nepal. Apa Sherpa, another very famous Sherpa has set the record of climbing the Everest the maximum numbers of times, twenty one. In 2011, he summited the Everest for the twenty first time. Another famous Sherpa is Phurba Tashi Sherpa, who equalled the record of Apa Sherpa of scaling Everest twenty one times. In May 2013 itself, he scaled the Everest two times, first time on May 10 while fixing up the rope, and the second time on May 24 while accompanying his client to the peak. The fastest climbing record on the Everest for reaching the summit from Base camp is only 8 hours and 10 minutes. This was also achieved by a Sherpa named Pemba Dorjie, who set this record in 2004. Another was Babu Chiri Sherpa (died in 2001 during Everest Expedition), a ten-time Everest summiteer, who spent twenty one hours on the peak of the Everest without supplemental oxygen. He slept there the whole night and set the world record of the longest stay on the highest point of the Earth that any human being has done till today. A young female Sherpa named Chhurim Sherpa, who met me during the Everest Base Camp trekking, summited the

Everest twice in 2012 and set the record of being the first female Sherpa to summit the Everest twice in one climbing season and recorded her name in the *Guinness Book of World Records*.' And many more such records go to the Sherpa community. They seem to be the true heroes on Everest.

With their extremely important role in assisting the climbers and the climbers' dependency on them for summiting safely and successfully, Sherpa are the real heroes in the mountains. But people hardly mention them after making a successful summit. Though they work for money they undertake enormous risks to their lives to earn their bread and butter. They are mostly covered by low insurance and their families suffer a lot when they lose them to death in the mountains. I had conversations with many of them about this and they had only one answer; that they would not send their children into this profession. They would send them to school and set them to work in another job where there was no threat to life. But ultimately many of them allow their children to enter the same profession because they earn good remuneration in spite of the serious risk to their lives.

This is the reason why Jamling Tenzing Norgay, the son of the legendary Tenzing Norgay said, 'I climbed the Everest so that my children wouldn't have to.'

20

The Last Preparations for the Triumph

'Cowards die many times before their deaths;
The valiant never taste of death but once.
Of all the wonders that I yet have heard,
It seems to me most strange that men should fear;
Seeing that death, a necessary end,
Will come when it will come.'
— **William Shakespeare**

The Everest is attempted during a lean period when the incoming monsoon pushes the Jet Stream further north and there is a gap when neither the Jet Stream nor the monsoons are in effect. At this point, the wind at the top is minimal. Otherwise, the Everest is affected by the Jet Stream and the wind speed at the top may be around 150 km per hour, which makes it impossible for a climber to go and return safely.

Therefore, attempting Everest in fair weather becomes one of the most important factors for successful summit as well as for a safe return. There have been major disasters owing to sudden worsening of weather while climbers were still uphill above 8000 metre zone. For example, 1996 Everest Disaster is famous for deaths caused due to sudden change in the weather where climbers were caught in a blizzard while making a summit attempt and 8 of them died on May 10 and 11, 1996. That's why, weather forecasting is of utmost importance for the expedition teams.

There are a few good forecasting agencies in the USA, Canada, Europe, and China, etc. Normally, each team hires an agency, which gives them regular weather updates, and according to this update, the team formulates a strategy for their climb. Although the weather forecast is taken into account for the journey beyond the Base Camp during the acclimatisation schedule, it is important to follow it for the final summit attempt. In the past, mass deaths have taken place due to the inaccuracy in weather forecasting. In fact, it is advised not to depend on a single forecasting agency but to get input from more than one by keeping in touch with different teams at the Base Camp. It is better to choose a common day out of the predictions from the different reliable forecasting agencies above. That's why, I was in touch with teams like the Indian Army, the North East team, and the NCC team in addition to our agency, which used to get inputs from a Chinese forecasting agency.

But generally, agencies conducting the Everest Expedition don't reveal weather forecast information to the people of other agencies unless they're in good faith. This is because of mainly two reasons.

The first reason is to avoid crowd on the slopes of the Everest. If the agency would reveal information about the best weather day, then most of the climbers would attempt on that day and it would be more chaotic with people trying to put more load on the fixed rope, increasing the chances of accident if the piton gave up. It also leads to traffic jam and would cause delay in climbing due to the availability of only one narrow route, especially above camp III. The delay is also caused by a few inexperienced climbers who join the queue and reduce the speed of advance because the pace of the queue would be the pace of the slowest climber in the queue unless somebody overtakes a slow moving climber climbing ahead. As mentioned earlier, overtaking is extremely risky on such steep slope at such high altitude. This can be dangerous, especially above camp IV because of the limited availability of supplemental oxygen bottles (3 bottles for climbers and 2 bottles for Sherpa guides) and if supplemental oxygen is exhausted then there is very rare chance of survival and returning back alive from such altitude.

The second reason is that the agencies have to pay a good amount of money to the weather forecasting companies. Agencies that want more accurate weather information take services of reputed weather forecasting agencies, which lead to a higher cost. Hence, they always hesitate passing valuable and expensive information to those who have saved on that aspect and have taken services of less reputed companies leading to less accurate weather information.

Therefore, to safeguard the weather information and plan of movement of their clients from being passed on to the other agencies, agencies at the Base Camp use different frequencies for the VHF communication. They also change the channel if their VHF Radio channel is leaked to other agencies. They keep the plan of movement of their clients a secret, so as to avoid other teams attempting the peak on the same day. In fact, there is a belief that lesser the number of climbers, the safer the climb, as there would be less traffic and no delay on the way.

Nature poses the biggest limitation. In May, there are a maximum of two to three clean days at a stretch, which appear mostly towards the second half of May. Some years in the past have also witnessed only one weather window. So, all the teams have to attempt the peak within the limited weather window and thus many teams plan to attempt on the same day, which falls either in the first or the second weather window and climbers have to experience huge traffic during the climb especially in the last stretch near the Hillary Step. Other than the main weather windows, there also comes one small weather window in the first half of May, when a group of route-opener Sherpa goes up to the top to fix the rope but climbers are not allowed to go along with them.

Weather forecasting is done for a maximum of five days in advance. It also takes about five days to reach the top. First day, climbers go directly to camp II. Second day, they take rest there. Third day, they go to camp III. On the fourth day, they climb to camp IV, and in the evening, they depart for the final summit push and reach the top in the morning of the fifth day and come back to camp IV by afternoon of same day. Some climbers come down directly to camp II by the evening of the same day and thus, reach in a safer zone within a time span of five days.

As the time for the final ascent was coming closer, I was continuously accessing my resources in order to deal with any drawbacks well in advance. This was because I was there all alone. I had come from Sikkim alone and was not part of a formal team, although Col. Rana had been helpful in terms of providing some medicines and we had stayed and moved together during trekking and acclimatisation, especially above the Base Camp. But in true sense, there was no team leader to take care of my general needs and instruct and guide me. Nor was there a doctor to carry routined medical check-ups. I had carried some medicine that the doctor at the Sonam Gyatso Mountaineering Institute (SGMI) had given me, and I was also carrying some of my own medicine like digestive pills from Patanjali Yogpeeth Haridwar, and some general medicines for fever, headache, diarrhoea, etc. My cousin Arun, a doctor, had prescribed those.

I was first told in Kathmandu that I was in the international team along with a pair of Indian twin sisters from Dehradun (who later bacame the first twins in the world to climb the Everest), and a Nepali film actor, Arjun Karki, along with some other foreigners, who seemed to be more experienced climbers. All these members had already arrived at the Base Camp a week before me. This international team was to be led by Commander Satya Dam. Later, I was put in the Indian team under the leadership of Col. Rana because I had said that Indian food was my priority and it was served in the Indian team.

This type of flexible approach is taken by the expedition agencies organising mountaineering expeditions for the comfort of the members, who pay a huge amount of money to the agencies as the expedition expenses. Even though such members are clubbed together to form a team under the leadership of a senior climber, but no leader has any direct control over members. Everyone is free to make individual decisions and decide their day of ascent. They listen more to their own guides the agency provide and who would accompany them to the summit rather than the team leader.

Col Rana the ex-principal HMI Darjeeling had arrived Kathmandu with his team the same day I had arrived. As mentioned earlier, they were seven boys from the Lawrence School and two girls, one from Maharashtra, and another from Rajasthan. When we had started trek from Lukla, the other two members from Nepal (Nisha Adhikari and Sanjay Pandit) had joined us as decided and arranged by our agency. Later, as we had trekked together for over a week, the agency decided to put all of us on one team, which would be led by Colonel Neeraj Rana. Although we were part of one team but naturally, it didn't give us that sense of team spirit which would have developed if a team had been formed much before the expedition and if we had trained together.

The original team of Col Rana, which consisted of seven boys and two girls from India, had been training together for many months. The boys from the Lawrence School told me that Col. Rana had selected the final team from many competitors, who competed in a series of physical test and then, had undergone an extensive five-month training from September 2012 to January 2013. During this period, they had undergone basic and advanced courses at the Himalayan Mountaineering Institute in Darjeeling and then, had undertaken a cycling expedition in the Thar desert, where they pedalled more than 1,000 km in nine days. This had been followed by a high-altitude training at over 6,000 metre in bone-freezing temperatures in Ladakh.

Over the period of these trainings, they had developed a good team spirit in addition to building up stamina. This original team had been completely under the command and control of Col. Rana and a few parents (who were retired defence personnel and who had been fit enough to make it to the Base Camp, and some even higher).

Out of three newly added members, Nisha Adhikari, Sanjay Pandit and I, Nisha Adhikari, was under the direct supervision of the Seven Summit representative, Tashi Sherpa, (Mingma Sherpa's younger brother, who claimed to be a six-times Everest summiteer) who had been staying at the Base Camp with us as well as her guide, Zangmu Sherpa, who claimed to be an Everest Summiteer ten times over. Sanjay Pandit, the Nepali marathon runner, was very enthusiastic and proactive about reaching the summit this time because he had tried unsuccessfully the previous year and this year, had faced a lot of difficulty in a getting sponsorship in contrast to Nisha Adhikari, who had got the sponsorship very easily. He was a lone decision maker and used to move ahead with his guide without caring about other members.

I had greater attachment with the Indian Army team under Major Ranveer Jamwal's leadership. The Indian Army team had camped just next to us and in fact, my tent was midway between the dining tents of the army team and our own. I used to often sit and chat with their members and had enjoyed meals with them several times. But the reason for my deeper attachment to the army team was Major Jamwal's helpful and cordial nature. I had known him before coming to Kathmandu. I had been introduced to the major by another Colonel in the Army, Col Subodh Kumar, the commanding officer of 225 Transit Camp at Thangu in North Sikkim. Another member of the army team, whom I had known since last year, was Subedar Major Mahabir. He had been a quarter master in the Himalayan Mountaineering Institute, where I had received basic as well as advanced mountaineering training and due to this bond, I always trusted the army team more about offering emergency support on the Everest slopes as they also had better infrastructure.

And so, for the final summit attempt, I started along-with the army team two days before the scheduled date for rest of my team (except Sanjay Pandit, who had started one day before me) and reached the summit on the same day and also met the leader like few members of the army team on the summit. On our way to the top, we could hardly meet because our agencies had put up a tent separately. Still, I had more confidence of emergency assistance with the presence of the army team in and around on the slope of the Everest.

Initially, my importance among the army team also increased because I was a link for them to establish initial contact with the Nepali actress, Nisha Adhikari. In Sanjay Pandit's words, she was like 'Priyanka Chopra or Bipasa Basu of India'. She was much more in demand at the Base Camp. Oh God, human nature wouldn't change even where everybody was completely at the mercy of nature. I could see the happiness on the faces of the army team the first time I had introduced Nisha Adhikari to them. I had had to persuade her to meet them to boost the morale of the Nepali army team who represented the pride of her nation. Sanjay Pandit and her guide Zangmu Sherpa had also come with her but I felt that the others had ignored them till I introduced them, as well. Nisha Adhikari didn't need any further introduction after my initial one. I was also happy to see the elation and laughter amongst members of the Army team and felt it had been worth it. The mountain is a treacherous place where everybody was completely at the mercy of nature and the whole Base Camp could even be swept away. I realized this after watching an internet video of a big avalanche that had occurred in May 2009. It had been triggered from Lola face nearby Khumbu icefall and had stopped just near the Base Camp.

Although every climber had their own Sherpa guide to accompany them to the summit of Everest, forming the team had still been a good idea as our tents were located together. We would eat in the same dining tent. Our acclimatisation schedule had been planned and mostly undertaken together. The training had been planned for all of us together. It consisted of ice-craft, training on how to use oxygen cylinders, and sometimes health check-ups that were held when Col Rana gave everyone the necessary medicines.

But in spite of all this, it is your own responsibility to take care of yourself and climb and descend safely. This is why I wanted to prepare myself well in advance for the final climb. I had prepared a checklist of all the essential items that I must carry with me from the Base Camp while going up for the final summit attempt. Some items were so important like the summit gloves, summit goggles, headlamp, etc., that it was not possible to make the final summit push from south col for the peak in absence of those. Earlier, I had heard that the mountain expedition had failed in the past just because the team had forgotten to carry a small item, like a matchbox. This happens because once you have gone up, there would be hardly somebody to lend their own items to you because everybody carries minimum essential items for their own use. Hardly anybody has anything extra for others. So, I had to be extra careful because I had to ensure that everything was in order before I leave the Base Camp for the final ascent.

For this reason I went to meet Commander Dam to discuss the food that I would carry for the final climb. In fact, the other members of my team, the Lawrence School boys, had asked for GU Gel chocolate from the U. S. A. Some others actually had the GU Gel Powder. This is a special product, which reenergizes you, giving you instant energy and it gets you through whatever degree of exhaustion you may be facing.

Although I had discussed food with the senior instructors in HMI Darjeeling when I was training in October–November, this GU Gel hadn't come up. Even while I had talked to Mingma Sherpa on the phone while booking my seat at Seven Summit, I had briefly asked about the food to be brought and he had mentioned this chocolate. But I had not found it in Kathmandu or even in Sikkim or Darjeeling, and there had been no time to get it from abroad. I told myself that it didn't matter if I had it or not, I just had to believe in myself. I thought that it would be worth it to get guidance from experienced mountaineers like Commander Satya Dam well in time to choose, what to carry from the food items I had. I had been carrying a lot of food from

India, which the HMI Darjeeling instructors and the director of Seven Summit Treks agency had advised me of. These included many kilograms of dry fruits like Kashmiri *badaam*, pistachios, raisins, *chhuhara*, *gur*, peanuts, maize *sattu*, *chanasattu*, *kaaju*, lots of chocolate, biscuits, some Haldiram namkeen mixture, Patanjali Chyawanprash, etc. It weighed more than 25 kg. Commander Satya Dam suggested that raisins, *gur*, fried peanuts, and chocolate are a source of instant energy, so I packed my rucksack accordingly with separate packets of these items, which were to be consumed while climbing, and other items in separate packets, which were to be consumed while our stay at the intermediate camps.

I had also packed few selected medicines like Lupidium tablets in case of diarrhoea, Diamox tablets for altitude sickness, but the most important of all medication for final climb was a steroid called Dexamethazone. It is either injected to the climbers or given orally in the form of tablets, when the climber gives up all hope of moving in the mountain due to health problems, like HACE or HAPE. It (Dexamethazone) is like a natural hormone produced by our adrenal gland and acts as its replacement when our body doesn't make enough natural hormone especially when climbers are suffering from high altitude sickness and are fully exhausted on the higher slope of mountain. Although I had read about this medication during the Mountaineering course but neither could I manage to carry it from Sikkim, nor did I remember to buy it in Kathmandu. Normally, it is the duty of expedition team doctor or leader to arrange for it and carry it. In my case, I had somehow managed to get one syringe and one ampoule of this injection from the Major Jamwal, after reaching the Everest Base Camp. I packed it carefully in the outer pocket of my rucksack so as not to break the glass cover of the ampoule as well as to make it easily available during emergency.

According to different forecasting agencies, the weather was going to be windy till the seventeenth and it was not recommended to attempt to summit. But still, a few climbers were trying with a very slim chance of success. Many were injured due to the chilly wind factor and the resultant frostbite. The weather was expected to improve by May onwards. May 19 to 22 had been forecasted to be the first good weather window. Overall, nineteenth and twenty first was considered to be the days with the best weather. Although the forecast from the Chinese agency was showing twenty first as the day with the best weather, a European agency forecasted that there was no such accurate prediction post May 20. I finally decided to attempt the summit on the twentieth as the Indian Army and the NCC team and most of the members of the international team in my agency had decided. However, my team leader Col. Rana had decided to attempt it on May 21. Later a new prediction arrived which said that there could be snowfall on the twentieth but this wasn't confirmed. I finally decided that I would start my journey in the early hours of May 16, i.e. one day ahead of my team and if, on the way, I found out that the prediction for the twentieth was correct, then I would make the summit attempt on either the nineteenth or the twenty first depending on when I received confirmation for the same.

21

The Final Journey

'The first question which you will ask and which I must try to answer is this, "What is the use of climbing Mount Everest?" and my answer must at once be, "It is no use. " There is not the slightest prospect of any gain whatsoever. Oh, we may learn a little about the behaviour of the human body at high altitudes, and possibly medical men may turn our observation to some account for the purposes of aviation. But otherwise nothing will come of it. We shall not bring back a single bit of gold or silver, not a gem, nor any coal or iron. We shall not find a single foot of earth that can be planted with crops to raise food. It's no use. So, if you cannot understand that there is something in man which responds to the challenge of this mountain and goes out to meet it, that the struggle is the struggle of life itself upward and forever upward, then you won't see why we go. What we get from this adventure is just sheer joy; and joy is, after all, the end of life. We do not live to eat and make money. We eat and make money to be able to enjoy life. That is what life means and what life is for.'

—*'George Leigh Mallory'*

The evening of 15th May was a happy one; I had ordered a cake in the bakery and it was wonderful. I cut it and everybody enjoyed his or her share. After this, I went to my tent at about 9 pm and set the alarm for 1 am, I slept for a few hours, leaving my worries behind, as my backpack was already ready. I had checked everything thrice in the day and had compared the essential items against a list. I had packed certain extra clothes and food that had to be left at camp II and were to be used on the return journey after making the summit.

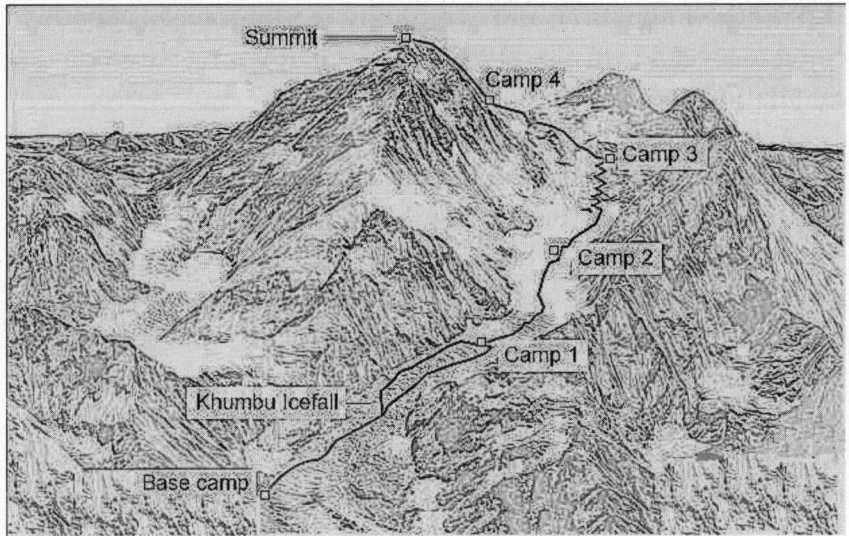

Route Map of Everest (South Col Route)

I woke just before my alarm rang. It is said that god has provided us with a wonderful clock in our minds, which never fails if you just tell yourself that you have to wake up at a certain time. Once inside the toilet tent, I felt a sense of relief that I was going to be saved from the morning and the evening routine of entering that closed toilet and defecating into a drum, irrespective of whether it was empty or almost full. Above the Base Camp, the only enclosed toilet facility is at camp II and we were free to do what we had to in the open in the other places. At least, I wouldn't have to inhale the unpleasant odour of the closed toilet, which always made me uncomfortable.

Finally, after freshening up and donning all my gear except the crampons, I went to the dining tent, which was the meeting point for the others who were going with me. They were the twin sisters from Dehradun (Tashi and Nungshi Malik) along with their guides. Although the planned time of departure was 2:30, the others were a bit late. So, I made glucose water with honey and started sipping it comfortably. When they finally arrived, we departed from the dining tent at 3:30 am. Commander Satya Dam, along with his clients, and the army as well as the NCC team had made a similar plan to move that very day. But they had set their own time and everybody would travel as per their convenience. So we also started moving upwards based on our calculations of pace and other conveniences.

Anyway, I was not in a mood to start with an experienced mountaineer like Commander Satya Dam. He was a mountaineer by profession, and his pace would be fast. If I started with them, I would have to race to keep pace, which would be exhausting and thus, was not recommended for the final climb. If I didn't do that and went at my own speed, then they would have moved ahead, leaving us behind. So I had decided that I would not race against anybody but would go at my own comfortable speed. I would maintain my own pace throughout my journey, because I was going to be alone in any case. I planned to start separately and a bit earlier along with a few climbers who kept a medium pace, so I would go at a comfortable speed, while the other people who had a faster pace would start a little later.

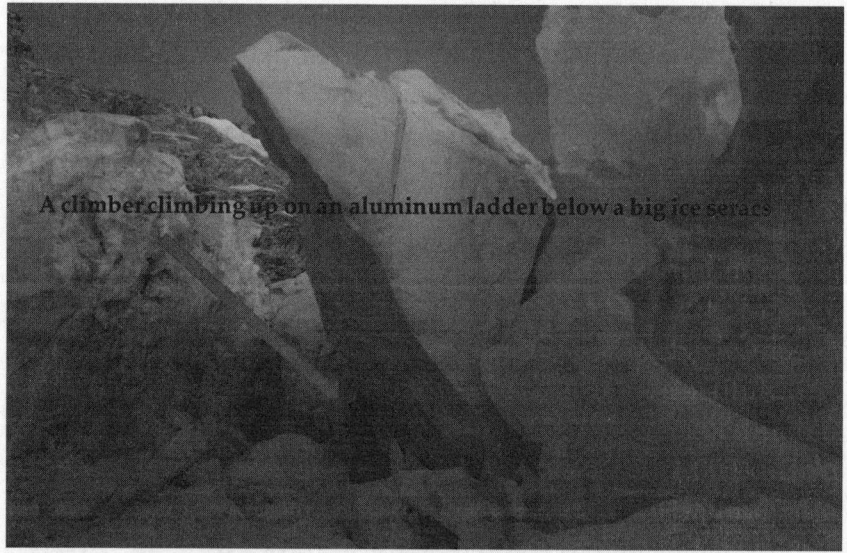

A climber climbing up on an aluminum ladder below a big ice seracs

A climber passing through Khumbu icefall

As usual, we went to offer *pooja* to Mother Chomolungma for the last time before we returned safely from the top and after making a clockwise circumambulation of Lhapso, we moved out, illuminating the darkness with the strong light from our headlamps. We reached the Crampon point as usual and we put on the crampons and continued our journey further upwards.

We moved at a comfortable pace. I was thinking of Mother Chomolungma as if she was calling me to come to the peak, and worship her. I imagined how she would appear in a different form as morning began with the sun rising and then at noon with the sun overhead, again in the evening with the sun setting beyond the horizon, and finally during the night, with the wind, cold, and silence all around the peak of the Everest. After a five-hour climb, we reached camp I at 8:30 am. We were exhausted, and our immediate target was to reach camp II.

Climbers climbing up in Khumbu icefall.

After getting some warm water and chocolate, we rested for some time in the open at camp I(all the tents were already full), my Sherpa and I left for camp II at 9:30 am. The path through the western CWM was usually tiring and I moved slowly but steadily. Once my Sherpa told me that if I moved so slowly then I wouldn't be able to reach the top, but I didn't care. I knew that as long as I was slow, I would be comfortable. However, once I increased my pace, I would become exhausted very fast and even though I would reach camp II, over-exhaustion might create problem during further climb towards higher camps and the final summit push for the top, so I preferred to store my energy for the final day by being slow and comfortable at that early stage. I remembered an inspiring statement by the ancient Chinese philosopher and the founder of philosophical Taoism, Lao Tzu,' Nature does not hurry, yet everything is accomplished, 'I continued at my slow pace without losing confidence and finally reach camp II at 12:30, after three hours.

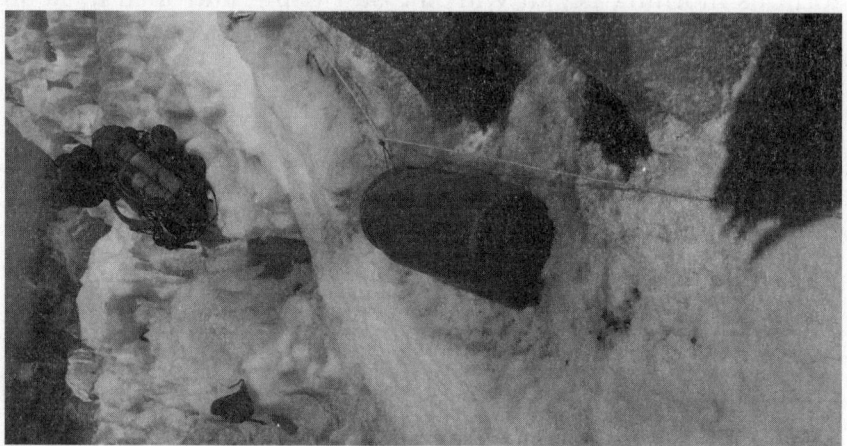

Medical Kit Drum kept on the route.

After settling my luggage at my tent, I was called for lunch. This time, the dining tent was further away. I was the only one from my team to have come here. So I had to go to the dining tent of the international team, where Commander Satya Dam and his clients, a Portuguese lady, the twin sisters from Dehradun, a forest officer from Haryana, two Pakistani siblings— a brother and a sister and some other foreigners were. Some of them were feeling normal and some were in bad shape at that altitude of about 6,500 metre. My shape wasn't either very good, or too bad. I was in a better condition than the last time we had gone there to acclimatise.

Commander Satya Dam spoke about the likelihood of snowfall on the twentieth and so, I made up my mind to go for the summit on the nineteenth. A summit attempt a day earlier meant there would be no extra day to rest here at camp II. Thus, I had to climb every day unlike many other members, such as,

Sanjay Pandit, the Pakistani siblings, and others who had arrived there a day earlier than and had had one extra day to better equip their bodies for further climb. But I decided to move ahead and Commander Dam also encouraged me to go for it.

Back in the tent, I prepared everything for the next day's departure, putting in all the essentials required until my return to camp II. This was the only camp beyond the Base Camp which had almost all the facilities that the Base Camp had, and was also safe. Above this, camp III at 24,000 feet was just a temporary shelter and camp IV at 26,000 feet was not a place to stay for more than 2 days in the death zone because it would have an adverse effect on the body.

Camp II is special because this is the last camp on the way to the summit and where cooked food and closed toilet facilities are available. It is also safe as opposed to camp III, which is located on the slope of the Lhotse face, considered one of the most dangerous routes as compared to camp IV because of its altitude and weather. In addition, a rescue from camp II would be easier because although rescue helicopters had been in service for camp IV, they are used in very rare cases, and were very expensive. Normally, if there is a sudden change in the weather above, the climbers return to camp II and take shelter there. After finalizing everything, I was all set to go up the next day.

Camp 2 at the altitude of 6500 meter

Camp 2.

On May 17, I woke up at 6 am as usual. After my morning ablusions, I donned on all the gear and was ready at 7 as Commander Dam had planned. At 7 am, I came to the dining tent but nobody was there and breakfast was not ready either. Anyway, the quality of food at camp II was not satisfactory. People were not satisfied with the meals. I was just comparing the food here with the quality of food at Base Camp and there was a huge difference. It wasn't deliberate;it was only a lack of management.

Anyway, my Sherpa and I satiated ourselves with whatever was available, and finally, started our journey for camp III at 9. As usual, I kept my own pace and never cared if people would overtake me. I was not competing with anyone there. I was competing against the mountain. I was there to conquer the mountains but not the people. I was in my own thoughts mostly looking down at the route; there were many cracks on the way and it was possible there would be hidden crevasses. I got some glimpses of the surrounding slopes; Nuptse on the right and the Everest and the Lhotse on the left. The Jumar Point, (the last point where we had come up to during acclimatisation) was a little ahead, after which we had to attach fasten jumar on the fixed rope, as the slope was steep and the blue ice was very hard, there were large chances of slipping.

I was thinking of one incident of a Sherpa (Lobsang Sherpa) from my agency. He had been my friend Sanjay Pandit's Sherpa, and he had slipped from the top on the Lhotse face and had lost his life on May 7. He had been a young and extremely strong Sherpa. I was moving ahead, paying attention to what was in front on the route and partly thinking about this accident when suddenly there was a hue and cry. Some of the people were shouting and alerting the others that a cylinder had fallen from the top and it was hurting with full force along the slope of the Lhotse. Suddenly, I saw that everybody had frozen in their places, especially those who were in the falling cylinder's way. I was almost out of the danger zone but it was alarming. If this fast moving cylinder hit somebody then it would be an unfortunate incident at this initial stage of final journey. Sherpa and many climbers considered that type of unfortunate incident, which happened before moving to the Sagarmatha (or Everest), ill omened. Thank god, the cylinder finally passed between the people who had scattered. Nobody was hit.

Earlier, I had heard many stories from the Sherpa in my agency about the risks on the Lhotse slope and about incidents that occurred, but this was a real one that I witnessed. However, there was nothing to worry about. There will always be threats but all of them would pass like that cylinder. Thinking this, I continued my journey, till I reached close to the Jumar Point where some climbers and Sherpa were taking a short rest to regain their energy. I took some rest too, ate some chocolate, and started for the climb along the Lhotse face with the jumar attached to the fixed rope. From that point onwards till camp III, I had to climb the entire route on the fixed rope.

The Lhotse face is around 3,700 feet high from its base (bergschrund) to the top and has a pitch of 40 to 50 degrees with some occasional bulges of 80 degrees. Camp III is located about half way up this ascending glacial wall of blue ice. Climbing the next ten metre, I understood why it was considered so difficult to scale the Lhotse face. The climbers were following the trail along the fixed rope, where the hard ice had become comparatively loose after repeatedly being pierced by the points of the crampons of hundreds of climbers who had already passed. But I could feel how hard the blue ice was whenever I tried to dig front point of my crampon in a little harder to get a better grip and then looked on both sides of the trail, as it offered a better idea of how hard the ice was. I could only imagine how hard it must have been for the first party of the year who came to open the route and how hard it must have been for Tenzing Norgay and Edmund Hillary and their team to climb this hard slope in 1953.

There was literally enough weight on the fixed rope. If the piton gave away, it was unlikely that the climbers would be able to balance on their feet. We had been advised not to carry our ice-axes because it would not be required. Still, many of the climbers had carried them, not in their hands but attached to their rucksacks on their backs. So using the ice-axe to arrest one's fall was out of the question on this slope.

My guide advised me to wear a helmet while climbing this slope, as small chunks of ice and small particles of rocks were always falling down.

Without a helmet, there was a fair chance of receiving a head injury if any big chunk hit your head. At the Base Camp, I had been advised not to secure the rucksack tightly to my back. In case any big piece of ice or rock falls down from the slope, we could take off the rucksack and use them as shields to hold in front of ourselves to save ourselves.

Climbers climbing on Lhotse Face towards Camp 3

After the initial climb of about fifteen to twenty minutes, I adjusted myself to this slope and to the prevailing condition of falling ice chunks and the heavy weight on the fixed rope. I became a little comfortable climbing this slope. Although my pace was slower on this slope than my normal rate, but still, it was better than few climbers and thus, I continued overtaking and being overtaken though it was not very often. Overtaking on this slope was very dangerous and it was nearly impossible to arrest your fall once you lose your grip on the rope. But the speed of ascent depends on the slowest member in the queue, and I was definitely not the slowest. So, I had to overtake a few climbers in order to maintain my own pace. Initially during the first half of the climb on the Lhotse face, I was quite comfortable and enjoyed climbing at this altitude though it was for the first time in my life. During acclimatisation, we hadn't come to camp III as the other teams normally do.

But as I was gaining altitude and sometimes looking down the steep slope, a shiver would run across my spine. I could only think what would happen if someone lost their grip, and couldn't arrest the fall. I started to avoid looking down as it was making me feel terrible. Also, as the time passed, exhaustion took over and I was eagerly waiting to reach camp III and rest in the tent. I was not overtaking anymore. It would be too dangerous. I met the leader of the Indian army team who was leading from behind and motivating his team to continue their journey without giving up. We continued together at the same speed as the slowest member in the queue. You can see thin rows of tents pitched on the Lhotse slope from the valley below, from a location away from the Lhotse base as you are coming upwards from camp II. But when you actually start the Lhotse face, the camps are no longer visible until you reach a certain point after which you can see that they seem near.

When we reached that point, I first saw two isolated tents and after some distance, a group of tents that had been pitched. The sight made me feel relaxed. We slowly kept moving. When we were near the two isolated tents, I saw Mirza Ali and his sister, the siblings from Pakistan, who were from Seven Summit Treks and part of the international team. We had become good friends. They were sitting with their rucksacks on the ice. I felt so happy thinking that I had reached the Seven Summit Treks tents, and was ready to take off my rucksack, and rest in one of the tents. But the next moment, my face fell when the siblings told me that they were just resting there for some time, where the Seven Summit's tents were up where the tents of the other companies were. It was like starting a new journey although the distance was not much, hardly 200 metre. However, at that altitude and in that condition, 200 metre was a matter of half an hour. There was no option but to continue. I decided not to rest and to complete the journey.

Finally we completed this stretch and reached camp III at 24,000 feet around 2 pm with the army team whom we had met along the way. My company's tents were in the first rows and then the Indian Army team had set up their tents further up hill in the rear row. Saying goodbye to Major Jamwal, I unclipped myself from the fixed rope and stepped aside. But a Sherpa from my company told me to clip on to another fixed rope on the side and sit down balancing the crampon on the ice so I could be more stable on the slope.

I sat down and took a look all around. I noticed how the steep slope had been cut into a small plain portion to pitch the tent so that there was extra support from outside. In fact, there was no flat surface on that slope except inside the tents. Looking at the surroundings, I could tell why this camp was considered one of the most dangerous. If there was snowfall in the night, the fresh snow fell so thickly that the almost frictionless slope couldn't hold the weight, and the fresh mass of the snow would start sliding down as an avalanche. If this happened then there was no chance that anybody on this lonely slope could survive.

Camp 3 on Lhotse face at the altitude of 24000 feet.

That was one of the reasons Sherpa didn't like to stay at this camp in the night. There were also many superstitions amongst them about the presence of the souls of climbers who had died at this camp before. That very month, one Sherpa from another agency had died there on May 5. He had fallen sick and died in one of the tents.

Normally when members come here, the Sherpa employed by the company keep the tents ready. But as it was a big agency, Seven Summit Treks was managing seventy three climbers that year and there were some drawbacks in their management. When I reached, they had not received the news that I was coming up. My team was supposed to come later and no tents had been kept ready. Although some tents were empty, the agency representative there said that they were reserved for other people who were on the way; they were some Chinese and some Korean climbers. Other people from the same agency who had come with me got their tents. Whatever the case was, I should not have suffered because of the agency's lack of management, and because they didn't pass the information up.

Climber resting inside tent at Camp 3 situated on Lhotse face at the altitude of 24000 feet.

After waiting for some time, I took the walkie-talkie and started calling Base Camp and camp II. Although the communication was not clear, I requested them to manage one tent. At that altitude and after climbing for five hours, I desperately needed immediate rest to regain the energy for the next day's tough climb to camp IV. I noticed that anger was overcoming my calmness. During our training, we had been told that it was normal for you to get angry at high altitudes and you had to control it. Finally, after about one and a half hour of waiting, I told my Sherpa to enter an empty tent, which was reserved for a Chinese climber. My Sherpa hesitated but I told him not to worry, and that I would talk to the company's chief later. Then the person in charge there agreed to accommodate three people in that small tent. Normally two to four people are accommodated in a small tent, which is meant to house one person comfortably, given the camp's location on the dangerous Lhotse face.

Now, I had wasted a good amount of energy because of my anger about the mismanagement in the agency. Once I was settled in the tent, I came to know that the agency had not arranged for any food except for soup. Down at the Base Camp, we were told that the agency had kept lots of juice and other food suited for high altitudes for the climbers. I was not worried about this as my guide and I had carried enough food to survive for the next five days. However, I was surprised that the agency (which was famous at the Base Camp for its bar and bakery and wonderful food) had not arranged anything to eat at this high altitude except soup. You need the best food at this altitude so the climbers can get the energy to climb further. In fact, it should have been just the opposite.

I decided not to waste any more energy in thinking about all this; it would yield no results. The three of us in the tent adjusted inside and enjoyed my homemade *sattu*. It was delicious and effective at that altitude, after the light breakfast in the morning and a five-hour climb. Later, we lay down with our legs folded to spend the whole night in the same position. We folded our legs because there was not enough space. We kept our helmets on because on this slope, nobody knew when a big stone could hurtle down along the hard, frictionless ice slope and enter your tent tearing the fabric apart and smashing your head. When one climber had been resting in his tent during acclimatisation, a big stone had come, torn through the tent and had passed by after just brushing his face.

We woke up at 5 am the next morning. We had planned to leave early and reach camp IV early so we had more time to rest, recuperate and be ready to start the final attempt in the evening. The next thirty six hours were going to be the toughest part of the whole journey. It would take about seven to nine hours from camp III to camp IV. Then, following a few hours of rest in the afternoon after we had reached, we would have to start for the final summit in the evening. We would have to climb the whole night to reach the summit in the morning. After taking photographs on the summit and having some food to re-energise our bodies, we would have to start the return journey to camp IV around noon or afternoon. So, except for a few hours of rest at camp IV, within the next thirty six hours, I would have to keep moving up or down on the exposed slope of Mount Everest with a load on my back in the sub-zero temperature and thin, oxygen deficit atmosphere.

Climbers climbing steep slope enroute from camp 3 to camp 4.

After waking up in the morning, it was my routine to finish my bathroom routine but today I did not feel like going to the toilet. I donned the outer shoe and crampon, which was removed while resting inside the tent and got ready with my rucksack on the back to move further up. As planned, we started moving upwards at 6 am. From now, as we moved higher, the risk in overtaking or being overtaken, increased. The day before, we had had the fixed rope on the second half of the route between camp II and camp III, i.e. only on the Lhotse face part of the climb. But today there would be fixed rope along the whole route. So there would be much less overtaking on this slope than there had been the previous day; but there was another challenge.

There was only one narrow route on which only one person at a time could climb. But there were people on both sides, who were going up, and others, who were returning (although the people coming down were comparatively fewer). Whenever people crossed, it was very risky and extreme precautions were taken. If you look uphill along the fixed rope then generally, the people coming down would cross from the left side of the rope and the people going up would keep on the right side, because there was only an upward climb during that phase.

As we continued climbing uphill on the ice, we encountered a rocky patch. It is the first time that climbers encounter any such rock above Base Camp. I could guess it was the Yellow Band. It is a layer of sedimentary sandstone rock, which runs horizontally at an altitude of about 25,000 feet along the Lhotse face as well as the surrounding mountains. The rocks in the Yellow Band consist of inter-layered marble, phyllite and semi schist. The climber needs about 100 metre of rope to traverse it. It is not an easy task because the rocky face is a challenge to climb with crampons on because there is hardly any grip between the rock face and the crampon. The grip depends on whether the pointers of the crampon receive some support in the tiny depression on the rock face. At some places, almost all your muscle power is used to pull your body up with the help of the jumar as there is hardly any support from the crampons. In case you slip, the jumar will hold your body weight, provided it is rigged properly. But there is always a chance of injury to the knees because in that sub-zero temperature, even a light jerk to the knee would cause severe pain. Luckily, nothing of that sort happened to me.

As usual, I maintained my comfortable pace and kept up the journey till we reached the traverse, where I got a break from the ascent and felt more relaxed. We had to traverse from the Lhotse face to the Everest side. Here, the people coming down kept to the valley side of fixed rope while crossing climbers going up. Those climbing up would keep on the peak side or higher side of the slope. We continued moving ahead till we reached Geneva Spur, which comes just after completing the traverse. A spur is a lateral ridge projecting from a mountain or a mountain range. The name Geneva Spur was given to this one during the 1952 Swiss expedition. It is an anvil shaped rib of black rock, nearly vertical and is another challenge to the climber.

Row of climbers climbing Lhotse face enroute from camp 3 to camp 4

Row of climbers climbing from camp 3 to camp 4.

There I took a five minutes break to regain energy to ensure a smooth climb on the near-vertical face, but fixed ropes as well as my rock-climbing technique made the task comparatively easier. I crossed this hindrance easily where most of body weight is put on the leg resting on the tiny foothold on the rock face while keeping the body straight and parallel to it. The hand is used to get minimum support to keep the body close to the rock face. Hanging the body on hands and pulling the body upward with the help of arm pull is avoided unless no foothold is available, so it saves lot of energy and keeps the climbers in a comfortable condition to continue further climb.

Finally after crossing the Geneva Spur and climbing further, a Sherpa from the Seven Summit Treks Agency met me on the way. He showed me a big rock ahead at about 50 metre distance on the left side of the route and said that there had been dead bodies lying on the other side of that rock for many years; but I did not have enough energy nor did I want to deviate from the route and discourage myself seeing the dead bodies. I continued and reached camp IV or south col at an altitude of 26,000 feet at 2 pm after a climb of eight hours and with that, I entered the death zone, which continued till I returned back from the summit and descended down from this area. Climbers are not advised to stay in this zone for longer duration due to adverse effect of prevailing atmospheric condition, i.e. very low temperature, very low atmospheric pressure, low oxygen level, etc. on the body.

Camp 4 at the altitude of 26000 feet.

22

Welcome To the Death Zone

'This tent nearly takes off when the wind blows, it must have a speed between 150 and 250 kilometre. And it's minus 50 degrees. The tent flaps so noisily that we have difficulty understanding each other. "Yes – I do hope that tent holds out. How close death still is. Yet I am not becoming apathetic – the rattling of the tent keeps us alert. But if it goes, we are lost. ...."

"Alright. I have never known such cold. When I put up the tent, there was half a centimetre of ice all over my face, and after half an hour it was impossible to see or do anything anymore. If you stood upright, the wind blew you right over. "

Mingma is again lying perfectly still beside me, giving a fair imitation of being dead. I have to pinch myself as well, to make sure I am still alive. All my deliberations are very slow. I have the greatest difficulty in speaking. ....

Before night falls – the second night here in the Death Zone – I go outside the tent again and check the outside poles. My fingers freeze onto the aluminium. I remain outside in the storm for a while, waiting for... I am not sure what. Perhaps just for the cheer of a narrow blue stripe on the Horizon. But the world around is relentlessly grey. Nothing but cloud, snowdrifts, storm. Our plight will be hopeless if it is not better in the morning.'

– Reinhold Messner, **Everest: Expedition to the Ultimate**

The death zone refers to the area beyond 26,000 feet (or about 8000 metre), where there is lack of sufficient oxygen to sustain human life. Although the ratio of oxygen in air remains constant till the altitude of 100 kilometre above the surface of earth, but as atmospheric pressure decreases with altitude, so the amount of oxygen in the atmosphere decreases with altitude and it remains only about half from that of the sea level at the altitude of about 16000 feet (or 5000 metre) and only one third on the summit of the Everest. Normally, the human body adapts itself slowly to low atmospheric pressure and low oxygen level as the climbers gain altitude. That's why climbers go for a series of acclimatisation schedule above the Base Camp. But in the death zone, the amount of oxygen is so less in the atmosphere that the human body uses oxygen faster than it can be replenished and that's why it can't acclimatise in this zone. Therefore, an extended stay in this zone without external supply of bottled oxygen causes adverse effect on the human body and interrupts with normal functioning of organs due to lack of minimum oxygen required, which generally leads to unconsciousness and ultimately death.

Dr. Edouard Wyss-Dunant, the leader of 1952 Swiss Expedition to Mt. Everest, coined the term Death Zone. The Sherpa *Sirdar* of the expedition was Tenzing Norgay. Although they could not reach the summit but made phenomenal achievement by reaching near to the summit to a point only 348 metre below the top on May 28, 1952. Their climbers, Lambert and Tenzing Norgay, reached a height of 8,500 metre on the South East Ridge that day but were forced to return back.

Most of the deaths on Everest occur in this death zone i. e. above 26,000 feet and especially while descending after reaching the summit. This is the zone of Everest, where estimated over 200 dead bodies are lying, mostly preserved and intact due to extremely low temperature. Lack of sufficient oxygen and fatigue of climbers are two major causes of death in this zone.

Before 2008, deaths at an high altitude would occur because of avalanches, falling ice from Khumbu, or pulmonary oedema (accumulation of excessive fluid in lungs). In 2008, an international research team led by the Massachusetts General Hospital (MGH), which is the largest teaching hospital of Harvard Medical School that conducts the largest hospital-based research program in the United States, conducted the first detailed analysis of the causes of death during the expedition to Everest by collecting data on deaths occurred from 1921 to 2006. They focussed specially on deaths occurring in death zone.

The study identified two major categories of risk causing death of climbers during Everest climb: Traumatic and Non-traumatic. Traumatic deaths were caused by mountaineering falls, avalanches, and extreme weathers. Non-traumatic deaths were caused by over exhaustion, injuries, altitude-related illness like high altitude cerebral oedema (HACE) and high altitude pulmonary oedema (HAPE),etc. These deaths usually occur on the lower slopes of Mount Everest, including the Khumbu icefall.

They identified that the symptoms of high-altitude cerebral oedema (HACE), a swelling of the brain, happens due to the leakage of cerebral blood vessels in the brain. Low atmospheric pressure and low oxygen is one of the biggest threats, when climbers exhaust their limited supplemental oxygen bottles on the slope of the Everest. Absence of sufficient oxygen in the atmosphere causes vital organ failure leading to death. It causes cerebral blood vessels to leak fluid into surrounding brain tissue, triggering swelling, due to which, climbers develop symptoms like loss of coordination, confusion, lack of judgment, and they may even slip into the unconscious. The oxygen-deprived brain makes climbers unable to take a rational decision about life and death, such as whether to continue an uphill climb, or to abort the climb and turn around to descend safely. In such cases, wrong decision costs their lives.

Another important factor responsible for death was excessive fatigue. Due to over-exhaustion, climbers slow down and lag behind others and thus, reach the summit late in the day, much later than the safe turn-around time. This happens mostly because climbers focus only on reaching the top ignoring safety factor, due to the huge money spent on the expedition. While descending, they sit down on the slope for a brief rest due to over-exhaustion and then slowly drift into deep sleep and never wake up.

Other than this, some other factors were also responsible for deaths in the zone. These are snow blindness, due to which climbers lose eyesight temporarily,and conditions like frostbite. Another factor, which adds to number of deaths, is that rescue is almost impossible in this zone. Helicopter rescue is impractical above camp IV and carrying the injured person manually is extremely difficult in such condition and in such a terrain where climbers hardly carry their own body and move every step with great difficulty.

On reaching the death zone, to camp IV for the first time, I looked at the surroundings. I could tell I have reached very high. When I reached there, on my left side was the Everest slope and on the right side was the Lhotse slope. Behind and in front was a spectacular view of the valley opening on both sides and all the other mountain peaks projecting up from the clouds but they were at a lower altitude than the place I was standing. Before this, we had been passing through the Khumbu Ice fall and the valley of western CWM and even the Lhotse face. There are many peaks in the surroundings, which are at lower altitude than those lower camps but this spectacular view is not available over there until you reach camp IV.

With such spectacular view, the camp is basically a flat and rock-strewn wind-swept saddle of about a football-field-sized area between the Everest and Lhotse. Many colourful tents were occupying the area in the middle. I could see the discarded expedition equipment and old oxygen bottles littering the surrounding area. While some tents already looked occupied, the Sherpa were busy erecting some other tents. Fresh oxygen bottles were stacked outside some tents. This area is under influence of jet stream, which can uproot and blow away tents in the spur of moment, so I could notice the extra strengthening of the tent from outside, which was not visible at the Base Camp or even camp II. There, I was lucky enough to get a tent within ten minutes of arriving, although I was not very exhausted because I had already decided that I had to save my energy to climb the whole night. I had maintained a comfortable pace from camp III to camp IV. There were four people in that tent:

another climber and two Sherpa, along with me. The other climber was a forest officer from Haryana.

The first thing to do after entering the tent (other than having some warm water or juice) is to remove your shoes and put some napkins or toilet paper inside it to absorb any moisture deposited during the climb. This makes them moisture free for a hassle-free further climb. The next was to remove the socks and wipe out our feet with ice and then dry cloth (mostly toilet paper) to remove any salt deposited on them from sweat to minimize the chances of frostbite later as an old mountaineer had suggested. He had said, 'Normally what happens is that due to the salt deposit on the feet due to sweating, it becomes cold just after you start your climb and the risk of frostbite becomes higher. After wiping your feet, put on woollen socks when you are resting, or wear a new pair of summit socks. 'In general, it is advised to wear a fresh or new pair of socks so as to prevent your feet from becoming moist from the sweating during the final climb to the top. The general cause of frostbite is the inadequate blood circulation to the body parts, which are either farthest from the heart or are largely exposed to the atmosphere because the body restricts blood circulation to these areas on its own to preserve the core temperature to fight hypothermia. It can be due to extreme cold outside, inadequate clothing, wet clothes, or the wind chill factor. Frostbite can be extremely dangerous as third or fourth degree frostbite requires the body parts like nose, ears, fingers or toes be amputated.

We were told to wear new summit gloves for the final push to the top. So I did. The summit gloves are double layered gloves, which are made of better material and are relatively expensive and so they are used for the final push. Although I used the double layered gloves during the journey from camp III to camp IV, they were of a slightly inferior quality. For safety's sake I was carrying two pairs of goggles too, because if by mistake, you lose one pair and you don't have an extra, you can't come down as you will become temporarily blind due to the powerful reflection of the ultra-violet rays from the ice and the chances of survival become very low. So I took out a new pair of goggles for the summit. In fact, I was advised to carry extra gloves, goggles, and head lamps to minimize the risks in case the original pairs were lost. I had carried them with me from the Base Camp but had left the headlamp at camp II. It was too heavy to carry an extra torch. At high altitudes above 8000 metre in the mountains, you think twice before carrying even an extra 100 grams. A100 grams at sea level would seem to weigh more at this altitude because of less oxygen. Even if you use supplemental oxygen, you are still in adverse atmospheric conditions. After adjusting all this and taking out the extra items, I finally got my bag ready for departure and then shifted my focus to other things.

Here as usual, I didn't expect any better food from the agency as I had made up my mind not to expect much from them because there had been mismanagement. In case, my expectations were not fulfilled, it would add to my frustration, and I would waste more energy. So I was happy with whatever the company provided and ate up whatever I was carrying but this definitely, added to my fellow climber's frustrations. Though, we had shared whatever I had brought, he asked his Sherpa to prepare something for him. But his Sherpa was quite negligent and didn't give him anything. The climber didn't express his concern at that time. I would openly express concern about why something had not been done if they had been promised earlier. The next day, to my surprise, when I returned to camp IV after a successful summit, I didn't see my tent mate from the previous day. I enquired about him and learned that he had returned the previous night because he had been feeling neglected and annoyed as his Sherpa hadn't given him the food he had asked for. So he hadn't gone for the summit. Thus, he lost the chance to summit that year. (a very big loss for him)

I was happy eating the food I had brought from home and then some soup the company had provided. Once the food had been eaten and I was in a comfortable state, I started doing a final check for the equipments before leaving for the final push. Here, even one mistake could be disastrous. It could either cost me my life or result in a cancellation of the summit push. In case anything happened, there was nobody except my Sherpa to take care of me. Though I knew members from the Army and NCC teams and even the international team of my agency, once you come to this altitude, every team selects its own place for their tents, so we are physically separated, and it's difficult to look for and just walk into someone else's tent at that altitude. Generally, once climbers enter inside their tent on arrival from lower camps, they come out of the tent only to depart for the final summit. The movement becomes very slow in this adverse condition. Anything has to be caught or held over thick layer of gloves on fingers. Even if you want to step out of your tent, you need to have a thick layer of down suit on the body, a long heavy climbing boot in the leg, thick gloves covering hands and thick goggles on the eyes, and oxygen cylinder at the back with a mask over the face with the oxygen on. In contrast to this, we may remain inside a warm sleeping bag inside the tent only in thick thermals on the body, socks and gloves and nozzle of oxygen cylinder.

The Army and NCC Teams were being managed by different agencies than ours and their VHF Radio channel was also different than ours, which they used to establish contact among members and with the Base Camp. The members of the international team of Seven Summit Treks were supposed to be somewhere around but I had not seen them after the departure from camp II except the siblings from Pakistan, who met on the way to camp III. Neither did I have any idea regarding the whereabouts of Commander Satya Dam nor did the twin sisters from Dehradun. They might be resting inside some tent.

Consequently, although I knew many people climbing on the same day, we were completely disconnected, and I was feeling all alone in the big mountain and had to take care myself because expecting help from them in emergency was foolish unless somebody spotted you by luck. During the final journey to the peak, all the climbers are covered from head to toe in similar clothes, which are mostly orange, or red coloured, so recognizing them becomes difficult. This happens especially after camp II when everybody donned their down-suit there, what would cover their bodies till they would return back to camp II after reaching the peak.

Met Korean climber Kim Chang-ho at Camp 4, he is the first Korean to summit the Himalaya's 14 peaks without using oxygen.

The advantage for members of a team is that they start together and they are in touch with each other by radio, and they also recognize the other members' body features because they have spent a long time together in spite of wearing similar clothes, so recognizing team members becomes easy. But this was not an option for a single person like me as my team was scheduled two days behind me and was at some lower camp. Therefore, I had written words like my name, Sikkim, and IAS on conspicuous places on my suit so that in case of a mishap, I could be easily recognized. Due to this, people would recognize me on the way. I would respond to anyone I did not recognise by waving my hand thinking that it was somebody I knew.

But even this was not the substantial solution to various problems, which might be encountered uphill. The slope of Everest is so cruel that even if other climbers recognize you in distress and even try to save you, they won't be able to and you would be left behind to die in this open burial ground amongst hundreds of dead bodies.

I could very well recall the incidental death of an American female climber named Francys Arsentiev, the first American women to reach the summit of Everest without the aid of bottled oxygen in 1998. While descending down after the summit, she caught snow blindness and landed on the side of a steep cliff. Her husband and fellow climber, Sergei Arsentiev, was descending ahead of her. When he noticed that his wife was missing, he started returning uphill to search for his wife, although he knew that he didn't have enough oxygen to last. On the way, he met a team of Uzbek climbers, who said that they had tried to rescue Francys but had to abandon her because their own oxygen became depleted. During the uphill climb, Sergei was beginning to get frostbite but he continued uphill and ultimately, Sergei found her wife on the cliff as she screamed for help. He tried to descend towards the cliff and reach his wife but unfortunately, fell down the slope and died leaving behind his pick-axe and rope as clue nearby his wife.

Next day, the two climbers, Ian Woodall and Cathy O'Dowd, spotted the woman, who was still alive as she cried for help, 'Please don't leave me behind.' Both of them climbed down to her and administered oxygen and tried to provide assistance but her condition was too poor to be moved. So they were forced to leave her behind to die alone and came down without risking their own lives. These two climbers again came back to Everest nine years later in 2007 to give her a makeshift high altitude burial and covered her body with the American flag.

While I was fully absorbed in my own thoughts and was busy visualizing how the American lady might have died when she was left alone, a sudden jolt to my tent due to a gust of chilled wind brought me back to the present and I struggled to get rid of the negative thoughts. I must only sustain positive thoughts and visualization during those hours in the death zone when I had to start my climb for the top a few hours later, and had to pass through the zone of many dead bodies. Over the years, I had learnt to come out of such hopeless situation by reminding myself of the teachings of great saints and teachers of the world. I remembered Buddha.

'No one saves us but ourselves.
No one can and no one may.
We ourselves must walk the path.'

I suddenly remembered that an experienced mountaineer had suggested me to keep one extra bottle of supplemental oxygen at camp IV to be used in emergency or in case of delayed stay at camp IV. Normally, the company gives five bottles to each climber, two bottles for the lower camps (camp III and the route between camp III and camp IV) and three bottles for camp IV and above. Three bottles were the norm, which all climbers use but each team always keeps some extra bottles of oxygen, which are used in case of emergency. I had also heard about a few cases of delayed stay of climbers at camp IV due to various reasons, including weather delay and a delayed stay at an altitude of 8,000 metre or above, means extra supplemental oxygen.

I had also heard about the case of climbers dying above camp IV when they had lost their gloves, goggles, or because their oxygen had finished and nobody had given their own share. Nobody will give you supplemental oxygen especially if you are above camp IV unless he or she is ready to risk his/her own life and sacrifice their own chance of summiting *and* surviving. People move up with limited oxygen, which lasts for about 22 hours if it is taken at 2 litres per minute and the time varies depending on the rate of consumption. Although the Sherpa consume lesser than climbers, they are provided with only two bottles, so chances of assistance from a Sherpa are also very few. Therefore, if your oxygen is finished above camp IV, then chances of survival are very few unless additional help arrives from below.

As I had come here ahead of my team, so I, myself, had to ensure that extra bottle of oxygen, as suggested by the experienced mountaineer, was available for me at camp IV before I left for the final climb to the top, so that if there is shortage of oxygen up, then the standby Sherpa of the agency at camp IV could be contacted to bring the bottle reserved for me without any further delay.

Few days before the departure from Base Camp, I had already talked to Seven Summit's Base Camp manager, Mr Tashi, about their providing me with an extra bottle of oxygen, which would be kept as a standby. He had agreed but demanded an extra USD 600 for it. However, I reminded him that before coming to Kathmandu, his brother and the boss of the company,

Mr Mingma, had promised me that he would provide extra oxygen and the amount I had paid was enough to cover all that. I still told him not to worry about the money and keep one bottle as a standby. If I used it in case of emergency, then I would pay if required. However, he had insisted on the carriage charge of the bottle, which was about 100 USD for taking it from the Base Camp to camp IV in case I was not using the bottle. Then I had replied that I would pay whatever the charge would come to, not to worry,and to keep the extra bottle. When I enquired about the extra bottle at camp IV, I learned that there wasn't one for me. I didn't know exactly whether it was deliberately not done because as I had not paid in advance, or it was a mistake, but I was only concerned with the fact that the oxygen bottle was not available there as expected causing extreme mental agitation at that point of time.

I thought this was worth mentioning to alert new climbers who might get carried away by the promises of the commercial agents saying that they will provide many facilities until you pay the amount and then changing their colours. This happens in everyday life as well and I found the mountains are not an exception. The only risk is that in everyday life, you are cheated out of money but in the mountains, there is a fair risk of losing your life. I had also heard about incidents of climbers' deaths in the past where agency couldn't provide emergency rescue because payment was not clear. The only suggestion to the new climbers who are reading this book is that whenever you are going through private agencies, make everything crystal clear and draw up a written agreement specifying the amount and quality of each item including the quality of food they would provide for you during the whole journey, before transferring the amount to their account.

Though, I had also thought to do it before handing over money to the agency but I couldn't do it because of paucity of time in the first week of April, when the decision was taken at the last moment. I had moved ahead without any written agreement by trusting the agency owner, Mr Mingma Sherpa, based on the feedback given about him by the veteran mountaineer Sri Kushang Sherpa. The latter was very well respected in the

Sherpa fraternity and they knew me and my service background very well. So, I suggest you to be completely objective when you are defining terms and conditions as you deal with companies.

The absence of extra oxygen was alarming. In the last few days, there had been many delays due to bad weather and people had had to wait at camp IV an extra day. This had been the case with the majority of the members of the North East team when they had to return to camp IV a few hours after starting for the top when the weather had worsened. But they had taken extra oxygen, so they managed their extended stay at camp IV. I had to ensure I had extra oxygen within the next few hours before leaving for the top. Once again I had to shout over the VHF radio calling Mr Tashi terrible things without even knowing whether he was actually listening or not. Finally, I received the news from the Base Camp that the company was ready to give an extra bottle if I paid 600 USD. Frustrated, I ordered two extra bottles and they were ready in my tent within the next ten minutes. I left them in the tent while moving up in the evening as they were to be used in an emergency and I went up in the evening with my normal quota of three bottles of oxygen.

As luck would have it, this was the last struggle against injustice. I had fought for my rights in Gangtok, camp III, and at camp IV, in order to realise my dream of reaching the highest point of the world. After settling everything, I tried to control my annoyance and anger at Mr Tashi and tried to regain my energy for the whole night's climb, thinking that losing precious energy at this juncture was certainly not wise. I had already lost substantial amount of energy at camp III the previous day, as well as there at camp IV that day. I must save it as energy is what I would require the whole time, and in the hour of need. I remembered an inspiring statement by the ancient Chinese philosopher and the founder of philosophical Taoism, Lao Tzu, who said more than two and a half thousands years ago,'The best fighter is never angry.' So, I thought of god and left everything to him and tried to relax as much as possible to revitalize myself for the final push up for the summit a few hours later.

After about an hour's rest in the tent, it was time to start donning all the mountaineering gear to be ready and depart for the top. Here, I had to wear two pairs of gloves, one inner and one outer. The inner ones were thin and skin-tight and outer ones were thick, double layered gloves. After putting them on, it seemed difficult to operate the karabiner or open the buckle of my rucksack to take anything out. Even during the climb from camp III to camp IV, I had used only one pair of double layered gloves and not two pairs but my guide suggested me to put on both the inner and outer gloves to avoid chances of frostbite in the extreme cold of minus twenty to minus forty degree temperature uphill during further climb. So, I had to do it but in order to avoid frequently opening my rucksack to take out water or eatables, I had put a small bottle of water, most of my eatables, and even my camera in the pocket of my down suit. I had kept most important and frequently needed items like some eatables and water and my camera in the outer pocket and the remaining items in the inner pockets for which you needed to open the main zip of the down suit. I had heard that last year one climber could not take photos on his own camera because he kept his camera in the inner pocket of the suit and later, the suit's zip had jammed as ice had frozen on it.

Pakistan's sibling Samina Baig and Mirza Ali at camp 4- Samina Baig is the first female from Pakistan to climb Mt. Everest.

After putting everything on and getting ready, I stepped out of my tent. It seemed very difficult; I had a thick cap to cover my head, an oxygen mask, a head lamp and big goggles on my head and it was difficult to even turn my head freely to look down, left, or right. I adjusted the goggles and the head lamp several times so that neither would fall down. If any thing fell, I had to postpone my climbing further or think about returning safely somehow. While I was carrying extra goggles (without which you can't even imagine going up or down because of the strong reflection of the ultraviolet rays) I only had one headlamp because it was heavy. Anyway, I could return during the daytime without a headlamp.

Ready in all aspect, I mentally told myself that the final ascent was going to be smooth and the D-day was not very far when I would be standing on the highest point of the Earth and the long-cherished dream would be realised in the next about ten to twelve hours. I was fully determined to reach the top and nothing could stop me on the way.

23

The Eternal Ascent

'For life–which is in any way worthy, is like ascending a mountain. When you have climbed to the first shoulder of the hill, you find another rise above you, and yet another peak, and the height to be achieved seems infinity: but you find as you ascend that the air becomes purer and more bracing, that the clouds gather more frequently below than above, that the sun is warmer than before and that you not only get a clearer view of Heaven, but that you gain a wider view of earth, and that your horizon is perpetually growing larger.'

— *Endicott Peabody*

My Sherpa, my tent mate, his Sherpa, and I started for the top at about 8 o'clock in the evening. We started moving slowly across the rocky surface of camp IV like astronauts moving across the moon. During the first hour of the journey, the slope had been gradual and, there was a lot of overtaking. Although there was a fixed rope on the route but the climbers were not using the jumar and the karabiner on the fixed rope as the route sloped gradually, so it was easy for one climber to overtake another person moving slowly but as usual, I set my own comfortable pace. Though there were lot of people overtaking me and a very few people for me to overtake, I didn't care about it at all.

I kept moving at my own speed focusing on the route below and sometimes looking at the surroundings, which could give me some idea of where we were. But in the darkness of the night and wearing big, dark goggles, not more than a few metres were visible. Far on the opposite slope across the valley, I could see a long line of tiny lights running across a long distance. I indicated for my guide to look at them and he told me they were the lights from the headlamps of climbers climbing the Lhotse face. Lhotse is adjacent to Mount Everest and it is the fourth highest peak in the world. It was a magnificent sight and I thought that they must be watching the same big line we were making as the many of us climbed the slope of Mount Everest.

The journey continued in the same way. I climbed calmly, like Buddha walking in a meditative state, the image of which I had pictured while reading *Old Path White Clouds* at the Base Camp. Later, when the slope became steep and we started climbing, every climber had to engage their jumar and karabiner on the same rope; then overtaking became rare and everyone had to maintain the same pace because overtaking at an altitude of over 8,000 metre on a steep slope was extremely dangerous. Everyone was climbing at the pace of the slowest climber in the queue unless some rare overtaking took place sometimes when some climbers moving ahead became extremely tired, and were overtaken because they were too slow. Therefore, during the silent night everybody seemed like they were moving very calmly and gradually and the silence was only interrupted by gusts of cold wind.

I was advised to take sips of water frequently and eat a small piece of chocolate almost every hour (which would keep up my energy levels) rather than eating it after a long five or six hour climb which would exhaust the body. So, at one hour or one and a half hour intervals (as I mentally approximated), as I was taking off the gloves to change the karabiner and the jumar at the anchor point, I would quickly open the pocket's zip and have a small piece of *gur* (jaggery). I had found *gur* to be more effective than chocolate a while ago. On the way, I saw many tall people returning and I was surprised at how they had climbed to the summit so quickly and were now going back. But when I calculated the approximate time I doubted that they had summited. The next day I confirmed with my Sherpa after returning to camp IV that they had given up on the way; about twenty five to thirty of them had come back.

When we started from camp IV, I was slow and my Sherpa was fast. Though my Sherpa wanted me to be a bit faster, I guessed this and signalled for him not to hurry as I had started slowly but maintained my pace. Later, I felt I needed to increase my pace, because overtaking would not be possible that night and I had read a lot about the crowds that would cause a hold up at Hillary Step. So, I asked my Sherpa to increase the flow of oxygen from one to two litres per minute. Normally, people start from camp IV at one and half to two litres per minute but I wanted to keep the rate less initially and increase it when the slope became steep so that I could maintain the same pace.

As the slope became steep and we started climbing, I noticed that although I was comfortably maintaining my pace, my Sherpa(who was just ahead of me) seemed very tired and was struggling to move forward. I was a bit surprised as he was considered very strong, he was a bit mentally slow. I started wondering what would happen if he felt sick and wanted to go back down, leaving me alone. Climbing alone is very difficult because a Sherpa becomes handy in taking out the empty oxygen bottles of climbers and changing to the new bottles. They also carry extra oxygen bottles depending on the climber's strength and wants and charge heavily for the same.

In short, they risk their lives while accompanying the climber to the top as everybody is equally vulnerable to nature on the slope of the Everest, irrespective of their strength or experience. I knew a few experienced Sherpa who had died during this very expedition. The heavy price they ask is more to compensate them for the risk to their lives than for the actual help they provide. Finally, at one convenient point on the slope, I signalled to him with my hand to ask him what had happened and if there was any problem; he said that he was alright. I was still doubtful and asked what his oxygen setting was. To my surprise, he said that he had started with half a litre per minute and it was still the same. I just saluted his courage and strength. I told him to stop and increased his flow to one litre per minute without asking him whether I could do it or not.

I don't know whether he wanted to save some oxygen for me for an emergency or to sell it off later at a very high cost to someone who needed to survive on that slope. I had heard few cases of selling of oxygen bottles at very high cost at this altitude because in fact, it is not the oxygen bottles which are sold when somebody badly needs it to survive at this altitude when his/her oxygen bottles are exhausted but it is direct sale and purchase of somebody's life. So, any higher cost is justified.

I remembered very well about the incident mentioned in the famous book on the 1996 Everest Disaster, *Into Thin Air,* written by one of the eyewitness climber of the expedition Jon Krakauer. A well known guide from New Zealand, Rob Hall, got stuck on top of the Hillary Step while descending down the Summit along with his client Doug Hansen in the afternoon of May 10, 1996 because his client ran out of oxygen. A storm hit the Everest. Another climber of his team, Andy Harris, was at the South Summit with full oxygen canisters, at a distance that is typically covered by descending climbers in less than thirty minutes. He requested the Sherpa *Sirdar* of another team, who was descending down the summit, to help him carry the oxygen canisters to his friends on Hillary Step and he would pay him five hundred dollars for his assistance but the Sherpa declined to do it saying he had to catch up with his own client, who was another famous mountaineering guide from the USA, Scott Fischer, and was struggling to descend down the southeast ridge alone. In absence of external assistance, the climber alone struggled to carry the oxygen canister to his friend on Hillary Step. The book doesn't clarify whether he did it successfully but later, Rob Hall reached the South Summit from the Hillary Step and he had two full oxygen canisters with him, but he couldn't use it to save his life because the valve of his oxygen mask was chocked with ice, which he couldn't clear even after several attempts. Ultimately, all the three climbers lost their lives life on the slope of the Everest.

Whatever may be the cost of an oxygen bottle at that altitude, I was sure that my Sherpa would lend it to me in case of need because after staying at the Base Camp for over a month, we had developed a good understanding. I respected the whole Sherpa community for their tough life in the mountains, their courage and determination. I often felt that the same was being reflected back by many good Sherpa through their helpful attitude. After adjusting my Sherpa's oxygen flow, I told him that I had made it one litre per minute and we continued our journey. Now he told me to move ahead and he would follow me and we went on.

Around midnight, we reached a flat place and I guessed that it might be the balcony about which I had studied a lot. It was a small platform located at an altitude of 27,560 feet (8400m) on the southeast ridge and climbers could rest there. I was right which I learned as I enquired about it from my Sherpa. I had been waiting to reach here and had been looking towards this point for over an hour. It seemed like the top of the peak because in the dark, as I was looking at it from below, the line of light from the head lamps of climbers ahead of me was stopped at this point.

I guessed that after this point, there was probably a horizontal surface and I planned to have water and some small piece of *gur* when I had reached it. In fact, it seemed like a small flat surface where the climbers could take a small break to change or replace their oxygen cylinders. I saw a few stationary headlamps in the dark indicating that few more climbers were stopped and taking a halt there, and few more were sitting on the mountain side of the fixed line along the route, which lay ahead with a gentle upward slope. They were resting while being anchored to the fixed rope so as to be properly secured to the line and at the same time, not obstructing the route of climbers. Climbers were passing from the valley side of the fixed line and they had to disengage and engage their karabiners on the fixed line when passing each sitting climber. Because of this change in slope in the route, and also that the route took slight left turn after Balcony, the line of the light from the head lamps of climbers which had been on the slope seemed to be ending if we looked up from below.

I had been climbing continuously at a gradual pace but it was very cold and the wind was chilly. My throat was completely dry as I hadn't taken water for over two hours, although during the initial part of my journey, I drank almost every hour. I wanted to take out my water bottle from the outer pocket to have a sip of water but I found the zip of the pocket was partly frozen and was difficult to open. Then I saw that the main zip of my down suit, which I had to open to reach the inner pocket, was completely frozen. The water dripping from the oxygen mask had frozen with the zip. After trying for some time, the outer pocket's zip opened and I took out a big chunk of *gur*, one chocolate, and the water bottle. *Thank god!* I had kept my essential items in the outer pocket but the next moment, I noticed that the whole bottle was frozen.

There was no choice but to squeeze out some ice from the bottle and put it in my mouth. The ice went down my throat after melting a bit, partly wetting my completely dry throat. I had to be satisfied with this when my Sherpa took out a water bottle from his bag, which was not frozen but had chilled water, obviously better than mine. I quenched my thirst. After a short break, we resumed our journey and went ahead of some people who had come just behind us but had gone in front earlier and were still resting. This made me a little confident that at least I was in a better state than many others. After crossing Balcony and climbing the gentle slope for some time, the slope became steep again.

At the pace we were going, it seemed that I would reach the top during the dark; we had discussed all these possibilities in detail and I was assured that even if we reached when it was dark, we could take photographs with the summit marker without the other peaks in the background. This would be sufficient proof for the Nepal Government official to be convinced that I had climbed to the top and he would then issue me a certificate as they have been seeing these photos for many years. Obviously, I would miss the view of the surroundings. For a long time, I had been imagining how the Earth would look from the highest point. I finally consoled myself thinking that if Mother Chomolungma was calling me to give me her blessing, I would have faith in her, not worry about anything, and focus on the climb.

After an approximately four-hour climb following the stop at the Balcony, the sky seemed to be changing a bit and the darkness seemed to be fading. I was happy to see this as it was a sign that morning was coming soon. I was just thinking how fast the whole night had gone by and I hadn't even felt it. The sky began turning from blue to red, when I was on the last slope of the South Summit. This was a fully exposed slope on the ridge and it seemed that we were very close to the peak. I had read the story of the first successful expedition to Mt. Everest by Sir Edmund Hillary and Tenzing Norgay. It said that when they had reached the top, they had found that there was one more peak higher than this one, at some distance ahead. So this one was not actually the top and it was later named the South Summit.

It is a ping pong-table-sized dome of ice and snow at an altitude of 28,700 feet (or 8750m), which has traditionally been used for changing oxygen bottles so that climbers could go for the final ascent with a fresh oxygen bottle. However, I was happy that after reaching the South Summit, mainly three obstacles would remain on the way to the summit: the Cornice Traverse, the Hillary step, and the final slopes to the summit. Also, the next slope would be gradual except the single big obstruction in the form of the Hillary Step, a big challenge for a climber to scale,since it is almost vertical, 40 feet high at 28,740 feet (8760m) altitude and extremely risky. Also, there would be a delay due to the waiting period. Only one climber can go up or down at a time and the others have to wait for their turn.

By the time, I reached the South Summit, it was 6 in the morning and the view all around was clear. I saw no sign of my Sherpa as I looked behind towards the South Summit. People have to descend about 50 feet before the knife-edge ridge, called the Cornice Traverse starts leading to the Hillary Step. But I saw a long queue of people waiting right from the South Summit up to the Hillary Step and others were crossing the Hillary Step one by one. I was no exception and after descending from the South Summit, I also stood in the queue, waiting for my turn as if I was waiting outside a cinema hall at the ticket counter. Just after descending from the South Summit, I was standing at one of the narrowest sections of the ridge, and a sharp slope was visible on both sides of it. On my right, I saw the near-vertical face of the mountain going down, it was Kangshung face.

It was completely white below. They were either white clouds or white snow-capped peaks poking out from behind the clouds. The scene below seemed similar to the Samudramanthan episode in Hindu mythology, in which a peak had jutted out of the sea water. It was beautiful and I took out my camera and clicked a few photographs. At the same time, the scene reminded me of my location and I realised how high I had reached! However, there was no sign of my Sherpa, which added to my worry because I had changed my oxygen cylinder around midnight and I had to check how much oxygen was remaining. The next section of the Cornice Traverse (which we had to cross before reaching the Hillary Step) was the most exposed section of the South East Ridge climb. On one side, there was an 8,000-feet drop along the South West face and on the other, an 11000-feet drop along the Kangshung face.

Although there were many people ahead of me and behind me in the queue, I didn't know any of them, so I couldn't take the risk of assuming their mental health was good enough to properly undertake the task at hand. I knew that in the past, people had set the oxygen flow of their fellow climbers incorrectly due to their mind's slow responses at that altitude. As a result, the oxygen had been almost shut off, leading to near dizziness in an extremely dangerous zone of the traverse. Sometimes people had increased the oxygen flow so much that the oxygen had been used up along the way down before they could reach camp IV.

So as the waiting period increased, my anxiety increased. I was also worried that if my oxygen cylinder was suddenly empty and was not immediately replaced with a new bottle then I would surely die. I was feeling all alone there and I was not carrying a spare cylinder because it was with my guide. But I couldn't see him within my eye sight range. I couldn't expect help from anybody else at that altitude. The top of Everest was about a hundred-metre higher than the place I was standing at and I had read earlier that if a human being were taken directly from the ocean-side and deposited at the peak, he or she would immediately fall unconscious and die within minutes. This statement made me even more cautious.

I recalled the incident Atul Karwal Sir (the first IPS Officer to climb Mt. Everest) had mentioned in his book, *Think Everest*. While climbing from camp III to camp IV, he had found that his oxygen bottle was suddenly exhausted just before reaching the Geneva Spur and neither he nor his team members had been carrying spare oxygen bottles. He had tried to continue without oxygen but was unable to move even a single step forward. He had been lucky that a Sherpa had been coming down with a full spare cylinder,which he had taken and had moved ahead. His case had been different because he had exhausted his oxygen at a much lower altitude, so he could survive without supplemental oxygen for some time. But I was almost near the peak and it was not possible for me to survive without oxygen. Without waiting any longer, I asked the climber standing behind me to read my pressure and he told me that it was just below hundred. I confirmed this with the climber standing ahead of me and felt a bit relaxed.

After waiting for about an hour, and advancing only a few steps, we finally moved ahead and reached the Hillary Step at an altitude of 28,750 feet. There, I saw that the people were taking turns in going up and coming down. Although one person crossed it at a time, normally one group going up or coming down finishes, and then another group starts. When I reached near the bottom of the Hillary Step, I saw many ropes hanging along the near-vertical rock. I had heard that the climber has to climb up the crack in the rock at the Hillary Step. But with two pairs of gloves, it was very difficult to climb. Though I was advised to pick a new rope to climb as the old rope could break, it was difficult to identify a new one. It took me a few seconds to decide which one to pick. Then I clipped my jumar in my right hand and the karabiner on one rope and gripped four to five ropes in my left fist and pulled myself up. But in the middle of climbing the rock, I was swung to the left side and was near the edge where the drop starts on the left. As I tried to balance myself and bring my body towards the right, to avoid risk on the left, I found that one more person was climbing on my right.

It was possible that while I had been thinking for a few seconds and had been deciding which rope to pick, this climber had started from the safer side on my right. Or perhaps he had lost the patience because of the long waiting period and had taken the risk of climbing with another person. Finding myself on the risky side, I put all my stamina in pulling myself up and I quickly found myself on the top before the other climber could reach. Even though you are tired, once it comes to saving your life, you get a tremendous amount of energy. Your adrenaline and your will saves you in the direst of situations.

On top of the rock, I was confused. There was nobody in sight and there was thousand-foot drop on my left side and a big boulder at the front obstructing the way. On careful examination, I found that there was a very narrow trail on the left side of the boulder and a small passage to its right. Guessing that the passage on the right could have been the way up, I took a few steps,but suddenly remembered that there was a vertical drop on that side of traverse as I saw earlier while standing on Cornice Traverse and so, it might not be the correct route. I stopped and returned back and moved to the left side of the boulder, shielding my sight from the thousand-foot drop on the immediate left. I was right. There were many climbers just a few meters ahead. They were standing in the queue, waiting for their turn, not making any noise. I went to get in line behind them. I came to know later that one of my friends had first tried the other way, seen the horrible vertical drop of the Kangshung face and had come back. Luckily, I escaped that horrible scene.

There was also about a fifteen or twenty minute wait as people were returning from the peak. Everest's peak was not visible from that point. There are more small hills that block the view. Although the gradient of the path ahead from that point is not steep,it still demands a lot of physical effort because of the adverse atmospheric conditions. We had to walk on the narrow path created by the continuous movement of the climbers on the soft snow. On the left, was a steep slope down, which went on for thousands of feet, and on the right were large snow cornices in unique shapes created by the prevailing winds. I continued upwards with slow but energetic steps as I had regained some of my energy while waiting in the queue. There was still some fatigue (which I wasn't feeling at the moment) because I had climbed the whole night. Finally I saw the peak, the top covered with *khadas* and the Nepalese flag on an aluminium pole in the centre.

24

The Feel of the Top

'Climb the mountain not to plant your flag, but to embrace the challenge, enjoy the air and behold the view. Climb it so you can see the world, not so the world can see you.'

—*David McCullough Jr.*

The top of the world is not flat but a slope, which culminates at a place covered with many ceremonial scarves (*khadas*) and other offerings by climbers to the Mother Goddess. You will also see few discarded oxygen bottles scattered around, littering the sacred place. There is an aluminium pole in the centre on which the Nepalese flag is hoisted. It is said that this summit marker (or aluminium pole) marks the international boundary between Nepal and China. The summit is covered with snow over ice over rock and the thickness of snow varies from year to year. Below the summit, there are three steep faces of Mt. Everest going down on three sides: North Face towards the Tibet side, South West Face towards the Nepal side and the most dangerous East or Kangshung Face. The summit is not a big area but it is enough to accommodate around fifteen people without compromising the climber's safety due to overcrowding. Because of limited area, people come here in groups and when one group goes down another comes up. Climbers are advised not to go too far on the east because there is an 11,000-feet drop along the Kangshung face below the massive cornices at the east edge of the summit.

I had learnt that people don't stay here for a long time. The normal duration of a stay on the top of the world is about thirty minutes but there are people who have stayed for more than an hour. The reason for avoiding a longer stay is the hurry to return to a safe place at lower camps because the mountain weather is highly unpredictable, especially in the day time. And at over 8000 metre, another reason to return is to minimize the harmful effects on the body, which is not accustomed to such high altitudes. But when I learnt about so many people and the waiting period at the Hillary Step I thought that it was also not ethical to stay here for a long time (especially during the days when there was a window of good weather) because you would be wasting the time of another climber waiting for their turn at the Hillary Step.

On reaching the top, I first chose a safe place on the slope alongside the fixed rope and sat there with the karabiner hooked on to the rope. I opened my bag and took out my second water bottle expecting hopelessly to find some water in it but ended up satisfying myself with some ice in my mouth and tried to quench my thirst. Then I ate a small chunk of *gur* and rested for about five minutes. I looked around as I sat. Suddenly, I heard my Sherpa's voice. He had reached about fifteen minutes after me.

The first thing I told him to do was to check the pressure in the oxygen bottle. He said that it was around 50 bars. Then I asked him whether I needed to change it here or somewhere on the way down. He said that it would be better to do it on the way down at the South Summit. Sometimes I would just go by his advice; he was an experienced climber and he knew the Himalayas better than I did. It didn't make much difference whether you remained without oxygen for some time on the top of the Everest or on the South Summit. Anyway, I was going to take off my oxygen mask while drinking water or eating or while giving a statement on video recording, but sometimes logic should not be used so much. So without questioning, I simply agreed.

**For few minutes, I removed my oxygen mask and enjoyed fresh
air on the top of Mt. Everest.**

He also took a place near me and I waited till he had had some
water. Then I stood up for the photo. I held the Indian tricolour in
my hand and posed. I felt proud for the first time. I was literally on
top of the world. The sense of achievement in holding the tricolour
and representing my country there, is immense. Until now, all my
focus had been on recovering from the fatigue by eating something
and drinking some water as I had to keep my body on the move
during descend for the next five to six hours. After my Sherpa
had clicked many photos and had taken small videos, it was my
turn to click some of him. After we had both finished with our
photography, and after recovering enough to be able to smile, I was
ready to enjoy the view of the world from the highest point.

I went closer to the summit marker and without keeping my feet on any of the *khadas,* I looked down at the world below. It was a magnificent view. The whole of the Earth seemed to be white except the blue sky. There were white, snow-capped mountain ridges on all sides and clouds floating below. The peaks were jutting out from the clouds and were white as they were covered with ice. The Earth seemed to be made up of clouds with a few peaks jutting out from them. The world lay below these clouds. I tried in vain to find out where exactly Nepal ended and India started. Then suddenly my thoughts took a turn and I was absorbed in another train of thought about how uniform the Earth looked with the white clouds and peaks. Below this uniformity,were many divisions in the form of international boundaries all created by humans, the sole disruptor of peace on Earth. Mother Earth doesn't recognise wired, marked boundaries. I wondered how peaceful the Earth would be if it was actually like how it was seen from the top.

South Eastern view of the world from the top of Mt. Everest.

Fully absorbed in the serenity of the surrounding and the enchanting natural beauty of Mother Earth, I took off my mask to feel the freshness of the surrounding. The atmospheric pressure as well as the oxygen content in the atmosphere on Everest is one third of that at sea level. So, the moment you remove your oxygen mask, you start feeling the lack of oxygen. Brain cells are very sensitive to lack of oxygen and start dying if starved of oxygen for a short while. So you lose substantial amount of brain cells if you remove your oxygen mask for just a little while on top of Everest. For someone like me whose whole professional life depends on using the brain, one could imagine the risk I was taking by taking off my mask in such an oxygen-deficient atmosphere. But sometimes, joy overcomes all logic, and that was the case when I was on the top of the world. I was comfortable taking the oxygen mask off my face even though I remeasured all the probable effects.

Southern View of the surrounding from the top of Mt. Everest.

I also removed those thick, dark goggles to enjoy the beauty with my own naked eyes, not worrying about the risk of UV radiation. I was in heaven, I believed; the abode of God and nothing would happen to me. I was just enjoying the beauty of the surroundings with my naked eyes and breathing the fresh air of Mother Chomolungma's abode, which was completely untouched by the pollution of earth. I could reach there because She had called me there. If she does not wish it, nobody can reach however strong they are. I had read about a few incidents of climbers returning from being within a few metre of the top of Everest. This was my privilege to be there after so much perspiration and toiling for months on the mountain slopes. I enjoyed each and every second of my stay on the top of the world.

**With Army Team leader Maj. Jamval and deputy
leader on the top of Mt. Everest.**

I just wondered how beautiful it would be if I had a hut there and I opened my small door every morning to come out to witness the first rays of the sun before they could reach other people. I would have the privilege of soaking in the sun rays completely pure and unadulterated by human beings. I wondered if Mother Chomolungma would allow me stay here in her abode. The illogical dreaming was taken over by logical thought which started rationalising that my wish could be fulfilled if my body was immune to the effects of low oxygen, low air pressure, sub-zero temperatures, the ultra violet rays, and if the Everest remained as windless as it was at the moment (a gentle breeze was playing with the Nepalese flag on the aluminium pole). Then I could stay here without thinking about any of the harmful effects of the prevalent atmosphere on my body. Then I suddenly found that my visualization was not illogical because it was quite impossible to stay on the peak of Everest. I recalled that it was already done in the past as quoted by one Sherpa at the Base Camp during one such conversation.

A famous Sherpa named Babu Chiri Sherpa of Nepal had already spent one night on the peak of Everest without using bottled oxygen. He had reached on the peak on May 6, 1999 morning without using bottled oxygen and stayed there continuously till the next morning for twenty one hours. During this period, he slept there inside his specially designed tent, which was specially made to beat any strong wind at the top of the Everest. He used a specially-designed sleeping bag and and mattress to sleep in such adverse condition. So, if he could do then so do I. I was really thrilled to think that my imaginary hut would be replaced by a specially-designed tent which was used by Babu Chiri, if I would get a chance to do so in future. This mere thought brought a large smile on my face and I said to myself how modern science always sets limitation but human beings always turn the limitations around.

The stream of thoughts, which absorbed me for some time, would have continued and I would have dreamt much more, but they were interrupted when my Sherpa signalled to start the departure. My thoughts can be best described in the following words, which I wrote down immediately after returning from the peak:

While standing on the highest point in the world, it's extremely fascinating to see the round Earth without boundaries. Facing India, on the left, you see the mighty Mount Kanchendzonga and a little to its right, Mount Makalu. Behind, is the vast Tibetanplateau. The limitless horizon is on all sides, under your own eyes, making you think that Mother Earth doesn't know her boundaries. If only it could have been a reality, an ever so peaceful Earth without countries or boundaries...

It was already over half an hour since I had been on the peak and it was time to leave as the sun was bright in the sky. The previous evening, someone from the agency had advised me to return early as the forecast had said that the weather could be bad in the afternoon. I made up my mind to start my departure. But before that I wanted to take a few more photographs with the view of the valley in the background. I knew that my Sherpa was not a good photographer, so I asked another climber to capture the beautiful moment. He took two photos, which remain my lasting memory along with two others taken with the leader and the deputy leader of the Indian army team (who had come when I had just started the journey downwards). Later, I discovered that my Sherpa had taken photos of me while wearing dark goggles and so had captured either only my waist or chest or head etc. None of the photographs he had taken made sense.

As I have already mentioned, when I started moving down after spending about forty minutes on the top of the world, I saw two people coming up and I could make out that they were the leader of Indian army team, Major Ranveer Jamwal and the deputy leader, Major Joshi. Our meeting was warm and we congratulated each other and took group photos.

Expressing happiness on meeting Indian Army personnel on the top of the world.

25

Down the Hill: Descending the Abode of the Dead

*'You cannot stay on the summit forever; you have to come down
again. So why bother in the first place? Just this: What is above
knows what is below, but what is below does not know what is above.
One climbs, one sees. One descends, one sees no longer, but one has
seen. There is an art of conducting oneself in the lower regions by the
memory of what one saw higher up. When one can no longer see, one
can at least still know.'*

—Rene Daumal

I moved down along with my Sherpa. But again there was a
queue you had to wait in just before the Hillary Step and there
were no exceptions, so I joined it. While standing there, I enjoyed
the surroundings and took out my camera to click some more
photos. Taking out your camera and clicking photographs is also
a big task at that altitude. There was bright sunshine everywhere
but as the waiting period kept on increasing, I kept thinking about
the bad weather expected in the afternoon as told to me by one
Sherpa at camp IV the previous day. Although the weather seemed
very clear at that moment but it can change any moment. It was
already 9:30 am and I was still standing in the queue and had not
yet passed the Hillary Step. I also had to change my oxygen bottle;
but thinking that the Indian Army team was still behind me at
the top of the mountain, I felt a bit relieved and planned to talk to
them about the day's weather once they came down.

Around 9:40 am, the queue moved ahead and we went
towards the South Summit. There, I changed my oxygen bottle.

By that time, the army team had also returned from the top and I asked about the weather forecast for the day. Major Jamwal said that there had not been any predictions of bad weather. I was a bit relieved on hearing this good news.

Climber descending down after reaching top.

Until this point, the slope had been gradual except for the Hillary Step. After the South Summit until the approach to camp IV, the slope is very steep and the route is completely open to the wind and weather as it follows a ridge. When I reached the point from where the steep descent starts, I looked down, and was shaken by the steepness, realising the dangerous point I was standing at. I felt like I was on a bamboo tip and I had to get down safely because about seventy percent of accidents in the mountains take place while people are descending. I had never experienced such a height and such steepness during a descent. The route, and thus the line of descent, were almost a straight line with just a little bit of a bend midway. In the dark of the night, new climbers don't realize where they are going when they are climbing, in spite of watching so many movies about the Everest. Their range of sight is only a few metres by the light of their head lamp.

But while returning in the daylight under the bright sunshine, they realise the dangerous location they are in.

I was shocked that I had reached here after the whole night's climb and I couldn't even comprehend it. Then, I told myself that it was better that climbers climbed in the night, because if it was during daytime then many would return if they looked down to assess their position while climbing this slope. This left me feeling as if I was in a different world and I had to reach another world at camp IV. It was hidden behind the clouds below because all I could see was the treacherous slope and the clouds spread around the slope, blocking camp IV from my line of sight.

Another point to note was that while climbing upwards, climbers use the jumar and the self-anchor (karabiner) hooked on to the fixed rope. The jumar arrests an immediate fall resulting from any slips, or other mishaps, provided it is hooked properly and the teeth of the jumar and the rope are both free of ice. In case the jumar gives up for some reason and climbers start falling down, the self-anchor arrests the drop at the last anchor point, where the fixed rope is secured to the ground with ice piton. So although climbers might be severely injured, they mostly stay alive in spite of this.

On the downward journey, the jumar is not used and we only hook the self-anchor to the fixed rope. In fact, climbers have to use the strength of their hands to grip the rope and descend. In case, the climber lost his balance and lost his grasp on the rope, he would start falling and could only be stopped at the next anchor point, provided the screw karabiner (preferably) was used to self-anchor, because it doesn't come off the fixed rope. So the overall risk was higher while descending. The slope was so steep that it was difficult for me to put each foot firmly on the ice. I had to put a considerable amount of my body weight on the rope, gripping it with my hands. In case my foot slipped and my hands failed to take the full weight of my body, it could have been dangerous. Although I had recovered to some extent after resting while waiting in the queue, I still had to descend in the same way for about the next four hours and my hands would be tired. I thought and thought for a solution to arrest my fall in case there was a mishap and suddenly I thought of using the descender. I told my Sherpa and he agreed. I used a descender and started rappelling down, putting almost my full body weight on the rope.

Normally, it is advised to put as little of your weight as possible on the rope because once the rope is fixed on the slope of the Everest, it is used by many climbers, and there is no system to regularly check the rope after it has been secured the first time. The only test was that as long as it was holding the climbers moving up and down, it was considered okay, but once it gave up and broke or the ice pitons came out, the climber could be injured or could die. But while rappelling downwards, we can't avoid putting body weight on the rope. Anyway, it was the fastest method to go down in the prevailing circumstances. It was not scary because my back was facing downwards as I looked up. I was moving down fast, stopping for a few seconds at each anchor just to change the descender to the following rope and continuing the journey while my Sherpa was coming down slowly using the normal method of descending on foot while being anchored to the fixed rope.

I was enjoying this new method; it was just like a game. But when I stopped at the anchor points(to access the way to the next anchor point) and looked down, if by chance I could see till the cloud below I found it alarming; if the rope gave up and broke then there was no chance of remaining alive on the slope. The drop would be almost like falling from a plane flying many kilometers in the air. It would be like a direct fall with no chance of gripping or holding anything on the way to save your life. It would be like the longest bungee jump without any rope tied to the leg. But I shook my head to get rid of all the negative thought my mind was getting clogged with. There are risks everywhere and I shouldn't think too much on that aspect. In fact, I had practiced something similar while training in HMI where the breaking of the rope could also have led to similar results (although the height to be climbed then was much less).

Without giving any further room to negative thoughts, I simply began enjoying the moment and kept descending nonstop till I reached the Balcony where I waited for my Sherpa. When he reached, both of us had some chocolate and some ice to quench our thirst. I did not realise that there was an old, dead body lying just behind the ridge of the ice where I was sitting. I came to know about it later, but thankfully, I hadn't seen it.

One more peculiar phenomenon, which occurred while descending, was how much I was panting. Although it was not at all tiring compared to the previous day's climb, I was still panting non-stop while descending. Later, at camp IV, I enquired about this with Major Jamwal and he said that it was normal and that he had been panting too.

After the balcony, the route was not as exposed to wind and weather as it had been before, so I was a bit relaxed and I slowed down. I also started switching between rappelling and descending, depending on the degree of the slope and how comfortable I was. But after sometime, the visibility reduced and suddenly it was almost zero. I was descending alone on the slope, by tracing the fixed rope. My Sherpa had told me at the balcony to continue my descent and that he would come later. I knew why he had said this. He wanted to pick up some empty oxygen bottles from the balcony to give to any of the agencies located below. They paid a handsome sum for each empty oxygen bottle that had been brought from the higher slopes of the Himalayas as an environmental protection measure. But as I had already told him to stay with me and not to disappear to collect bottles, he was hesitating. In fact, I had told him that I would pay him the same amount that he would get from selling bottles because I knew that simply talking to him without mentioning money wouldn't hold any weight. Sherpa come to this altitude, risking their life only for money. Still, as it is human nature, he stopped at the Balcony and I was climbing alone on this lonely route with zero visibility. There was no room for mistakes. I slowed down and waited for him or for the visibility to improve. Luckily, after some time, the visibility did start improving. It seemed a big patch of cloud had been passing by. Then, my Sherpa also looked to be hurrying down with his rucksack full of oxygen bottles.

The next unforgettable and horrifying experience on the way down was the sight of a dead body. At first, I thought that someone was lying face down, fatigued, but my next thought was that his back was uncovered and it had turned white. Whoever it was he couldn't be alive with bare body exposed to the prevailing sub-zero temperature. I passed it at a distance of about 10 metres and my heart almost sank at the sight of the dead body. I thought to capture this sight in my camera, but I gave it up the next moment. Something inside me didn't allow me to do this. When it was out of sight, I sat down to rest for some time without moving further down and mentally saluted the hero, who seemed still alive and sleeping comfortably without any disturbance in the lonely lap of nature. Somebody had truly said, 'Death is opposite of birth. Death is not the opposite of life. What takes birth dies but the life continues.' Although his body had been lifeless for many years lying on the slope of the Everest, he still lived in the minds and hearts of the climbers passing by.

As mentioned earlier, an estimated over 200 dead bodies are lying in this area of the Everest Dead Zone, between the summit and camp IV, mostly preserved and intact due to the prevailing extremely low temperature. Many of those are fully intact with climbing boots and down suit on their bodies and the climbing rope still around their waist. Others are found at various stages of decay. Some dead bodies may be as fresh as only a few days old belonging to climbers who died during the same climbing season, but most of them would be many years old. Many of them would be even many decades old. The dead body of the legendry climber George Mallory is the oldest one found till date, which was discovered after seventy-five (75) years of his death on the northern slope of the Everest. He died in 1924 and his dead body was lying on the slope of the Everest for more than seven decades till it was identified in 1999. Some dead bodies are lying in open on the slope, some partly covered under ice. Some are lying a little away from the climbing route, where, only a distant view is possible but some are lying just alongside the route and climbers, over the years, see them while climbing up and descending down. In fact, many dead bodies have become landmarks and climbers use them as route markers to determine their locations.

They lie there for years, sleeping in silence, motionless, without being disturbed by the climbers, sending a silent message to them climbers passing by.

One may ask why the bodies aren't moved, or recovered. It is because it's extremely risky, difficult, and a time-taking process to do so due to the extreme environmental conditions, limited oxygen bottles available with the climbers, and thus limited time available with them to stay at such altitude. Also, it is extremely risky to approach some dead bodies due to their dangerous locations. In such conditions where, climbers struggle for each and every step of their own bodies, pulling or pushing the extra weight of a dead body seems quite impractical. But still, some of the experienced mountaineers have tried in recent years to bury some of the dead bodies lying in the accessible locations, or at least to push them down the cliff in order to avoid direct sight. And some are moved by the ice and the wind, when part of an ice cliff breaks, or is blown away by high wind, and bodies lying on such cliff find their way down the slope and go away from the sight.

I had heard about the dead body of a female German climber, Hannelore Schmatz, that had been lying about 100 metres above camp IV, where our tents were erected. Although it was no more in sight that year. She died due to over exhaustion while returning down after a successful summit of Everest in 1979. Her frozen dead body was sitting and leaning against her rucksack for years, when any climbers passing by could see her eyes open and her brown hair blowing in the wind. In spite of her dead body being so close to the climbing route and so exposed and visible, its recovery was not done for years. In 1984, two climbers tried to recover the dead body but fell to their death. Later, the wind had blown her remains over the edge and down the Kangshung face.

When I started again, there was another patch of bad visibility accompanied by snow fall; we still had more than an hour to go to reach camp IV. We continued in the snowfall as there was no other option. Although, many people were probably behind us, everyone whom I met on the way, like the members of the Indian army team, had already overtaken us and had gone ahead.

Finally we reached camp IV at 2 pm. I was not very tired as I had come down at a comfortable pace. I was, however, very thirsty. When I reached my tent, some Korean climbers were inside and were vacating it. They came to camp IV that day and would be leaving for the final summit push in the evening. They were from my agency, which hadn't been able to arrange for enough tents to accommodate all the climbers due to the sudden surge in the number of climbers because of a good weather forecast. I requested a member of the Korean team who was about to leave the tent to give me some water if she had any. She said something I couldn't understand but came back with half a bottle of water mixed with some energy drink, which was very helpful at that time. Later I met the same Korean girl on the way back to Kathmandu from the Everest Base Camp and expressed my gratitude also my condolences; the deputy leader of her team had lost his life after summiting the peak.

To rejuvenate further, I ate small pieces of gur that I had been carrying in the pocket of my down suit. I feel that our Indian *gur* is much more effective than any GU Gel from abroad because while returning from the peak after summiting, I had met the leader of the Indian Army expedition and I descended with his team for some time when he offered me one GU Gel chocolate; I found that I didn't affect me as much as *gur*.

After returning to camp IV, some climbers generally continue their descend after short break and reach camp III camp II, especially those who reached camp IV early, but I was not in a mood to do so. I had reached there in the afternoon and wanted to take sufficient rest by spending the night, which was a common practice. So my attention went on two full oxygen bottles, we kept the previous day as reserve but it wasn't there. Somebody had taken it. Anyway, I was not worried any further on the matter because there was sufficient oxygen left in my third bottle that I had started using from South Summit. While descending down, I used only one litre per minute and while resting in the tent at camp IV, I was consuming only half litre per minute, so the remaining oxygen in the bottle would be sufficient for the whole night. For the following day's downward journey, I would use the oxygen bottle, which I had used during the previous day's journey from camp III to camp IV, and there was sufficient oxygen available in it to make us go for the way. Still, as a precautionary measure, I told my Sherpa to check the surroundings, if any discarded bottles had any gas because many climbers threw used up oxygen bottles with some gas in them. After some time, he came back with two bottles and measured the content. In one bottle, the gauge showed 100 and in another, it was 80. I was very happy because I had enough oxygen in hand to spend the night comfortably and descend down the following day.

In the evening, I wanted to talk to my family. I had informed them about my scheduled summit attempt and they would have been waiting for the news. Although I had given the agency a list of a few important people who had to be informed, after witnessing the mismanagement in the higher camp, I couldn't trust that they had informed my family. I had given important contact numbers to the doctor of the army team,but I wasn't sure whether he got the news of my summit. So, I went to the army camp to use a satellite phone to call up my district collector. I had given him the list of all the remaining important people to be informed. The army camp was a little away from our camp but even a small distance matters at camp IV.

I was warmly welcomed by Major Jamwal, and enjoyed a meal of *rajma* and rice. Although it was pre-cooked and packed, which was heated and served (because cooking is extremely difficult in the thin atmosphere), I will never forget the delicious dish that I ate for the first time after leaving camp II. After having a little bit of the food, I called up my district collector and then returned to my camp. By this time, it was already dark outside and all the tents, in fact the whole area, seemed completely silent, although there must have been more than one hundred people in that small, flat area.

This night was comfortable because firstly, the weather seemed good with almost negligible wind and clear sky. I thanked god recalling the difficulties the members of North East Everest Team had gone through, at the same place a few days ago. Sometimes, weather at this place is so bad that a strong wind could uproot your tent and you would be left in open fully exposed to the bad weather and left to die. Secondly, there were only two of us in the tent; another climber and his Sherpa were supposed to have shared the tent but had already left for the lower camp after suspending their summit attempt the day before.

26

Towards the Plains

'Until one is committed, there is hesitancy,
the chance to draw back. Always ineffectiveness.
Concerning all acts of initiative (and creation)
there is one elementary truth,
the ignorance of which kills countless ideas and splendid plans:
that the moment one definitely commits oneself,
then providence moves too.
All sorts of things occur that would never otherwise have occurred.
A whole stream of events issues from the decision,
raising in ones favor all manner of unforeseen incidents and meetings
and material assistance which no man could have dreamt
would come his way.
I have learned a deep respect for one of Goethe's couplets –
"Whatever you can do or dream you can, begin it.
Boldness has genius power and magic in it.'
—**W. H. Murray, The Story of Everest, 1921-1952**

The next morning, I was ready by 6 am and came out of the tent wearing all my gear. The weather still seemed to be fair to our luck with a clear sky and no wind. Outside the tent, my friend Sanjay Pandit, was standing very happily and was ready to depart. At the same time, a Sherpa came out from his tent and he seemed happy too. He revealed that a climber had been trying to jump from the top of the world but his Sherpa had saved him with the help of a few other Sherpa. I believed him because I had heard earlier that people reached there after so many trials and hard work, and when they reached, they became so happy, they lost control and indulged in nonsensical activities like shouting, crying, or attempting to jump down. One of the reasons for the suicide attempt could have been the effect of HACE. In absence of sufficient oxygen, human brains get dull and are unable to take rational decision about life and death, and climbers don't realise the impact of the crazy actions, which lead to loss of their lives.

I was happy to see Sanjay Pandit, who made to the top successfully although his face was swollen and he was coughing and feeling weak. This had been his second attempt. The last time he couldn't make it to the top for some reason and had to return empty handed. This year, I saw he had been very eager and very concerned about his success because, firstly, his young guide of twenty two, Lobsang Sherpa, had slipped from the steep Lhotse face while descending from camp IV, and had slipped into a crevasse and died. Secondly, his former guide had died in another incident at Mount Makalu the previous year also. So, he found it difficult to get a guide as no Sherpa was ready to serve him. Sherpa considered him unlucky in their own beliefs and superstitions. Finally, a Sherpa had agreed to work with him. Although he was on my team under the leadership of Col. Rana; he too, had started his journey well before the rest of the team. He had even started one day before me but had summited the same day and at around same time though I hadn't seen him on the top.

We all started at 7 am and passed the Geneva Spur and then crossed the traverse, and then the Yellow Band. We encountered many climbers on the way who were coming up to attempt the summit. I met the remaining members of my team below the Yellow Band. They included Col. Neeraj Rana, Nisha Adhikari, the seven boys from the Lawrence School, and the girl from Maharashtra. I also had a brief conversation in a few statements with some of them because the queue halted as we stopped to meet each other along the fixed rope.

While talking to one of the Sanawar boys, Guribadat Singh, I could understand the impact of that short conversation.

He, who scaled the peak the following day, recalled and told me that when he asked me how the situation was uphill and if could make it. I told him, 'There is nothing so tough there as we had imagined. It's easy. Don't listen to other's talk about difficulties up. Focus on your climb with cool mind and you will make it.' He was grateful to me that my statement motivated him a lot whenever he felt tired, so he continued and made it to the top although a bit late. I felt that it was my duty to project an image of easy route up in his mind, which may repeatedly appear in his mind and may make his journey comparatively easier because mental hindrance is the biggest hindrance. He had always believed in me and had also taken some suggestions previously at the Base Camp. If I would have talked about real difficulties up then he would have visualised the same and might have restrained his movement.

Anyway, as we parted after very short meeting, I noticed that I didn't see Saachi Soni, the other girl in the team, who was from Rajasthan. All of them were fully covered from the top to bottom and it would have been difficult to recognize them if they hadn't marked their down suits with symbols especially the boys from the Lawrence School.

A little later, I was surprised to see Commander Satya Dam who I had thought would have probably scaled the summit and returned because I hadn't seen him after leaving camp II. He congratulated me and said that his client was not feeling well that day so he had delayed his plan.

His client, Maria Conceicao, had come to climb the Everest for her social motive. Maria Conceicao is the founder and head of The Maria Cristina Foundation, a non-profit organization based in Dubai. She has dedicated her life for the welfare of the poor, especially slum dwellers, by providing them with quality education. Her organisation supports many underprivileged students by enrolling them in private schools and colleges in Dhaka, Bangladesh, and provides them with their daily needs such as transportation, food, accommodation, medical facilities, etc. Her quest to Mount Everest was an effort to raise funds for her organization, which was running short of funds due to the intake of a large number of students by the organisation.

She said to me later after returning from the summit that she was fully exhausted and was about to give up and return back, one moment during the final climb. But when she remembered that her success or failure was not her personal achievement and involved the future of hundreds of children in need. She regained her energy and she started taking each uphill step on the name of each of her students and thus, she made it to the top.

Later, even some experienced Sherpa shared their opinions with me that they were surprised how Maria could make it to the top because she was not looking fit and she also got sick at camp II. I could understand that, in spite of being fully tired physically, she could climb because she had a beautiful heart. Her cause was extremely good and the love for those children allied her momentarily and made her climb to the top.

After meeting them and having a brief conversation, I felt re-energized and continued my journey downwards. Around 11 am, I reached camp III, and after a short break there, continued further down. I had been panting the whole way but still kept up my pace and moved comparatively faster than the other climbers. Below camp III, my pace increased and so did my panting. I had to stop frequently so I could catch my breath. I reached jumar point (the base of the Lhotse face) at about 12:30 in the afternoon. There I took a good break to have some water. My throat had been dry for a long time. I had some water punched with energy drink, which my Sherpa had arranged from one of his Sherpa friends. I continued on and someone from the agency was waiting with warm apple juice midway between the base of the Lhotse face and camp II. I was a bit sarcastic about this. The company's arrangements at camp III and camp IV had not been satisfactory at all when good, sustainable food was required. But now, after returning to as low as camp II, they had arranged some juice. But I enjoyed nonetheless, thinking that nothing would change even if I didn't accept it.

After the two drinks I was feeling a little lethargic, as I was tired, and my stomach was full. I walked lazily and at 2 pm, reached camp II. There, the Lawrence School boys' parents welcomed and congratulated me. Saachi Soni, the girl from Rajasthan came out from one of the tents and was happy to see me, although she looked completely exhausted. Her face looked as if she had been sick for quite a long time.

After about half an hour, my friend Sanjay Pandit also arrived and everybody congratulated him. The last bit of trouble from the company was the search for my luggage. While my Sherpa and I had climbed to the top, we had left extra clothing and some food in what was supposed to be our designated tent at camp II. Later, somebody else from the agency came and stayed there and our luggage had shifted to another place. I came down from camp IV thinking that I would freshen up after changing from my down suit into fresh warm clothes because I had been in the down suit for the last four days. Actually, climbers put on the down suits at camp II while going up towards the summit and continued wearing them till they returned to camp II from the summit, and so did I. In between, we changed only our warm thermals, which could become wet from the sweat during the long climb.

So while leaving camp II for the upward climb, I had a total of two sets of thermals: one that I was wearing and another in the bag. The one I was wearing became soaked while I was climbing upwards from camp III to camp IV. I put on the only extra set of thermals for the final climb from camp IV onwards. It was fine when I returned from the top as there is negligible sweating after camp IV due to extreme cold. But the final set of thermals was spoiled while I was descending from camp IV to camp II. Presently, I had nothing fresh to wear and all the clothing I was wearing, and even the clothing in my bag, was wet.

When I asked the Sherpa, he said that somebody had put the bag somewhere else and nobody knew where, not even the cook who had been at camp II the whole time. Finally in the evening, I got my clothing but I had to stay in wet clothes at camp II for five hours. This could have otherwise made me completely lose it at the company's mismanagement. But by this time, I had started treating it as normal when I encountered many examples of the agency's mismanagement. I kept calm.

Although these type of minor mishaps aren't of much significance, but I prefer to mention it so that any reader aspiring for the climb would be careful during their expedition.

I was ready at 6 am the next morning so I could depart for the Base Camp. I left my tent, went to the dining tent and received news that two of the Lawrence School boys had made it to the top; but one of them had become sick and had had to avert his summit attempt. Col. Neeraj Rana had also averted his summit attempt due to some problem. I congratulated the father of the Lawrence School boy who had made it to the top and gave my condolences to the father of the other, who had had to return. Before starting the journey for the Base Camp, I enquired with my Sherpa about whether the radio was working. He said that he had forgotten to charge it here (at camp II) after returning from camp IV the previous day, so it had completely lost charge and was not working. It was dangerous to cross the Khumbu icefall without a working radio but it was not a good time to tell him off. Finally, I decided to start the journey because we were going in a group with a few members from the international team of the same agency.

I started my journey to the Base Camp at about 6. 30 am. Luckily, when we came out of our camp area and reached the main route, we met members of the army team, who were also going down after all of them had successfully summited. We descended together at a normal pace and comfortably reached camp I. Here, we took a few minutes' break to have some water and continued the journey down. While descending through Khumbu, I thought to myself that this was the last journey of the season through the treacherous Khumbu as nobody knew who would face death on this route. It is full of danger and considered one of the most hazardous stretches on the south east route to

Everest. The day before, at camp II, I had heard about the death of a veteran Russian climber named Alexey Bolotov. He had died in Khumbu on May 15, one day before I had crossed it on the way up for the final journey. But I had been safe enough and had never had any problems above the Base Camp except the inconvenience due to mismanagement of my agency.

I wanted to overcome the last obstruction on the way back to the Base Camp as soon as possible and to sleep peacefully when we reached. I knew that after going to such a high altitude, where my body had withstood such a thin atmospheric conditions, the Base Camp would feel as comfortable as Gangtok. Although I recalled that everybody had developed severe headaches and sleeplessness at the same Base Camp after arriving there for the first time. As I was eager to cross Khumbu, it seemed to take longer and longer and the route seemed to be different as I couldn't find same seracs and the crevasses I had crossed during my last trip and had developed an attachment with. There seemed to be many more aluminium ladders than the last time. Finally, I asked my Sherpa about it. He confirmed that the route had been changed due to a shift in the glacier and that many more aluminium ladders had been put up to cover many new crevasses, which had been formed the previous week. There is actually a team of expert Sherpa called icefall doctors, who regularly survey the route in the icefall and repair or make changes when required so that climbers and other Sherpa can cross safely.

Finally at 10:30 am, we crossed the final stretch of the icefall, came out, and found many people standing at the foot of the icefall to welcome us. They had come from their camp till here to welcome us. The army team's support team was there to receive their group (who had been returning with us after a successful summit). There was no sign of anybody from my agency. It might have not been the agency's fault as my Sherpa hadn't communicated with them because the radio wasn't working.

But it didn't really matter whether anybody from the agency was present or not. After so many interactions with the army team, whose camp was just adjacent to ours, there were many friends. I was welcomed with equal warmth. We took group photographs, had some eatables and I was invited to celebrate the successful summit at their camp. All of us moved out from the foot of the icefall towards our camps. As usual, before entering the camp, we went to the Lhapso and offered prayer to Mother Chomolungma; then I moved towards my tent, which was en route to the army camp. I kept my luggage inside my tent, changed into light clothes and went to the army camp to be part of the celebration. There, I was very happy to see the grand welcome ceremony arranged by the army's support team. It was a sunny day and they had arranged stalls with various snacks, soft and some hard drinks out in the open. We sat on the chairs, which were laid in a semicircle with the snacks and drinks stalls in the front. We sat soaking in the warmth of the sun under the open sky and enjoyed the drinks and then, had our lunch. Finally, after 1 pm, I returned to my camp.

Relaxing at Army Camp after returning from Top.

Here, many Sherpa were waiting in the dining tent as they sat and listened to the VHF Radio on which news of the climbers' successful climbs was being broadcasted. They greeted me warmly and one of them innocently mentioned that he was very happy to see me alive which surprised me. I had not had any physical problems like many other climbers who had suffered from frostbite, and others who had died. He also informed me that there had been no communication with my Sherpa after we had left camp IV for the final summit and everybody had been worried. They had tried to call me on the radio many times but there had been no response, so they had started thinking of the many possibilities. They had also enquired with many other people who had been climbing the same evening but were told that we had not been seen. Finally, they had received a call from a Sherpa from another agency. He had said there was one lone climber asking for help as he had finished his oxygen and was saying that he was from Seven Summit. On enquiring further, they had realised that it was a young Indian boy and he had come alone from India and had been asking for immediate help so his life could be saved. They had assumed that it was me as I had come alone from India. They had told the Sherpa to save the boy at any cost. Later, they had assumed that my Sherpa had slipped from the slope and had died but that I was safe.

They had continued to believe this till 2:15 pm when my Sherpa called them on the radio and gave them the news of our successful summit after we reached camp four. They were surprised to hear my Sherpa's voice as they had assumed that he was dead. Upon enquiring, my Sherpa replied that the radio had run out of charge and there had been no communication. I was listening to this conversation between my Sherpa and the people from my agency at Base Camp, so I could think and analyze why my Sherpa hadn't used the radio to call. I had told him to communicate with the Base Camp from the peak and inform the agency that I had succeeded so that they could inform my family members in turn. He had not told me about all this lack of communication. I had been completely unaware of all these developments, thinking that I did not have to worry about this as he was an experienced Sherpa and was very aware of reporting and the minor precautions that were expected from a Sherpa.

Anyway, I let bygones be bygones. I didn't say anything to him in spite of two big blunders, the first being my photos and the other being the communication problem. He hadn't charged the radio at camp II either. I thought that he at least had come all the way down with me from the summit in spite of the slight deviation on the way to collect the empty oxygen bottles. Many Sherpa just leave the climber after helping them reach the summit as if their responsibility has come to an end and they are not responsible for the climber's return.

However, I forgot all this on hearing that my team members had successfully reached the summit two days after I had. Out of a total of ten members (Col. Neeraj Rana, seven boys from the Lawrence school, the girl from Maharashtra, and Nisha Adhikari) who had gone up for the final leg of the journey; six boys (Raghav Joneja, Guribadat Singh, Prithvi Singh, Ajay Sohal, Fateh Singh and Shubham Kaushik) from the Lawrence School and the Nisha Adhikari had made it to the top. Only one boy from the Lawrence school named Hakikat Singh, and Col. Neeraj Rana couldn't make it for some problem. The girl from Maharashtra, Priyanka Mangesh Mohite, also couldn't make it to the top that day but she would go for her second attempt that evening. Thus, a total of nine out of thirteen in the team had made it to the top. Seven scaled that day, Sanjay Pandit and I had scaled two days earlier, and one (Priyanka) was waiting at camp IV to make her second attempt. Overall, it was grand success for the team.

Later, I busied myself in informing the well-wishers and family members of the news and called up my district collector in Gangtok, our counsellor in the IAS Academy Mussoorie, my *Mamaji*, Capt. vv, etc. I was very happy to receive a call from the director of the IAS academy just ten minutes after my conversation with my counsellor.

The evening was relaxed and the agency arranged a cake to celebrate the successful climb that Sanjay Pandit and I had completed. We enjoyed the cake, played a few games of chess and I won all them, again. At about 9 pm, I disappeared into my tent and that was the end of the day.

The following day May 22 was relaxed, as usual. I spent it chatting, packing my bags for the final departure, taking a bath after a long time and putting on fresh clothes. But in the afternoon, I got news of two deaths. The previous day, May 21(the day I returned back to Base Camp and the day, Sanawar boys had summited the peak), two people had died on their way down after a making successful summit of the Everest that day. One was the member of Korean Team of our agency and another was a Bangladeshi climber of some other agency.

The death of the Korean climber Mr Sung Ho-Seo was shocking to me because I knew him before. His team, with the expedition name *Zero to 8848 expedition* was going through the same agency, Seven Summit Trek. They had started their expedition from the Bay of Bengal at sea level kayaking, then biking, and trekking to the Everest Base Camp. He was the deputy leader of his team. His team leader, Mr Kim Chang-ho, was another veteran climber, who had already summited thirteen out of the eight thousanders without supplemental oxygen and he came to summit the Everest as his last eight thousander without the aid of bottled oxygen. I had close interaction with both while he and his team leader had visited our dining tent few weeks ago. I also met few of his team mates at camp IV two days earlier, one of whom gave me juice when I had just arrived to camp IV back from the summit. Mr Sung Ho-Seo was a young amiable man in his thirties. I was literally shaken by his death because he was an experienced climber and had already climbed twelve out of the total fourteen eight thousanders. Mt. Everest was his twelfth eight thousander peak, which he summited without using supplemental oxygen. One Sherpa from our agency, who was present there that day, told me that the health of Mr. Sung Ho-Seo had deteriorated while descending down after the summit. He died while resting at camp IV due to vital organ failure from lack of oxygen. His dead body was later recovered with great effort of our agency.

Another person was, Mr. Mohammed Khaled Hossain, a film director from Bangladesh. He was also in his thirties. He summited the Everest sometime around 10 am on same day and had died on his way down on the south east ridge. People were saying at the Base Camp that he exhausted his supplemental oxygen and then couldn't move ahead due to lack of essential oxygen, as well as fatigue. He sat down to rest while he was anchored to fixed rope on the route and then, lay down and never stood up.

Later on reaching Kathmandu, I heard that he was married and had a son. His wife came to Kathmandu along with some other family members to recover his dead body from uphill and to enquire about the cause of his death. But his body couldn't be recovered.

Later, while talking to one of the Sanawar boys, named Guribadat Singh, who summited the peak the same day around 12. 30 pm, I came to know that Mr. Hossain died somewhere between Balcony and camp IV. Guribadat, who used to be my chess mate at the Base Camp and a good friend, revealed that while descending down from the summit along with his Sherpa, he saw a person lying and resting along a fixed rope as he descended about one hour after Balcony. He also went and sat beside him for a brief rest as he was feeling very tired. But as soon as he looked at his face after sitting, he found that he was dead and he immediately stood up and departed from the place.

Anyway, till then, I had become used to all such death news in the Everest area and had learnt to carry on with day's activity after getting emotionally carried away for some time.

While the news of two deaths was still a matter of discussion, we heard that there was no news of Priyanka (the girl from Maharashtra) and her Sherpa after she had left for her second attempt for the peak along with her new Sherpa the day before. People at Base Camp as well as higher camps had been trying to establish contact with them on VHF Radio but no contact could be established. This was a sign of worry for all of us. Taking the matter seriously, our agency Seven Summit Trek sent four Sherpa along with few oxygen bottles for their rescue. But it took time for Sherpa to climb and reach uphill. When the rescue party reached camp IV around midnight, they found Priyanka and her Sherpa sleeping in a tent. The message was immediately sent to the Base Camp and we felt a lot relieved on hearing the news of her safe arrival at camp IV. It was also a wonderful success for the team as ten out of thirteen had made it to the top and more importantly, everybody was safe till then.

Later, Priyanka told me that her radio was dead because the battery was discharged and so, connection couldn't be established. She said that she had started for her second attempt in the evening of May 21, and summited at around 11.15 a.m. the next day. But on the way down, she exhausted her oxygen around Balcony. Luckily, her Sherpa managed some oxygen from another Sherpa and she could reach camp four at 7pm the same day. She said that she was totally exhausted by the time she reached back to camp IV. So, she entered a tent and slept like an unconscious person.

The next day was May 23, 2013. Although I wanted to stay at the Base Camp to meet the team mates who were descending down but representative of our agency suggested me to depart from Base Camp and meet the team mates later in Kathmandu. So I finally departed from the Base Camp towards Kathmandu. I was lucky to reach Kathmandu at a good time as I got a chance to meet two legendary mountaineers. The first one is Reinhold Messner, an Italian mountaineer, who is well known as the first climber to scale all the fourteen eight thousanders, and also as the first person to ascend Mt. Everest without using supplemental oxygen along with Peter Habeler. He, at 78, still had a deep attachment with the mountains and so, he was in Nepal for some other project related to Everest. The second one is Dave Hahn, an American climber of Japanese origin, who scaled Mt. Everest for the fifteenth time in 2013, the maximum for any non-Sherpa climber. While talking to him at the breakfast table in Hotel Yak and Yeti, he said to me that he was aiming to scale it twenty one times and thus, he was aiming to equal the record set by Apa Sherpa.

I felt great to be talking to them. I felt like an amateur before the great figures. Although I had scaled the Everest in my first attempt, which is also first peak of my life but still, my achievement seemed nothing after meeting them. Anyway, this marked the end of a chapter of my life, one I had been dreaming about and pursuing for months and months.

Happy to meet legendary mountaineer-Reihnold Messener in Hotel Yak & Yeti in Kathmandu.

With Mingma Sherpa - First person from Nepal to climb all 14 eight-thousanders.

27

All's Well That Ends Well

'Be the change that you want to see in the world.'
—*Mahatma Gandhi*

I summited the highest peak of the world and returned back safely. This was a very happy moment of my life; a happy conclusion to all the trouble and tribulations I had to go through. I didn't even get a single scratch on my body during the whole journey although a total of nine people died on the slope of the Everest during the same period, seven people on its south route and two more on its north route. I was really lucky in that sense because many good climbers couldn't make it including Mirza Ali, Col. Rana, Wing Commander S. K. Kutty, and many others. Mirza Ali from Pakistan seemed a very confident and strong climber but he returned back from camp IV, although his sister Samina Baig did it successfully and set the record of being the first Pakistani woman to climb the highest peak of the world. The leader of our team and ex-principal of HMI Darjeeling, Col. Rana had to return after covering a little above camp IV although most of his boys (clients) made it to the top including the young Raghav Jonega, who set the record of being the youngest Indian to climb Everest in 2013. Similarly, the climbing leader of the NCC Team, Wing commander S K Kutty had to return from about 8,200 metre due to altitude sickness after he had started from south col but most of his NCC boys made it to the top.

I completely believe that I owe my success to my positive visualization, and my positive attitude to successfully reach the top. I have always imagined myself standing atop the Everest, paying homage to mother Chomolungma and enjoying the serene beauty all around. I had never contemplated my return without a successful summit or any accident where I was injured or dead. But I had prepared myself for the worst-case-scenario in advance by taking extra insurance and informing the family about all my assets and liabilities.

During the expedition, many people were severely injured with frostbite on their toe, fingers, nose, ear, etc. Some of them would have to amputate their limbs because of getting third-degree frostbite. Their agonies were much bigger than mine. I had only suffered some minor health issues during my initial few days in the Base Camp, and while acclimatising.

My struggle for securing my name in the Sikkim Everest Expedition team and later, the inconvenience caused due to the mismanagement of my agency during the final climb did discourage me for a while. I can very well recall the degree of my frustration at the end of March 2013 in Gangtok when my name was cancelled off the Sikkim government Everest expedition team and there was no hope for being a part of any other expedition. The next was when I didn't find oxygen bottles at camp IV which could be fatal. But I am thankful to god that I was somehow able to quickly come out of those frustrating situations by one way or another. At such times, I would leave everything up to god and continue with my will to come out of it. I would compare my situation to someone in a worse condition. For example, I compared myself with the people climbing the more difficult Lhotse wall when I was about to give up on the way to jumar point during the last stage of acclimatisation. I would recall an extremely motivating statement by Helen Keller, the deaf-blind-mute American author,'I cried because I had no shoes until I met a man who had no feet.'

The magnitude of the seriousness of those situations might have seemed very big at that moment, but later, when I compared these with the great agonies of the ones, who lost lives, or someone who lost limbs, or someone who returned without summiting Everest, my problems seemed very minor. Still, I feel that those minor problems of mine could also have been overcome with the proper applications of positive visualization during such period especially by practising the technique – called as direct suggestion to subconscious mind by Advanced Positive Visualization technique in a meditative state' as mentioned initially in this book. But, it didn't happen because I didn't use it in those cases. The reason for not using it in those cases is only because I wanted to put all my focus on main target until its accomplishment and didn't like to dilute the focus by putting on something less important. I focussed on the main target and left all minor details, thinking that if the main target would be accomplished then minor tasks in the process doesn't keep much significance.

I clearly recall that few negative visualization culminated in the form of doubt in my mind. On analysing the whole scenario from the view of application of positive visualization technique, I very well recalled that I had doubts in my mind whether I could secure a seat in the government-sponsored Everest team. Similarly, I doubted the arrangement at the higher camps while going for the final summit, mainly because of two reasons: Firstly, there was an on-going politics and rivalry between the Seven Summit Treks agency and the Indian Army Team due to some previous issue, and I had more inclination towards the Indian Army Team and I think that the representative of my agency might not have liked it. Secondly, I went ahead of scheduled date during the final summit attempt, inspite of several suggestions of the leader to go along. Obviously, the leader would lose interest to ensure a proper arrangement at higher camps. Anyway, strong doubt in my mind turned into reality later which created all the hindrances and inconveniences.

Although I know visualizing more than one target at a time is very possible, but I preferred to go slowly trying to understand the process deeply because I am still experimenting with different hues of this power and still, I am in the process of understanding it fully. I am a learner and yet to gain perfection. As mentioned earlier, a perfectionist on positive visualization can accomplish anything in life.

I have always been someone with positivity brimming inside, from my childhood. Later on, while I became aware of the miraculous power of Advanced Positive Visualization, I tried to engulf myself more and more in this power, mainly to rid myself of all kinds of negative visions and thought. As a normal human being, sometimes I succeed and sometimes I fail. When I succeed, I would be immensely happy, and when I failed, I tried to overcome the pain by diverting my focus elsewhere or most importantly, finding the positive aspect of failure itself. For example, when I didn't succeed in clearing the civil services examination in my first attempt, I consoled myself thinking that it was better that my name didn't appear in the merit list in the last slot. Other wise I wouldn't have been given a choice to choose the type of civil service I wanted. Hence, I decided to appear for the examination once again with full effort to ensure a good rank in the second attempt. So, very soon, I came out of the sadness and focussed on the incoming prelims, that was hardly a few weeks away.

In any case, over the years, I learnt not to give up at any stage and continue to move ahead with an optimistic approach. I feel this is one of the most important factors behind my success.

There is also another angle, which I can't miss to mention and analyze here.

It is my faith in god. Although I reached the top of the world in my first attempt, I don't want to boast of myself on this success, because I believe that you can't reach on the top of the Everest unless mother Chomolungma permits you to do so. Many people may defer on my faith here. My faith in god, as like many others while climbing the peak, is a positive force that held me during tough times. Although I would always resort to positive visualization, I would still need to keep faith. I chose to have faith in Goddess Chomolungma. Such a belief gives me immense inner strength and courage and my faith in God, I would thus say, has helped me in every way of life.

As mentioned earlier, belief and faith is the matter of the subconscious mind. Once your subconscious mind has accepted that you would be safe during your journey to Everest, it will start executing it, irrespective of whether the source of your faith and belief is the rational visualization of your conscious mind or due to your faith in God. What is required is that you imagine about safe climb, you imagine about yourself being on the top of the peak, paying homage to God and rejoicing your success, you imagine about your safe descend and returning home and celebrating your success there. In this way, you are devoid of a fearful visualization about failure. You don't imagine about encountering an accident during the journey. You don't visualize about a condition when you die and your family members are sobbing. In short, your mind is occupied with only positive and constructive thoughts of success and a safe journey, and is devoid of any negative thought.

Swami Sivananda Radha in her book *Kundalini Yoga for the West* has mentioned, "Mind can then be seen as a screen on which the pictures emerge. . . . Worship when positive is a very helpful factor, contributing to personal development. ... In one's personal worship, a spiritual image can be created and visualized by the power of imagination. ... It sets some seekers free from religious aspects that may be undesirable. At the same time, substitution of various Gods and Goddesses is avoided, once the practice of concentration has been mastered.'

The human mind is very fickle. In the absence of such concentration and control over the conscious mind, you don't know when it would weaken or ruin your chance of success, by filling itself with negative thoughts about failure, accident, etc. and pull you towards failure even before you attempt such a great task.

The day at the Base Camp when I had tremendously low content of oxygen, the situation got quite risky. There was fair chance that I would have focussed more on the bad consequences, and may have stayed back at Gorakshep for some more days and given up my climb, which would have been a huge loss to me and my dream. But I moved ahead thinking that the oxygen would improve in next few days and never thought about any bad consequences.

Similarly, when my name was removed from the list of Sikkim Everest team, I still believed that I was going to climb it somehow without thinking too much on how, because I thought I had to pay tribute to mother Chomolungma on the peak of the Everest. I had a firm belief that mother Chomolungma had accepted my tribute while I was still in Sikkim and she was calling me to the peak.

Further, my whole journey was filled with some happy moments as well as some painful experiences. For a happy and peaceful life, it is necessary to take key learnings from such painful experience and then move on. It's better to remind myself of the happy moments of the past and feel like a winner. Because if I would continue reminding myself of the bad moments during that whole journey then it would unnecessarily draw more bad moments in my life in the future because the subconscious mind will actualize the thoughts in my conscious mind.

Life is not a bed of roses, and every human being passes through the crest and trough of pleasure and pain, but still some people with positive attitude change their lives. Oscar Wilde said,'We are all in the gutter, but some of us are looking at the stars.'

Thus, my appeal to all the readers is to read the subtext underlying in my attempt to pen down my story. My attempt would only succeed if you start believing in yourself and start exploring the unlimited potential of your mind, and use it for the betterment of your life and realise your dream. You try and develop a positive energy within yourself and strengthen your prevailing positive energy and belief inside you, which would further create a positive atmosphere in your surroundings leading to the happy society, which would further lead to the progressive country and pave the pathway to a peaceful world.

****

Glossary

Acclimatisation: The process of adaptation of body to changing atmospheric condition, explained in details in chapter 18: Much-needed Acclimatisation.

Advanced Positive Visualization: A process of visualization or creating image about your future in your mind. Detailed explanation is given in Chapter II *Advanced Positive Visualization*.

AIIMS: All India Institute of Medical Sciences.

Avalanche: It is a sudden fall or slide of a large mass of snow or ice along with rock particles down the mountain slope. It travels with great speed and has potential to sweep out and destroy whatever comes in the way depending on its extent and strength.

All India Services: Includes Indian Administrative Services (IAS), Indian Police Services (IPS) and India Forest Services (IFS).

Anchor: Refers to something used to hold something else firmly in place. In mountaineering, it is the point on the mountain slope where rope is fixed to the ground or rock at regular interval to provide stability to the climbers and to arrest their falls.

Ascender: A device used for climbing with the help of fixed rope. It can move in only one direction on the rope due to teeth provided, which stops its backward movement on the rope.

Balcony: A small flat place at the altitude of 27,560 feet (or 8,400 m) on southeast ridge of Everest. It lies between camp IV (26,000 feet) and south summit (28,700 feet).

Base Camp: Base Camp with reference to a Mountaineering Expedition means the main camp from where mountaineering expedition or any other particular activity starts. It acts as the main shelter, source of supply and communication or reporting point for higher camps.

Begusarai: A district in the state of Bihar, India, located in the Gangetic Plain. The district headquarter is a town named as Begusarai.

Bridge: This is control room of the ship from where ship is navigated. Also called wheelhouse because ship's steering wheel is located here by which ship is steered. While ship is sea, bridge is always manned by an officer on watch (OOW), who is in charge of navigation of ship and a duty AB (Able bodied seamen), who keeps look out. It is generally located at the second highest point of the ship only below the money island, so that all round look out of the ship and surrounding sea is maintained.

Bridge Deck: Deck or platform of ship on which the bridge is located. It also includes the bridge wing, which is open space on both sides of Bridge. Compass repeaters are located in both Bridge wings, with the help of which generally sun sight and star sight are taken under open sky.

Camp I: Set up at altitude of about 19,900 feet (or 6,065 metre). It is generally used as transit camp between Base Camp and camp II.

Camp II: Set up at an altitude of about 21,300 feet (or 6,500 metre) and considered the most safe camp and camp with maximum facilities above Base Camp.

Camp III: Set up at 24000 feet (or 7,315 metre) on the steep face of Lhotse. It is considered unsafe due to rare chance of survival in case of avalanche or slip and fall.

Camp IV: Set up at 26000 feet (or 7,925 metre). It comes in Death zone and is not considered a place to stay for more than two days because of adverse effect on the body.

Chatten: Chatten is a small village in North Sikkim District, which is located just before Lachen. It is known for the headquarter of Indian Army establishment in North Sikkim district.

Chief Officer: Chief Officer is managerial level deck officer on board ship. Master (also called as Captain) does overall command of merchant vessel. Chief Officer is just below him or second in command. There is also chief engineer, who is overall in-charge of running and maintenance of engine and machinery on vessel but he works under overall command of the Master.

Chomolungma: The Tibetan name of Mount Everest. The word 'Chomolungma' means the Mother Goddess of the Earth.

Chowrikiang: A place inside Kanchendzonga National Park in West Sikkim located near the Nepal-Sikkim border around the Kanchendzonga Base Camp area. It is situated at 14,000 feet above sea level and is used as the Base Camp for providing field training by HMI Darjeeling. It can be reached by three days of trekking from Yuksom.

Chungthang: It is one of the sub-divisions of North Sikkim district. The headquarteris a small town named Chungthang, which is junction point for tourists because route for Lachen-Gurudongmar axis and Lachung Yumthang axis gets separated from here.

Civil Services Examination: This is considered the most difficult competitive examination in India, which selects candidates for twenty-four civil services of Government of India including IAS, IPS, Indian Foreign Service, IRS etc. It is organized in three phases namely preliminary test, mains examination and interview and is conducted by Union Public Service Commission.

Col: A pass between two mountain peaks. It is basically the lowest point where mountain ridges coming down from two different peaks meet and a pass like structure is formed. Also known as notch, gap or saddle although it may have slightly different geographical features if compared in strict sense.

Cornice: Overhanging snow or ice along a ridge shaped like a curly thing or wave.

Cornice Traverse: It is only a few-feet wide ridge with the breath-taking drop on both sides and is located between south summit and the Hillary step on the southeast ridge of Everest. It is considered as the most exposed section of climb. On one side there is 8000 feet drop down the southwest face of Everest and on another side, there is 10000 feet drop down the Kangshung face.

Crampon: A metallic plate with spike or sharp tooth fixed to it. It is attached to the sole of climbing boot to provide proper grip on snow and ice while ice climbing or walking and to arrest slip. It comes in pair like boot, one for each leg.

Crampon Point: It is a place above Everest Base Camp where people don their crampons before entering into the Khumbu Icefall.

Crevasse: Crevasse is crack in the glacier, which is formed due to the internal tensile force. Its depth and width varies from few feet to several hundred feet. It is the main obstacle in the Khumbu Icefall where dozens of aluminum ladders are used to cross it. It may be open, where cracks are clearly visible to climbers or hidden where crack is covered with thin layer of snow and climbers may fall in it when they mistakenly put their foot on top of thin layer of snow covering the mouth of crack.

CWM: It is a steep walled semi circular or bowl shaped glacial valley. Also called Cirque. It is formed by glacier in high mountains. The most famous CWM is the Western CWM in the Everest region.

DAV Jawahar Vidya Mandir: DAV Jawahar Vidya Mandir, presently known as only Jawahar Vidya Mandir is a CBSE Board English medium co-educational school in Ranchi. Known as one of the best schools in North India, it imparts education from Nursery till Senior Secondary level. It is mainly for the employees of MECON, a subsidiary of Steel Authority of India but outsiders are also inducted depending on merit and availability of seat.

Death Zone: The death zone in reference to mountaineering refers to the area beyond 26,000 feet (or about 8,000 metre), where there is lack of sufficient oxygen to sustain human life.

Descender: A metallic device, which is used with rope for descending the steep slope of rock or ice.

Dexamethasone: It is a steroid, which is like natural hormone produced by our adrenal gland and acts as its replacement when our body doesn't make enough of it. It is used for treating high altitude sickness like HACE or HAPE.

DIG: Deputy Inspector General of Police.

DM: District Magistrate. Also known as District Collector or Deputy Commissioner or simply Collector is an officer and overall in-charge of revenue collection and administration of a District of India.

Down Suit: It is one piece full body suit filled with down for high altitude use. The quality of the Down Suit depends on the quality of down as well as the blends of feather and down in various proportion.

The Eider Down is an extremely rare and high end product. Then comes goose down and then duck down. Duck down has typically lower cost than goose down. Down Suit is also known as Climbing Suit or Expedition Suit or Dangri.

Eight thousanders: There are 14 mountain peaks in the world with altitude more than 8,000 metre. These are commonly called as Eightthousanders. These are Mt. Everest (8,850 m), K2 (8,611 m), Kanchendzonga (8,586 m), Lhotse (8,516 m), Makalu (8,463 m), Cho Oyu (8,201 m), Dhaulagiri (8,167 m), Manaslu (8,163 m), Nanga Parwat (8,125 m), Annapurna (8,091 m), Gasherbrum I (8,068 m), Broad Peak (8,047 m), Gasherbrum II (8,035 m) and Shishapangma (8,027 m).

Epigenetics: A branch of the Genetics studying the external modification to DNA caused by external environmental factors without changing underlying DNA sequence

Etrier: A short ladder made up of light-weight rope with few rungs of wood or metal.

Everest: The highest peak of the world. It comes under category of young fold mountain of tertiary period. It is 8,850 metre (or 29,035 feet) high and is located near the Nepal-China border. It is also known as Sagarmatha in Nepal and Chomolungma in Tibet.

Everest Base Camp: refers to the Base Camp for expedition to Mt. Everest. It is located at the altitude of 17600 feet (or 5364 metre). It is the largest flat area located on top of a glacier and surrounded by mountain ridge from all sides except a narrow entry/exit along the Khumbu River of ice. It is the place where tents are erected with all basic facilities and climbers are stationed for most of time except journey uphill for acclimatisation or final climb.

Figure of 8: A type of metallic descender, which looks like '8'.

Fixed Rope: A rope fixed to ground, rock or ice on the slope of mountain or in Glacier with the help pitons or other anchor.

Gangtok: The capital town of Indian State of Sikkim. It is also headquarter of East District of Sikkim.

Geneva Spur: It is an anvil shaped rib of black and nearly vertical rock, which comes as a challenge to the climber en-route to camp IV from camp III. It is located at about 25500 feet altitude and is above yellow band. Geneva Spur was given to this one during the 1952 Swiss expedition.

GPS: Global Positioning System. This is an electronic equipment to determine position in latitude and longitude based on input from satellite.

Gur: Also called jaggery, *gur*, is natural solid brown colored product of sugarcane, which is made by heating sugarcane juice until dry. It is more unrefined than sugar.

Harness: It is a supporting gear, which takes up the body weight while climbing or descending. It is combination of straps, bends etc. It is worn around waist and thigh of climber and all other safety gear and climbing equipment are attached to it.

HACE: High Altitude Celebral Edema. It is a form of severe high-altitude sickness, which is characterized by the swelling of the brain that happens due to the leakage of cerebral blood vessels in brain and is responsible for major deaths in the death zone of Everest. Absence of sufficient oxygen in the atmosphere causes cerebral blood vessels to leak fluid into surrounding brain tissue, triggering swelling, due to which, climbers develop symptoms like loss of coordination, confusion, lack of judgment, and they may even slip into unconscious. Persons with this sickness are often confused and may not judge whether they are ill. Loss of coordination causes staggering walk like intoxicated or drunken person. Immediate descent is the best treatment for HACE. Supplementary oxygen and Dexamethasone are temporary measures until sick person descends to lower altitude.

HAPE: High-Altitude Pulmonary Edema. It is another form of severe high-altitude sickness, which is characterized by filling of fluid into lungs. The hypoxia of high altitude causes constriction of some of the blood vessels in lungs, resulting in blood flow through only limited blood vessels, which are not constricted. This causes excessive blood pressure in these vessels and results in leakage of fluid from highly pressured blood vessels into lungs. A quick descent, supplementary oxygen, rehydration, rest, or medication, such as, Dexamethasone, are few prescribed treatments.

Heli-Rescue: Rescue by Helicopter

Hillary Step: The last obstruction before the summit. It is an almost vertical rock, 40 feet high at 28740 feet (or 8760 m) altitude and a big challenge for a climber to scale. It was named after Edmund Hillary who climbed it first.

HMI: Himalayan Mountaineering Institute located in Darjeeling, North East India. It is an institute of Government of India for training in mountain climbing and other adventure sports. It was founded in 1954 by then Prime Minister of India Pandit Jawahar Lal Nehru and Tenzing Norgay was its Director of Field Training for more than two decades.

IAS: Indian Administrative Services. It is the successor of ICS (Indian Civil Service), which prevailed during British rule over India. It is one of the three All India Services.

Ice axe: A mountain climbing equipment, which is shaped like an axe and is used for climbing the ice and snow surface.

Icefall: An icefall is fast moving glacier which is characterized by deep crevasse and big seracs. The difference between glaciers and icefall is similar to the difference between rivers and waterfalls. A glacier is like a river of ice that moves very slowly and an icefall is like a waterfall, which forms when a snow mass passes down a steep slope and so, its speed increases a little bit.

Icefall doctor: A team of expert Sherpa, who open the route between Everest Base Camp and Camp I through Khumbu Icefall and also regularly survey it and repair or make changes when required so that climbers and other Sherpa can cross safely. They use fixed rope and aluminum ladders to make the route safe and navigable.

IHCAE: Indian Himalayan Centre for Adventure and Ecotourism, a training institute for mountaineering and other adventure sports as well as for promoting Eco-tourism in the State of Sikkim. It is located at Chemchey, South Sikkim and Sikkim Government Institute.

IIT: Indian Institute of Technology

IPS: Indian Police Service. It is one of three All India Services.

Jumar: Same as ascender.

Kakarvitta: A small town in Nepal along Indian border of Northern West Bengal. It is adjacent to Siliguri and known for its airport, where tourists catch flight for Kathmandu.

Karabiner: A metal clip with a spring like catch on one side used for fastening rope to it or attach it to piton etc. It may be screw karabiner, which has screw type locking facility at spring catch or plain karabiner which doesn't have locking facility.

Khada: Sikkimese traditional ceremonial scarf. Also called Khata in Tibetan language as it is also used as traditional ceremonial scarf in Tibetan Buddhism. It is offered or presented at many ceremonial occasions like wedding, funerals, religious worships or arrival / departure of guests, etc.

Khumbu Icefall: Khumbu icefall is the icefall near Everest Base Camp. It is first obstruction for climbers moving above EBC on the way to Everest Peak. It is located at the head of Khumbu Glacier and is considered treacherous where many climbers lose life by falling in crevasse or buried under falling ice serac.

LBSNAA: Lal Bahadur Shastri National Academy of Administration, located at Mussoorie. It is the training academy of Indian Administrative Services (IAS) Officers. Also carries out some training courses for other services as well.

Lhapso: A temple like structure erected by Sherpa at the Everest Base Camp to worship goddess of Everest Mother Chomolungma. It consists of cubical shaped stone structure with a pole in the center. Many strings with prayers flags tied over it move out in all directions from the top of the pole in the center.

Lhotse: The fourth highest peak of the world with an altitude of 8,516 metre. It is located adjacent to Mt. Everest and camp III of Everest is located on its slope.

Lumsey: Small colony in Tadong area near Gangtok in East Sikkim District.

Magellan Strait: It is strait (sea route connecting Atlantic Ocean to Pacific Ocean) near the southern end of South American continent, which separates mainland South America with Tierra del Fuego.

Mangan: Small town in Indian State of Sikkim. It is also headquarter of North District of Sikkim.

Metaphysics: The branch of philosophy dealing with the relationship between mind and matter, substance and attributes, that is unanswerable to scientific observation or experiment.

Moraine: It is ridges on the sides or other extremities of glacier, which are formed by the debris (rocks, gravels, sand, soils and other sediments) brought down by the glacier and deposited at its edges.

Navodaya Vidyalaya: Refers to Jawahar Navodaya Vidyalaya. Founded in 1986, it is chain of fully residential and co-educational schools with over 600 branches almost all over India and is fully funded and run by Government of India. It provides free accommodation, food and education facility to selected students preferably from rural background.

NIT: National Institute of Technology located at Calicut, India.

Non-Sikkimese: All those people living in Sikkim but who don't possess a certificate issued by Government of Sikkim namely Sikkim Subject Certificate (SSC) or Certificate of Identification (COI) or Indian Citizenship Certificate (ICC), are called Non-Sikkimese. This certificate is required to get Government's benefit specially the quota benefit in educational institution and Government job. Non-Sikkimese doesn't get these benefits.

North East Cadre: It is general term used to denote all cadre states of North East India including Sikkim.

NPA: National Police Academy. It is the training academy of Government of India for training of IPS Officers and is located at Hyderabad.

Nuptse: It is a mountain peak near Mt. Everest and is 25790 feet high.

Param Vir Chakra: India's highest military honour awarded for bravery or self-sacrifice in the face of enemy. A TV Serial was made in late 1980's portraying the extra-ordinary deeds of award winners during their struggle against enemy.

Piton: It is metal spike mainly steel spike, which acts as anchor for fixed rope to assist climbers in climbing. It is pointed at one end and has an eyehole at other end to which karabiner or rope is attached. It may be ice piton or rock piton. Ice piton is mainly screw type and rock piton is mainly plain pin or peg type.

Poop Deck: The aftermost part of the main deck or weather deck of the ship, which is located behind engine room. If you see a ship from behind then the main deck above water level is poop deck.

Pranayama: *Pranayama* is a Sanskrit word consisting of *Prana* meaning fundamental life force or vital energy and *ayama* meaning extension or elongation. It is basically a deep breathing exercise designed to extend and control one's vital energy.

PTI: Physical Training Instructor.

Pulse Oximetre: A small pocket instrument to measure oxygen saturation in the blood as well as pulse of a person.

Rappelling: The process of descending a rock face or mountain slope with the help of fixed rope with or without descender.

Rishi: Rishi is a Sanskrit word. Also known as seer, sage or saints are divine human beings distinct from God, Demon or mortal human being. They, through Yoga, meditation and spiritual experience, had divine power and their teachings became the basis for spiritual culture of ancient India.

Sagarmatha: Mount Everest is called by another name Sagarmatha in Nepal.

Sage: Same as Rishi.

SAATO: Sikkim Association of Adventure Tour Operators
SAMA: Sikkim Amateur Mountaineering Association

Serac: A large block of glacial ice, which may be as big and high as a multi storied house. It poses threat to mountaineers crossing below it due to chances of its fall and resultantly mountaineers getting buried under it or injured.

Sherpa: They are hilly people who are born and brought up at high altitude in mountain and often work as mountain guide or carry loads or equipment during mountain expedition.

Sikkim: Tiny Indian State located in the lap of Himalaya. It shares international boundary with three countries namely Nepal, China and Bhutan. It is considered as seven sisters plus one in the North Eastern India and is busy tourist destination.

Siliguri: A city in northern West Bengal State of India. It acts as one of the biggest market in the whole area as it lies in a very narrow trip of land linking North Eastern States of India with rest of India.

SMA: Sikkim Mountaineering Association.

South Col: A plane field or pass like formation at the place where Everest slope and Lhotse slope meet at the altitude of 26,000 feet. It is used as camp IV during Everest Expedition for setting up tents.

South Summit: A ping pong table sized dome of ice and snow at an altitude of 28700 feet (or 8750m), which has traditionally been used for changing oxygen bottles so that climbers go for the final ascent with a fresh oxygen bottle.

Spur: A spur is a lateral ridge projecting from a mountain or mountain range.

SP: Superintendent of Police. SP is head of police force in the districts of India.

Star Sight: It is an ancient method to determine the location of the ship at sea by measuring the altitude (angle between the star and visible horizon) of the star with the help of sextant and azimuth (direction of star measured in angle with respect to north) of the star with the help of compass. Such altitude and azimuth of minimum three stars gives the accurate position of ship in latitude and longitude after certain calculation.

Stupa: It is Buddhist religious structure, hemispherical in shape. It contains the relics or remains of Buddhist monks or nuns and is considered as scared place and is used for meditation purpose. Some stupas are also linked to major events in Buddha's life.

Subconscious Mind: Subconscious describes something that is just below the surface of your awareness i. e. you are not aware of it but you can become aware of the information once you direct your attention to it and it can be recalled easily as memory.

Supplemental Oxygen: It is bottled oxygen, which is carried in lightweight cylinders especially made for climbing purpose. Climbers usually use supplemental oxygen above camp III of Everest. It is considered essential above south co,l i.e. in death zone and almost all climbers use it except few, who target to set record of climbing Everest without bottled oxygen.

TAAS: Travel Agents Association of Sikkim

Thangu: A place in North Sikkim at 12700 feet altitude. It falls on Lachen-Gurudongmar route and is known for Indian Army and ITBP camps. It also acts as transit camp for forces going to higher camps.

Traverse: Moving laterally or sideways rather than up and down in mountain. In Everest, two traverses come, first comes between yellow band and Geneva Spur while moving from camp III to camp IV. Second one lies between South Summit and Hillary Step known as Cornice Traverse.

T S Chanakya: Training Ship Chanakya. It is a training institute of the Government of India under Ministry of Shipping and Surface Transport to train deck officers for ships and is located in Navi Mumbai, Maharashtra. It is successor to Training Ship Rajendra (1972-1993) and Training Ship Dufferin (1927-1972).

TTE: Traveling Ticket Examiner. It is a post in Indian Railway.

UPSC: Union Public Service Commission. It is a constitutional body established under article 315 of constitution of India. It conducts examinations for recruitment for various posts under central government and also deals with disciplinary cases relating to different civil services of Government of India. CSE (Civil Services Examination) is one of the various examinations conducted by this body.

VHF Radio: A portable walkie-talkie, which works on very high frequency radio waves transmission and is used during mountaineering expedition for communication between climbers and agency. It can be used for communication within a limited distance in every case where mobile towers or landlines are not available.

Western CWM: Also called the Valley of Silence, it is a large, flat glacial valley between camp I and camp II of Everest. It's made from the ice and snow that comes off from the Everest, Lhotse and Nuptse face and gets accumulated in the valley.

Wheel House: Same as the bridge of ship. Defined earlier.

Yellow Band: It is a layer of sedimentary sandstone rock, which runs horizontally at an altitude of about 25000 feet along the Lhotse face as well as the surrounding mountains and is one of the obstructions for climbers climbing Lhotse face while en-route from camp III to camp IV.

Yeti: An ape-like Himalayan man. It is described in details in chapter *The Journey Begins.*

Yoga Nidra: A sleep-like state experience in Yoga. While doing Yoga Nidra, a practitioners' mind goes to a sleep mode where their bodies and mind pass through effortless relaxation. He/She is not actually asleep, but, it is a condition, where the body and mind is devoid of any tension or anxiety and fully relaxed while being aware of the surrounding unlike sleep, where people are not aware of surroundings. On completion of Yoga-Nidra, practitioners feel re-vitalized as if they have woken up after many hours of deep sleep.

Yogis: A practitioner of Yoga.

Yuksom: Yuksom is a historical town in West District of Sikkim. It was the first capital of Sikkim. It is starting point of trek in Kanchendzonga National Park.

References

1. Swami Satyananda Saraswati. Kundalini Tantra. Yoga Publication Trust, Munger, Bihar, India: 2013 Golden Jubilee Edition.

2. Swami Sivananda Radha. Kundalini Yoga for the West. Motilal Banarsidas Publishers Pvt. Ltd., Delhi. Reprint: Delhi, 2011.

3. Paramahansa Yogananda. Autobiography of a Yogi. Yogada Satsanga Society of India, Kolkata: Eighth Impression, 2013.

4. His Holiness The Dalai Lama. Beyond Religion: Ethics for a whole World. HarperCollins Publishers India, New Delhi. 2012.

5. Thich Nhat Hanh. Old Path White Cloud: Walking in the footsteps of the Buddha. Full Circle, New Delhi, India: Fourteenth Edition, 2012.

6. Jagadis Chandra Bose. Response in the Living and Non-Living. Kindle Edition.

7. Swami Yogananda. Scientific Healing Affirmations. Kindle Edition.

8. Jon Krakauer. Into Thin Air: A Personal Account of the Everest Disaster. Pan Books, 2011 Edition.

9. Reinhold Messner. Everest: Expedition to the Ultimate. Vertebrate Publishing 2014 (eBook), Sheffield, S11, 8UT.

10. Murray, W. H. and Robert Anderson. The Story of Everest 1921-1952. E. P. Dutton and Co., New York 1953.

11. John Hunt. The Ascent of Everest. Hodder and Stoughton Ltd., London 1953.

12. Atul Karwal, Anita Karwal. Think Everest: Scaling Mountains with the Mind. Viva Books Pvt. Ltd. New Delhi: Second Edition 2012.

13. Ed Viesturs. No Shortcuts To The Top: Climbing the World's 14 Highest Peaks. Broadway Books, 2007.

14. Reinhold Messner. The Crystal Horizon: Everest – The First Solo Ascent. Mountaineering Books, 1998 (Reprint edition).

15. http://www.xtreme-everest.co.uk/Everest2007

Personalities in the Book

(Note: It gives brief information about people mentioned in the book as prevailing at the time of the incidents described in the book. It may differ from their present profile.)

Abha Rani Singh: My cousin, an IRS (IT) Officer of 1996 Batch posted in New Delhi as Additional Commissioner Income Tax.

Abhijit Sinha: An IAS Officer of 2000 Batch of Nagaland Cadre posted in New Delhi as Private Secretary to Minister of State for Human Resource Development on central deputation.

Aishvarya Singh: An IAS Officer of 2008 Batch of Sikkim Cadre posted in Gangtok as Additional District Magistrate of East Sikkim District.

AK Singh (Aunjaneya Kumar Singh): An IAS Officer of 2005 Batch of Sikkim Cadre posted in Gangtok as the District Magistrate of East Sikkim District after January 2013.

AK Srivastava (Alok Kumar Srivastava): An IAS Officer of 1984 Batch of Sikkim Cadre posted in Gangtok as Principal Secretary in Social Justice, Empowerment and Welfare Department, Government of Sikkim.

AK Yadav (Arun Kumar Yadav): An IAS Officer of 1987 Batch of Sikkim Cadre posted in Gangtok as Development Commissioner, Government of Sikkim.

Arjun Karki: Nepali film actor, who came to climb Everest through same agency Seven Summit Treks. He successfully scaled the peak.

Arun: My cousin, an MBBS Doctor from NMCH, Patna.

Birendra: My younger brother.

BK Prasad: Braj Kishore Prasad, an IAS Officer of 1983 Batch of Tamilnadu Cadre posted in New Delhi on deputation as Additional Secretary in Ministry of Home Affairs, Government of India.

B. R. R. Kumar: An IRS (IT) Officer of 1995 Batch posted in New Delhi as the Additional Commissioner Income Tax and spouse of Mrs. Abha Rani Singh.

Capt. Pandey: Captain N. B. Pandey, the Managing Director of Pentagon Marine Services Pvt. Ltd., Mumbai. It is the shipping management company I worked with during my whole shipping career.

Champak Chatterjee: A retired IAS Officer of 1971 Batch of West Bengal Cadre, formerly the Secretary to Government of India. He was posted as the District Magistrate of Darjeeling from 1982 to 1984 and was an adventure lover.

Chanchal Kumar: An IAS Officer of 1992 Batch of Bihar Cadre posted in Patna as Principal Secretary; Culture, Youth Affairs and Sports Department, Government of Bihar.

Chandan Jha: My IPS batchmate of Jharkhand Cadre as well as my friend during prepararions for the Civil Services Examination.

Chewang Gyatso Bhutia: A Sikkim State Civil Service Officer and District Magistrate of North Sikkim District.

Chief Minister: Honourable chief minister of Sikkim, Sri Pawan Chamling.

Col Rana: Col Neeraj Rana, formerly Colonel in Indian Army and Ex-Principal of HMI Darjeeling. He was the leader of Everest Expedition Team of seven boys from Lawrence School, Sanawar, Himachal Pradesh, in which I and few other climbers was also added later in Nepal by Seven Summit Treks.

Col Niranjan: A Colonel rank officer in Indian Army and 2nd commandant of Brigade at Chatten, North Sikkim.

Col Parry: A retired colonel in Indian Army, who was father of one of the seven boys from Lawrence School Sanawar Hakikat Singh.

Col Sharma (Col. Satish C. Sharma): A colonel rank officer in Indian Army, who was the Leader of NCC Everest Expedition 2013.

Col Subodh Kumar: A Colonel rank officer in Indian Army and the commanding officer of 225 Transit Camp at Thangu in North Sikkim.

D. Anandan: An IAS Officer of 2000 Batch of Sikkim Cadre posted in Gangtok as the District Magistrate of East Sikkim District from June 2009 to January 2013.

DD Bhutia: A mountaineer, Everest Summiteer and Principal of Sonam Gyatso Mountaineering Institute (SGMI), Gangtok.

Dharmendra Singh Gangwar: An IAS Officer of 1988 Batch of Bihar Cadre posted in Patna as Principal Secretary; Personnel and General Administration in General Administration Department, Government of Bihar.

Dushyant Nariala: An IAS Officer of 1993 Batch of West Bengal Cadre posted as Joint Director in LBSNAA, Mussoorie on deputation to Government of India.

Dharmveer Acharya: A member of Gayatri Pariwar and a Social Worker.

GT Bhutia: Also mentioned as Director Chemchey in this book. He was director of IHCAE located at Chemchey, South Sikkim.

Guribadat Singh: One of the seven boys from Lawrence School, Sanawar, who summited peak on 21st May 2013.

K. Sreenivasulu : An IAS Officer of 1994 Batch of Sikkim Cadre posted as Managing Director, Government Fruit Preservation Factory, Singtam, Sikkim.

Kapil Meena: An IAS Officer of 2010 Batch of Sikkim Cadre and my immediate senior in the cadre.

Kazi Sherpa: A famous mountaineer from Sikkim and an Everest summiteer posted as Assistant Director in IHCAE, Chemchey, Sikkim. He was also the climbing leader of the first North East Everest Expedition 2013.

Kushang Sherpa: A renowned mountaineer from Darjeeling posted as senior instructor in HMI Darjeeling. He owns special record of climbing Mt. Everest from all three faces i. e. North face, South face and Kangshung face.

Kutty (Wing Commander Sudhir K. Kutty): A wing commander in Indian Air Force, who was the climbing leader of NCC Everest Expedition 2013.

Mamaji: My maternal uncle (my mother's eldest brother) Sri Shyam Kumar, retired IPS, Government of Bihar.

Mandeep Singh Tuli: An IPS Officer of 1999 Batch of Sikkim Cadre posted in Gangtok as Deputy Inspector General of Police (Range), Sikkim.

Manoj Tiwari: An IPS Officer of 2003 Batch of Sikkim Cadre posted in Gangtok as Superintendent of Police of East Sikkim District.

Maria Conceicao: A Portuguese female climber and social worker, who came to climb Everest through same agency Seven Summit Treks. She scaled peak under leadership of Commander Satya Dam.

Mingma Sherpa: Owner and Managing Director of Seven Summit Treks. He is the first person of Nepal to climb all fourteen eight thousanders.

Mirza Ali: A climber from Pakistan, who came to climb Everest along with his sister Samina Baig through same agency Seven Summit Trek.

Nisha Adhikari: Nepali actress, model, mountaineer and my extended teammate during Everest Expedition 2013. She scaled the peak on 21st May 2013.

Passang Sherpa: My guide during the Everest climb.

PK Jha: Prabhas Kumar Jha, an IAS Officer of 1982 Batch of Uttar Pradesh Cadre posted in New Delhi on deputation as Additional Secretary and Financial Advisor in Ministry of Consumer Affairs, Food and Public Distribution, Government of India.

Prabhakar Verma: An IAS Officer of 2007 Batch of Sikkim Cadre posted in Mangan as Additional District Magistrate of North Sikkim District.

Priyanka Mangesh Mohite: A female climber from Maharashtra, who was one member of the Everest Expedition team of Sanawar boys under leadership of Col Rana.
She scaled the peak on 22nd May 2013.

Raghav Joneja: One of the seven boys from Lawrence School, Sanawar, who summited peak on 21st May 2013.

Rajiv Ahir: An IPS Officer of 1996 Batch of Punjab Cadre posted as Deputy Director in Intelligence Bureau, Government of India on deputation. He was in-charge of Sonam Gyatso Mountaineering Institute, Gangtok, Sikkim.

Ranveer Singh Jamwal: A Major rank officer in Indian Army, a successful mountaineer and Everest Summiteer and he was the leader of Joint Indo-Nepal Everest Expedition 2013. His team had camped adjacent to us at Everest Base Camp.

Robin Gupta: A retired IAS Officer of 1974 Batch of Punjab Cadre, a formerly Financial Commissioner, in the rank of Chief Secretary, Government of Punjab and the author of book *And What Remains in the End: The Memoirs of an Unrepentant Civil Servant.*

Saachi Soni: A female climber from Rajasthan, who was one member of the Everest Expedition team of the Sanawar boys under the leadership of Col Rana.

Samina Baig: A climber from Pakistan, who came to climb Everest along with her brother Mirza Ali through same agency Seven Summit Treks. She summited the peak the same day as I did.

Sanjay Pandit: Nepali Ultra Marathon Runner, Mountaineer and my friend and and extended teammate during the Everest Expedition 2013. He scaled the peak same day as I did.

Satya Dam (Commander Satyabrata Dam): His full name is Satyabrata Dam. He is an ex-Indian Navy officer, an old mountaineer and an Everest Summiteer. He holds several records in mountaineering and climbing.

Subedar Major Mahabir: A member of Joint Indo-Nepal Everest Expedition 2013 under leadership of Maj. Jamwal. Formerly Quarter Master in HMI Darjeeling.

Tashi and Nungshi Malik: Twin sisters from Dehradun (India), who came to climb Everest through same agency Seven Summit Trek. They summited peak the same day as I did.

Tashi Sherpa: The in-charge of Seven Summit Treks at the Everest Base Camp and an Everest Summiteer. He is Mingma Sherpa's younger brother.

Tejveer Singh: An IAS Officer of 1994 Batch of Punjab Cadre posted as Deputy Director in LBSNAA, Mussoorie on deputation to the Government of India.

Vineet Vinayak: An IPS Officer of 1995 Batch of Sikkim Cadre posted in Gangtok as Inspector General of Police (Law and Order), Sikkim.

Vishal Chauhan: An IAS Officer of 1998 Batch of Sikkim Cadre posted as Special Secretary in the Rural Development Department, Government of Uttar Pradesh on deputation.

****

About the Author

Mr Ravindra Kumar is an ex-seafarer, an IAS Officer, an adventure-sports enthusiast, and a person with deep interest in social work. Born in a necessitous farmer's family in Begusarai District of Bihar in 1981, Kumar cracked some major academic levels like the IIT Entrance Examination in 1999 in his maiden attempt and later, the Civil Services Examination in 2011. Finally, he settled in his current job in the Indian Administrative Services in 2011 after working over a decade in shipping. But soon after, he went on to jump over the hurdle of climbing Mount Everest in 2013 and set the record of being the first I.A.S. Officer as well as the first seafarer from India to scale Everest. For his big feat, he was awarded the Sikkim Khel Ratna Award by the Government of Sikkim, Vishesh Khel Samman by government of Bihar, Kashti Ratna Award by the shipping fraternity, and many more such accolades.

In 2015, he led the First All India Services Everest Expedition, an expedition flagged off by the Prime Minister of India himself. The expedition was first of its kind with a group of All India Services officers to climb the peak of Everest with the slogan *Swachh Bharat Abhiyan* to raise awareness about health and hygiene in the nation from the highest peak in the world. But the Nepal earthquake and resultant avalanche shattered the attempt by killing and injuring many people at the Everest Base Camp. Kumar, with his indefatigable courage, managed to rescue a few lives in the menacing post-avalanche scenario at the Base Camp. The Himalayan Rescue Association had also appreciated his effort for the same.

Through his first book *Many Everests*, the author has presented the readers with invaluable tenets of success that he had followed in his life, with a strong hope to bring changes in many such lives like him. You can get more details about the Author or you may contact the Author directly to share your valuable feedbacks regarding the book on the following :

Email : ravindra.everest@gmail.com

Website : www.shriravindrakumar.com

****